【基金项目】江苏省社会科学基金项目“隐喻研究‘神经相关物’进路的哲学困境及出路”(19YYB005)

A Study of the Realrzation Mechanism of Metaphorical Categorization

隐喻性范畴化的实现机制研究

龚玉苗 著

吉林大学出版社
长春

图书在版编目（CIP）数据

隐喻性范畴化的实现机制研究 / 龚玉苗著. —长春：吉林大学出版社，2022.3

ISBN 978-7-5692-9231-2

Ⅰ. ①隐… Ⅱ. ①龚… Ⅲ. ①隐喻—研究 Ⅳ. ①H05

中国版本图书馆 CIP 数据核字（2021）第 221676 号

书　　名　隐喻性范畴化的实现机制研究
　　　　　YINYUXING FANCHOUHUA DE SHIXIAN JIZHI YANJIU
作　　者　龚玉苗 著
策划编辑　李潇潇
责任编辑　矫正
责任校对　李潇潇
装帧设计　杨西福
出版发行　吉林大学出版社
社　　址　长春市人民大街 4059 号
邮政编码　130021
发行电话　0431-89580028/29/21
网　　址　http://www.jlup.com.cn
电子邮箱　jldxcbs@sina.com
印　　刷　三河市华东印刷有限公司
开　　本　787mm × 1092mm　1/16
印　　张　15
字　　数　294 千字
版　　次　2022 年 3 月第 1 版
印　　次　2022 年 3 月第 1 次
书　　号　ISBN 978-7-5692-9231-2
定　　价　68.00 元

前　言

隐喻同探索人类意识本质的哲学前沿研究紧密相关,其挑战性在于回答隐喻何以作为人类概念形成和扩展的重要机制。在此追问中,最为广泛的研究切入点之一是将隐喻映射和范畴重组或范畴扩展机制结合起来。本研究将隐喻中本体和喻体在范畴层级中的转化过程定义为隐喻性范畴化过程。以往认知语言学研究对该转化过程多是基于具体语言的描述分析,对其具体的实现机制并未做进一步深入系统的研究,因此仍缺乏一个较全面系统的理论框架。本研究以类比理论中的结构映射理论和抽象图式归纳理论为理论分析框架,通过心理语言学研究范式考察隐喻的本体和喻体跨越常规范畴进入新的共属范畴的实现过程的认知机制,以期探索性地为隐喻性范畴化的实现机制提供一个较具解释力的心理语言学模型。

基于对文献和以往理论的分析,围绕隐喻性范畴化的实现机制,本文提出四个研究问题:一,隐喻性范畴化的中介是什么?二,隐喻的本体和喻体如何取得范畴联系?三,隐喻的喻体如何获得抽象的范畴指称?四,隐喻性范畴化具有那些制约机制?

针对这些研究问题,本研究以人类的类比机制作为理论分析框架,具体包括:结构映射以及双重性抽象图式归纳。基于这一分析框架,本研究提出的核心假设是隐喻的双重范畴化模型。包含以下子假设:其一,隐喻性范畴化基于本体和喻体之间的结构映射,因此其中介是关系结构相似性;其二,隐喻性范畴化的动态实现机制是基于发生在两个层面上的抽象图式的归纳。在微观层面,类比关系中取得匹配的论元之间取得范畴联系;在宏观层面,取得匹配的结构关系之间取得范畴联系。其三,隐喻性范畴化具有双重性,即隐喻所表述的范畴隶属关系取决于发生在宏观和微观两个层面的范畴联系的程度。其四,隐喻性范畴化和常规范畴化之间具有差异。基于这四个子假设,本研究形成五个研究问题,以汉语隐喻"甲是乙"(如"老板是鲨鱼")为研究语料,设计四个子研究系统地考察隐喻性范畴化的实现机制。

研究一(包括实验 1)考察第一个研究问题,即隐喻性范畴化的中介是什么。本研究假设结构映射是隐喻性范畴化中介确定的基础,因此隐喻性范畴化以关系相似性为中介。实验 1 对隐喻传达的相似性进行了严格控制,对比喻表达的句法倾向性进行了调查和统计。结果表明隐喻得以通过范畴隶属句的表述形式取决于隐喻的相似性的特征。具有关系相似的本体和喻体倾向于通过隐喻形式表述,而表面相似的本体和喻体倾向于通过明喻形式表述。这初步验证了结构映射作为隐喻性范畴化的中介——相似性的认定机制的假设。

研究二(包括实验 2 和实验 3)考察隐喻性范畴化的动态实现机制。具体回答第二、三个研究问题,即隐喻的本体和喻体之间如何取得范畴联系,以及喻体如何获得抽象范畴指称。本文假设这两个层面的范畴化基于隐喻中的双重性的图示归纳。实验 2 考察第二个研究问题,相应的假设是隐喻的本体和喻体之间范畴联系的取得基于二者之间的基于结构映射的微观的图示归纳。实验采用词汇判断任务记录分析反应时和准确率,结果发现与单一的语义加工任务相比,对本体和喻体的语义信息的结构匹配任务对本体喻体共属上义范畴有显著的激活效应,结果验证了隐喻性范畴化的结构映射的认知基础。实验 3(分作 3a 和 3b)分别从两个角度考察宏观范畴化过程,即喻体获得抽象范畴指称的认知机制。实验 3a 考察在具体的隐喻理解中,喻体获得抽象范畴指称的时程关系。相应的假设是,这一过程基于抽象图式的归纳。实验 3a 采用词汇判断任务记录反应时和准确率,结果表明抽象图式的激活基于早期的具体特征的结构映射,即具有"先映射-后归纳"的时程特征。实验 3b 在实验条件下考察喻体获得抽象范畴指称的历时性。结果表明与喻体具有关系相似的本体更能促进喻体的抽象范畴化，并具有历时性进展的特征；喻体和抽象图式的联系并非基于喻体和某一固定本体之间的重复记忆，而是基于和不同本体之间连用所产生的相同抽象图式的重复激活。

研究三（实验4）考察第四个研究问题，即隐喻性范畴化具有什么影响机制。我们假设由于隐喻性范畴化所基于的抽象图示归纳具有双重性，因此隐喻所表述的范畴隶属关系受微观和宏观两个层面的范畴联系程度的制约。实验4采用Stroop效应的语义变式考察隐喻表述范畴隶属关系的影响机制，将隐喻性范畴化的宏观层面和微观层面分别操作性地定义为喻体的规约化水平和隐喻的适当性水平。结果表明隐喻表述范畴隶属的程度取决于两个因素，即隐喻本体和喻体范畴隶属关系有两个条件：其一，喻体较本体具有较高的抽象性，即喻体的规约性水平较高；其二，隐喻具有较高的适当性，即喻体能够适当描述本体的重要特征。

研究结果总体支持“隐喻的双重范畴化模型”。其核心思想是，隐喻性范畴化以关系相似性为中介；隐喻所表述的范畴隶属关系基于双重性的图式归纳，因此隐喻性范畴化涉及两个层面的范畴化：在宏观层面，本体和喻体分别涉及的相似的抽象关系取得范畴联系；在微观层面，取得匹配的抽象关系所涉及的相对应的具体论元取得范畴联系。隐喻性范畴化的实现可以通过人类的一般认知能力得以解释，而与常规范畴化的脑机制的不同也可以通过一些现有的普适的语言加工理论得以解释。据此本研究支持认知语言学所执的隐喻是人类一般认知能力的一部分的基本观点。

尽管存在一些理论和方法上的不足，本研究仍然在以下几个方面做出一定的贡献：理论层面，其一，对隐喻性范畴化的理论建构以及对隐喻中的关系范畴的论证对现有的范畴理论是一项重要补充；其二，对隐喻何以可能所依赖的范畴错置的消解机制进行了深入系统的研究，在一定程度为这一长期困扰隐喻研究和范畴研究的这一重要课题提出了新的解释方案;其三,对隐喻与明喻的差异的本质提供了一个全新的阐释视角;其四,对隐喻性范畴和常规范畴的区别作了更深入的探讨;其五,本研究关于隐喻性范畴化所基于的关系相似性的论证为认知语言学所基于的体验哲学及主观主义意义观提供了新的佐证。实践层面,本研究对“隐喻能力”的培养、隐喻性多义词以及动词的教学具有重要启示。研究方法层面,本研究所采用的心理语言学和认知神经科学的手段顺应了当代认知语言学的理论创建和发展所必须进行的“实证革命”。

Contents

Chapter 1 Introduction

1.1 Research orientation

A metaphor[①] ("An x is a y.") is basically formed through juxtaposing two concepts conventionally belonging to two separate categories in a literally taxonomical fashion(or is a relation in logics) by using the copula be. This kind of metaphorical category juxtaposition, despite the entailment of a sense of deviation, is made felicitous by a recategorizing process in which the topic and the vehicle leap over the conventional category boundaries and join a shared superordinate category. The overarching goal of this dissertation is to provide a unified theoretical account of such a recategorizing process. More specifically, it attempts(1) to examine the mediator of the recategorization process, i. e., similarity between the topic and vehicle; (2) to look into the underlying mechanism of such a dynamic recategorizating process which includes two sub-mechanisms: A. the mechanism in which the topic and the vehicle leap over the conventional category boundaries and jump into a shared superordinate category, and B. the mechanism in which the metaphor vehicle dynamically obtains its abstract categorical referent; (3) to look into the constraints on the categorical inclusion relationship between the topic and the vehicle; (4) to explore the neural substrates of the categorization mechanism in metaphor. Based on the four specific aspects, this dissertation intends to provide a unified theoretical framework of

---

① This study takes strict distinctions between metaphors and similes in terms of their grammatical forms, i. e., a metaphor has the identical grammatical form with a literal category inclusion statement(e. g., "An x is a y." as "A dog is a pet."), while a simile has the identical form with a literal comparasion statement(e. g., "An x is like a y." as "A lime is like a lemon.").

metaphorical categorization. This study will hopefully shed some new light on our understanding of the nature of metaphor comprehension, fluidity of categorization and the philosophical implications regarding the role of metaphor in category extension.

1.2 Research rationale

Due to its pervasiveness in language use (Pollio et al., 1977) and semantic ambiguity in nature, metaphor has been traditionally a hot research topic for theories of meaning and language comprehension. The growing recognition of the importance of metaphor in language and thought (Lakoff and Johnson, 1980) has resulted in a proliferation of studies on the cognitive processes involved in metaphor comprehension.

Beyond the influences of metaphor on studies of semantics and human cognition, a much more significant landmark is that the strong cognitive approach to metaphor study has constituted a revolution in philosophy (Lakoff and Johnson, 1999). In contrast to the traditional objectivism, which assumes that reason is abstract and disembodied and primarily based on propositions that can be objectively either true or false, the embodied philosophy recently put forward by Lakoff and his colleagues claims that human reason has a bodily basis, and that imaginative aspects, such as metaphor, metonymy, and mental imagery, are central to human cognition. In both the two philosophical views, categorization is taken as the main way in which human makes sense of experience and in terms of which conceptual systems are organized. What distinguish the two views from each other are their distinct assumptions concerning the role of metaphor in categorization. According to the objectivist philosophy, things are in the same category if and only if they share certain properties in common, i.e., a category is defined on necessary and sufficient conditions, and imagination including metaphor, metonymy plays no roles in categorization. The embodiment philosophy, however, posits that category boundaries are fuzzy, and metaphor and metonymy are two basic mechanisms in category extension (Taylor, 1995). As a result, the study of the relation between metaphor and categorization has long been regarded as the testing ground of these two dramatically different philosophies(Lakoff and Johnson, 1980; Lakoff, 1987). The significance of such studies has been well recognized, as Gibbs(1992: 577) noted: "the challenge for experimental psychologists is to find other empirical methods that can assess how, and to what degree, conceptual categorization is determined, and perhaps constituted, by metaphor."

The study of the relationbetween metaphor and categorization has been centered on two more specific research topics in cognitive linguistics. First, in the stream of category study, most work has been conducted on the dynamic nature of categorization and the role of metaphor in category extension. In this field, researchers have relied heavily on descriptive linguistic data, especially metaphorical polysemy. For example, based on several detailed case-based observations on metaphorical polysemous senses of propositions (e. g., over), modalities (e. g., must), and nouns (e. g., mother) (Sweetser, 1990; Taylor, 1995), it is concluded that polysemous meanings emerge as categories with fuzzy boundaries, and the relatedness of these polysemes is most often motivated by metaphors. Second, the significance of the relation between metaphor and categorization also find its way in the studies of the nature of metaphor and metaphor comprehension. A metaphor is generally considered to be "a juxtaposition of two concepts conventionally belonging to two distinct categories in a taxonomical(or is a) fashion" (Qian, 1979; Shu, 2000, 2008, 2009), or "replacing the fourth term of a proportion with the second" in a proportional analogy(Ricoeur, 1977). In both views, categorical conflict or deviation between the topic and the vehicle is taken as the basis for being a metaphor, and the tension evoked by metaphor(or metaphoricity) is caused primarily by the disparate nature of the two concepts being combined.

Besides the nature of metaphor per se, researchers have also relied heavily on the relation between metaphor and categorization in explaining metaphor interpretation. It has long been believed that metaphor comprehension can be accounted for through the mechanism in which the tension arising from category conflict in metaphor dispels between the topic and vehicle. For example, in cognitive linguistic tradition, the two most widely recognized metaphor theories, i. e., the mapping theory(Lakoff, 1993) and the blending theory (Foccornaur, 1985, 1994; Foccornaur and Turner, 1998), despite their many different basic hypotheses concerning metaphor, both agree that metaphors essentially involve some kind of interaction between two different categories[①].

In psycholinguistics tradition, researchers have also centered their analyses on the relation between metaphor and categorization. In fact, the three major psycholinguistic models of metaphor build their basic theoretical assumptions on the categorical relation between the topic and vehicle. The comparison model (Malgady and Johnson, 1976; Miller, 1993; Ortony, 1979, 1993; Tversky, 1977; Verbrugge and McCarrell, 1977) argues that metaphor topic and vehicle belong to two distinct categories and metaphors are comprehended through a pragmatic three-stage mechanism. The categorization model (Glucksberg and Keysar, 1990, 1997) posits that the metaphor vehicle has dual-referent in nature, that is, a literal concrete referent and simultaneously an abstract categorical referent. Metaphor comprehension is hence the same as property attribution in literal categorization. The recent career model (Bowdle and Gentner, 1997, 2005) attempts to reconcile the two previous competing models, positing whether metaphors denote category violation or category inclusion depends on the conventionality level of the vehicle. In this view, the abstract categorical referent is not the inherent nature of the vehicle, but the outcome of a reinforced association between the vehicle and a categorical referent.

In contrast to the strong philosophical observation concerning metaphorical mechanism in human categorization discussed above, it must be borne in mind that there are severe criticisms undermining this cognitive linguistic approach. The first criticism concerns the issue of language-thought language circular reasoning in descriptive research (Murphy, 1997; McGlone, 2001, 2007). Lakoff's claim that metaphors transcend their linguistic forms to influence conceptual structure rests solely on these manifestations. For example, as for the famous example of conceptual metaphor ARGUMENT IS WAR, how do we know that people think of "arguments" in terms of "wars"? It is because people often talk about arguments through using war-related expressions. Why do people often talk about arguments using war-related

---

① Instead of the term "category", the term "domain" is used in Lakoff's mapping theory of metaphor, and the term "mental space" in Foccornaur and Turner's blending theory. The present study does not take strict distinctions among the three terms as they are all cognition oriented.

expressions? It is because people think of arguments in terms of wars. Using only linguistic analysis evidence to argue for the functional relationship between thought and language will definitely cast doubts on the scientificity of the theory. The second criticism concerns the issue of simplicity in linguistic sampling. Lakoff and Johnson (1980) have notably based their studies on conventional metaphors and confounded conventional metaphors with novel ones, with the latter having been seriously neglected. The simplicity in linguistic sampling has definitely endangered the strong version of metaphor cognition relationship because it is commonly recognized that conventional and novel metaphors involve different processing mechanisms (Leezenberg, 2001).

Based on the above mentioned criticisms, both the metaphor theory and category theory in modern cognitive linguistics have to further extend their evidence ground. Firstly, in addition to exclusive linguistic evidence, further argument of the relation between metaphor and categorization should rest more on evidence derived from critical empirical studies in other fields, especially psycholinguistics. In fact, the significance of psycholinguistic experimental evidence for both linguistic and cognitive theories has been explicitly pointed out by Croft and Cruse (2004: 329): "There is considerable scope for further interaction between cognitive psychology and cognitive linguistics, in particular for critical experimental testing of cognitive linguistic hypotheses, and a refinement of the linguistic assumptions behind the experimental design of cognitive psychologists."

And more recently by Geeraerts (2006:21): "The future of linguistics is likely to be determined by methodological issues: whether linguistics will be able to turn its current theoretical chaos (however creative it may be) into a situation of cumulative development will crucially depend on the possibility of finding a common ground that allows competing accounts to be compared in an objective way."

In addition to the recognition of the significance of psycholinguistic empirical evidence, it is increasingly widely recognized that further metaphor study should diversify its linguistic samples to include metaphors with different semantic characteristics, such as "conventional" "frozen" or "dead" metaphors which mostly interest philosophers and linguists, and "novel" "imaginative" or "creative" metaphors in poetry and literature. The importance of appropriate choice of linguistic samples has been noticed by Stern (2000: 25): "theories of metaphor are often a function of their authors' examples." It is assumed that a specific theory of metaphor can only account for certain groups of metaphors with specific characteristics, and there is still much room for further investigations into different kinds of metaphors.

In contrast to the plethora of studies on the relation between metaphor and categorization, there are virtuallyrare experimental studies that have explicitly attempted to find evidence on the role of metaphor in the process of categorization. In this regard, the present study intends to provide some psycholinguistic evidence to the relation between metaphor and category, and hopefully, to develop a psycholinguistic model concerning how categorization is constituted by metaphors. In addition, as the competing metaphor psycholinguistic models contrast with each other in terms of the basic assumptions concerning categorization processes in metaphor comprehension, a deeper look into these processes will shed some light on our understanding of metaphor comprehension. Besides, since metaphor has been assumed to be an important source of polysemy extension, this study can also shed some new light on the motivation underlying diachronic metaphoric polysemous sense extension, which will definitely have some pedagogical implications to the teaching of metaphorical polysemes.

1.3 Scope of the study

Metaphors in the simplest form "An x is a y." (e. g., "A boss is a shark.") are frequently referred to as "nominal metaphors", in which the first noun is termed as the topic (e. g., boss) and the second the vehicle (e. g., shark)①. The scope of this

① The two nouns are termed variously according to different weight on different aspects of human cognition or language. In cognitive linguistics tradition, Richards (1936) termed x as "topic" or "tenor", and y as "vehicle" or "ground"; Black (1953) termed x as "the principal subject" or "frame", and y as "the second subject" or "the focus of the metaphor"; Lakoff and Johnson (1980) termed x as "target", and y as "source"; Ortony (1979) termed x as " target" or "tenor" and y as "base". This paper will adopt "topic" and "vehicle" as they are more conventionally used in psycholinguistics literature (Holyoak, 2004) on analogical reasoning which is taken as the theoretical framework for the present dissertation.

study is limited to such nominal metaphors due to the following considerations: (1) most of the existing models of metaphor thus far are developed on the basis of investigations into the "be" relationship between the topic and the vehicle; (2) nominal metaphors are comparatively easier to manage without sacrificing the quality of being representative. It is commonly assumed that metaphors in more complicated forms, such as predicative metaphors (e.g., "The sun has a big smile.") have the same mechanisms as nominal metaphors (Glucksberg, 2001: 49), thus the study of the simplest form can serve as a good starting point for future complex study without the risk of confounding the results with additional semantic and syntactic variables; (3) since the focus of the present study is categorization mechanism in metaphor, the categorical juxtaposition form of nominal metaphors (e.g., "The boss is a shark."), which is identical with the syntactic structure of literal categorization (e.g., "The animal is a shark."), can offer a good digging point for a deeper understanding of potential similarities and dissimilarities between metaphorical and literal category statements. Once reliable results are obtained based on these simplest materials, they can be applied to test metaphors with more complicated forms, such as those with adjectives or predicative metaphors, or even those which are embedded in sentences or discourses, and so forth.

1.4 Structure of the study

The rest of this book unfolds as follows.

Chapter 2 provides a comprehensive argument to justify and define the notion of metaphorical categorization. In Chapter 3, the author presents a thorough review of previous studies on the relation between metaphor and category. Some remaining problems are also pointed out. Chapter 4 presents the theoretical analysis framework, the research questions, the general hypotheses and the subsequent empirical research design for the present study. Chapter 5—8 are four separate albeit related studies designed to seek the answers to the research questions through testing the specific hypotheses. Specifically, Chapter 5, consisting of Exp 1, looks into the mediator of metaphorical categorization. Chapter 6, including three sub-experiments, investigates the core dynamic process of metaphorical categorization. Chapter 7 specifically looks into the duality of metaphorical categorization. Chapter 8 provides a general discussion on the findings emerging from the previous experiments. In the final chapter, some conclusions are reached, and some limitations and the recommendations for further research are also put forward.

Chapter 2 Defining metaphorical categorization

This chapter is devoted to a theoretical definition of the overarching concept of the present study, i. e., metaphorical categorization. Firstly, in Section 2. 1 the author explores the logical sense of a nominal metaphor with the grammatical form of "An x is a y." Then in Section 2. 2 attempts to explore the notion of conventional categorization against which metaphorical categorization is discussed. Finally, in Section 2. 3 explicitly elucidates the definition of the core concept, i. e., metaphorical categorization.

2. 1 The nature of "An x is a y."

As a nominal metaphor has the same linguistic form as a literal category inclusion statement "An x is a y.", an exploration into the nature of metaphorical categorization can begin with a look into the logical nature of "An x is a y.". From the very beginning, researchers have been intrigued by the logical sense of the copula be in metaphorical "An x is a y.". According to Davison (1977), metaphors have no figurative senses other than their literal senses. So what does "An x is a y." literally mean? Several researchers have attempted to offer kinds of accounts. Shapiro (1997: 83) proposed four distinct logical senses denoted by be in the structure "An x is a y."; (1) numerical identity, as in "Cicero is tully."; (2) class inclusion, as in "Iron is metal"; (3) intertheoretic-reduction, as in "Temperature is the average kinetic energy of molecules."; (4) role-occupancy, as in "Mel Gibson is Wallace." in the famous movie Brave Heart.

Besides the four senses suggested by Shapiro, Hintikka (2001) puts forward a fifth logical sense: counterpart correspondence, as in "This cobble is Beijing.". To interpret this utterance, just imagine the speaker is showing the positions of various cities on a map illustrated by cobbles on the floor. The equivalence between the concept of cobble and the name of a city is realized by the notion of counterpart correspondence, which is based on the theory of possible world semantics (Perry, 2008; Zhou, 2004; An and Guo, 2007). According to this theory, the actual world which we inhabit is one of the many possible worlds. Our actual world is related to other possible worlds in one way or another. One kind of possible relationship is the existence of correspondence between counterparts in different worlds. The establishment of this kind of correspondence is through analogical reasoning which draws on analogical mappings. Again in the case "This cobble stone is Beijing", what determines the meaning of the sentence is not the correspondence between the properties of the stone itself and the geographical name of a certain place, but rather the correspondence between two relational structures, i. e., the relation between certain cobbles and the relation between certain cities.

Among the five proposed senses pertaining to the nature of "An x is a y.", we assume that two of them can possibly speak for the logical sense of a metaphorical one. First, the be relation in metaphors (e. g. "A boss is a shark.") has a completely identical meaning as in literal categorization (e. g. "An apple is a fruit."), indicating a class inclusion relationship. This argument is consistent with Glucksberg's (2001) proposal that the vehicle inherently has dual referents. Second, as Hintikka (2001) proposes, the metaphorical sense of be in metaphor "An x is a y." denotes a kind of analogical counterpart correspondence relationship.

Besides these views of the relation denoted by be in metaphors, Xu (2008) argues for a more unified account for the sense of be in metaphors. That is, be denotes the inheritance of denotation and connotation from the vehicle domain to the target domain, and this kind of inheritance happens between concepts at different levels on taxonomic type hierarchy. That is, concepts at the subordinate level naturally inherit all the denotations and connotations of the ones at the superordinate level[①].

This dissertation will take a unified view of the nature of metaphorical "An x is y" based on the senses discussed above, and define metaphorical "An x is y" as a category inclusion (taxonomical or is a) relation which relies on a recategorizing process in which the topic (x) and the vehicle (y) extend the conventional category boundaries and join a shared superordinate category. Our assumption is grounded on the following rationales. First, based on the fact that metaphor "An x is y" is irreversible and the vehicle y diachronically gains more abstract polysemous meanings, we argue that "An x is y" conveys a sense of class inclusion. However, different from Glucksberg's class-inclusion view (Glucksberg and Keysar, 1990; Glucksberg, McGlone and Manfredi, 1997) which holds that y inherently refers to the abstract superordinate category, this dissertation assumes that y dynamically and diachronically acquires the abstract superordinate category. Second, this study argues that y dynamically obtains its abstract superordinate category and x can be included in the category through analogical mapping and abstract schema induction.

2.2 Conventional categorization

To avoid irrelevant theoretical connotations and confusions, this study will adopt the more common and neutral terms "category" and "categorization" in cognitive linguistic tradition in place of "set" which is conventionally used in mathematics, or "collections" and "type" in logics, or "class" in other fields. Categorization is defined as the process by which objects or events are grouped into categories — collections of objects treated in some respect(s) as equivalent — for the purpose of making sense of the world. First of all, the author believes that the overarching concept of this study, i.e., metaphorical categorization, can be elucidated more clearly by first sketching the counterpart notion against which it is set — conventional categorization.

In order to have a look into the notion of conventional categorization, it is

① A more comprehensive description of Xu's account is offered in Section 3.2.3.

necessary to firstly explore the notion of conventionality. As conventionality in linguistics mostly originates from cognitive science, the author would like to mainly follow the cognitive linguistic tradition when discussing it. Specifically, the author mainly follows Croft's (2000) understanding of conventionality which is generally based on Clark's study (1996) and Lewis' study (1969). According to Croft (2000), convention refers to regularity in behavior that is partly arbitrary and that is commonly grounded in a community as a coordination device for a recurrent coordination problem (communicating a meaning). In practice, to be conventional usually seems to mean the same as to be fixed or preset in the minds of the speakers. In other words, it means to be entrenched in the speakers' minds and not created online or on the fly.

As the present dissertation is psycholinguistics-oriented, we will rely more heavily on the analyses of the notion of convention in psycholinguistics literature, which provides definitions of conventionality with more operational value. Bearing this in mind, by conventional category, this study will mainly follow Barsalou's argument (1983) in terms of a very similar notion, i. e., common category and its connotations. According to Barsalou, common category has two central psychological properties. The first is the property of graded structure which has three aspects: better example (or typicality) phenomenon (Rosch and Mervis, 1975), the presence of unclear cases (McCloskey and Glucksberg, 1978), and variation in similarity of nonmembers to the category concept (McCloskey and Glucksberg, 1979). The second is that common category has *well-established* representation in long-term memory. We believe the second aspect is closely related to the cognitive linguistic notions of entrenched, fixed or preset concerning conventional categorical relation aforementioned. As the central interest of the present study is dynamicity and fluidity in categorization, which is closely related to the issue of strength in knowledge representation, we will here take a closer inspection into the second property, i. e., "well-established".

According to Barsalou (1983), "well-established" categorical relation involves three aspects of associations in long-term memory. The first is concerned with strong category-to-instance associations①. That's to say, category concepts easily activate category instances. Such top-down associations are empirically found when one is trying to generate category member during category production tasks or trying to recall information from a category list. For example, the superordinate category "furniture" might activate the subordinate categories like "chair" "table" "desk", and so on, as shown in many classic studies on category (Rosch and Mervis, 1975). The second aspect is strong instance-to-category concept associations②. Such bottom-up associations exhibit when one is categorizing single instances or organizing multiple instances of the same category. For example, perceiving the words "oak" "maple" and "pine" may activate superordinate "tree". The third aspect is pertaining to strong associations between a concept and its properties and between the properties themselves. For example, on the one hand, presence of "bird" can more automatically activate the properties such as "wings" "flies" "features", and so on; on the other hand, these properties themselves can highly activate each other.

Besides the three association criteria, it should be noted that there is another criterion, i. e., context dependency. That is, for a category concept to be well established in memory, it should be easier to locate in memory in that it can be retrieved independently of any extra linguistic context. The three types of association tasks discussed above should be independent of any specially biased context.

2. 3 Metaphorical categorization

According to the notion of conventional category relation discussed above, out of any context, "man" more automatically activates "human" than "wolf" as its superordinate category. Yet in the sentence "A man is a wolf." which serves as a minimal metaphorical context, "man" is included in the superordinate category

① The classic experimental paradigm in examing category-to-instance association strength is exemplar generation technique (Barsalou 1983, 1985; Rosch and Mervis, 1975)

② The classic experimental paradigm in examing instance-to-category association strength is category generation Task (Barsalou 1983, 1985; Rosch and Mervis, 1975).

"wolf". This gives rise to a question: how is it possible to juxtapose two concepts conventionally belonging to two distinct categories in a category inclusion fashion? To this question, there have been proposed a number of solutions, one of which has been considered to be the most convincing, that is, the dispelling of the deviation arising from the misjuxtaposition of categories relies on a recategorizing process in which the metaphor topic and the vehicle leap over the conventional categorical boundaries and join a common superordinate category, and the vehicle obtains its abstract categorical reference denoting this superordinate category (Xu, 2008). The present study tentatively terms this kind of recategorization process which metaphor topic and vehicle undergo as metaphorical categorization.

This study argues that metaphorical categorization in its own right comprises three sub-mechanisms. First, the mechanism in which the mediator of recategorization, i.e., similarity between the topic and vehicle is identified. Second, the underlying mechanism in which the topic and the vehicle conventionally belonging to separate categories gets categorically associated. Third, the mechanism in which the metaphor vehicle dynamically obtains its abstract categorical referent(s).

In contrast to conventional categorization, we argue that such recategorzation is dynamically processed. That is to say, the metaphorical category relations are not entrenched or well-established in the long-term memory, and the categorical associations between the topic and the vehicle and the shared superordinate category are created on the fly in the course of metaphor processing. This position has the following two corollaries. First, metaphorical category relations are context-dependent in that the categorizing process can only be realized in a metaphoric context even in the minimal form "An x is a y.(e.g., A boss is a shark.)". For example, out of a metaphor context, "man' is conventionally associated with the superordinate category "human", and "wolf" with "animal". In the metaphor "A man is a wolf", however, "man" can be included in a superordinate category denoted by the vehicle term "wolf". In this sense, metaphor itself or the topic and vehicle pair serves as the minimal linguistic context in which metaphorical categorization occurs. Second, metaphorical category associations are created dynamically on the fly of metaphor processing, that is, categorical relations are established only in the process of metaphor comprehension as the byproduct of abstract schema induction[①]. This point distinguishes our notion of metaphorical categorization from that of ad hoc category theory (Glucksberg and Kay, 1990; Glucksberg, McGlone and Manfredi, 1997), which argues that ad hoc categorical association between the metaphor vehicle and the abstract categorical referent (s) is the basis or starting point of metaphor comprehension. In our view, metaphorical categorization is the outcome of metaphor processing rather than its starting point.

Besides the two properties which are distinct from conventional category association, we claim that metaphorical categorization also has two basic properties which are the same as conventional category association. On the one hand, metaphorical categorization also relies on similarity as the mediator of the categorization. Metaphor topic and vehicle can only join the shared superordinate category on the basis of their similarity. On the other hand, metaphorical categories have the same internal structure with conventional categories. According to principles of categorization (Rosch and Barbara, 1978), the greater the inclusiveness of a category within a taxonomy, the higher level of abstraction it is at.

① This notion will be fully described in Section 4.1.3 which elaborates the theoretical framework for the present study.

Chapter 3 Literature review

This chapter reviews previous theoretical and empirical studies on the relation between metaphor and category, thus paving the ground for the theoretical analysis framework for metaphorical categorization. In Section 3. 1, the author explores the relation between metaphor and category with more weight on theoretical considerations from both a cognitive linguistic(Section 3. 1. 1) and a psycholinguistic point of view (Section 3. 1. 2). In Section 3. 2, the author specifically focuses on previous studies on metaphorical categorization. Three related issues are discussed: the mediator of metaphorical categorization(Section 3. 2. 1), empirical measurement of the category relation between the topic and the vehicle(Section 3. 2. 2), and some theoretically hypothesized proposals concerning the dynamic process of metaphorical categorization (Section 3. 2. 3). After a critical review of existing theoretical views on the relation between metaphor and category and related empirical studies on metaphorical categorization, the study will arrive at some critical reflections on some remaining problems(Section 3. 3), which provides the motivation for the present study.

3. 1 The relation between metaphor and category

The relation between metaphor and category can be explored through investigations into the category theories and the metaphor theories respectively. As category is more studied in cognitive linguistics and metaphor is more studied in psycholinguistics, in the following sections we will take a look in the relation between metaphor and category from the two independent yet related perspectives.

3. 1. 1 A cognitive linguistic perspective

Categorization is fundamental to all higher human cognitive activities, as noted by George Lakoff(Lakoff, 1987:5):"there is nothing more basic than categorization to our thought, perception, action, and speech".

The definitions of categorization in literature boil down to three major aspects: the ability to see similarity in diversity (Taylor, 1995); a mental process of classification on which conceptualization is based(Ungerer and Schmid, 1996:2); and the outcome of the juxtaposition of two conceptual structures(Jackendoff, 1985: 87). Contemporary studies of the way human beings actually categorize things indicate that categorization is a rather complex matter which reflects deep philosophical positions. In order to provide a comprehensive description, it is necessary to distinguish two major current category theories, i. e., the classical theory and the prototype theory. Since the relation between these two schools of theories have been extensively reviewed elsewhere(Lakoff, 1987; Taylor, 1995) and the focal interest of the present dissertation is the relation between category theory and metaphor, it is only necessary for us here to provide a thorough discussion of different views held by the two theories related to metaphor.

3. 1. 1. 1 The classical theory: metaphor as category violation

Since Socrates, philosophers have struggled with the issue concerning how things are categorized in the world and represented in the minds. The ancient Greeks thought that the world is composed of a certain number of primary elements(i. e., fire, earth, air, and water). In ancient China, there is also a thought hold that the substantial world is composed of some definite primary elements(metal, wood, water, fire, and earth). When plato put forward his theory of forms, the field of category was born. However, it was not until aristotle that a more pragmatic science of categorization emerged. The classical theory of categorization began with aristotle and continued into the modern period, and has had deep influence on the development of analytic philosophy or objectivist philosophy (Chapman, 2000). In analytic philosophy, category membership is defined in terms of a theory based on the notion of "substance", which does not "admit of variation of degree", so the basic assumptions of the Classical Theory of categorization are: (1) the world is made up of a definite number of categories; (2) category members have equal status, thus, no members are more central than others; (3) categories have sharp boundaries, which are defined by certain definite common properties.

In this objectivist tradition, concepts by definition exclude all nonobjective influences. Meaning is based on a metaphysical account of reality, which is made up of objectively existing entities with properties and relations among them. Meaning has nothing to do with human being. Consequently, pragmatics — the study of what speakers mean by what they say, is segregated from semantics — the study of meaning. In this view, metaphor, metonymy, and mental imagery are banned from the realm of meaning study (Lakoff, 1987: 165), instead, they are considered as study topic in pragmatics, i. e., the study of speaker's meaning. As semantics is assumed to be central and pragmatics peripheral, semantics must be understood first before pragmatics can be approached. Within this tradition, the essence of metaphor is captured by the notion of violation of selection restriction, thus category mistake (along with compressed simile and forged equation) is considered as the most common definition of metaphor. So a metaphor like "That boy is a pig." can only be interpreted in a sequential manner. Firstly, it is recognized as a semantic anomaly, because "pig" possesses the feature (-Human), a person cannot therefore predict the feature "to be a dog" to belong to an entity (i. e., that boy) which has the feature [+ Human]. Secondly, an alternative nonliteral meaning will be derived to make sense in certain context. This assumption echoes with the comparison model of metaphor comprehension in psycholinguistic study (which will come to the fore in Section 3. 1. 2).

The classical theory of category has served over two millennia of scientific and philosophical research although it eventually proves to be descriptively inadequate. First, as Wittgenstein (1953) points out, it fails to explain categories which can not be defined by using necessary and sufficient conditions. A second major problem with the classical theory is its failure to explain gradient membership in a category (Rosch and Mervis, 1975). A third criticism against the classical theory is its insufficiency in explaining fluidity of human cognition. Although the classical approach to category well maintain the structural stability of a category in that a category by definition always has the same set of properties, it can not account for flexible adaptability of category and human cognition. The reason is that with strictly clear-cut boundaries and membership, categories can not accommodate new, hitherto unfamiliar data and expressions in the changing world(Sloutsky, 2003).

3.1.1.2 The Prototype Theory: Metaphor as Category Extension

Based on a series of case studies in various disciplines①, Eleaneor Rosch(1975) first provided a thorough challenge to the classical theory of categorization, and initially through experimental paradigm established the study of categorization as a subfield of cognitive psychology. In prototype theory, category boundaries are no longer as sharp as assumed in the classical theory. Categories are defined by best members, family resemblances, feature weightings, and central tendencies rather than by criteria attributes. The prototype theory is a major advance over the classical theory, particularly in terms of its ability to deal with the psychological aspects of real-life categorization.

There is now overwhelmingly rich literature documenting the motivation for the shift from the classical theory to the prototype Theory②. Here the present study only provides a brief description with more emphasis on the hypotheses held by the prototype theory towards metaphor. Prototype Theory of categorization is closely related to the Embodiment Philosophy(Lakoff and Johnson, 1999). According to the Embodiment Philosophy, metaphor is regarded as a basic cognitive tool to conceptualize abstract concepts rather than merely a linguistic phenomenon. One of the major challenges to analytic philosophy which asserts that concepts are literal and disembodied is the importance attached to the role played by imaginative processes, especially metaphor, metonymy, mental spaces, etc., in human conceptualization and

---

① These pioneer studies mainly include: Wittgenstein's study on family resemblances (1953) and Austin's study on word meaning (1961) in philosophy, Zadeh's fuzzy set theory (1965 in mathematics and artificial intelligence), and Berlin and Kay's work on basic color terms(1969) in anthropology.

② Readers may refer to Lakoff(1987) for an extensive review on this issue.

reasoning.

In this view, a metaphor is possible in that the metaphor vehicle serves as a category to include the new data or expressions that are termed as the topics. This mechanism is followed by two essential notions of the prototype theory of category. First, categories have fuzzy boundaries so that the vehicle as a category has the potential to accommodate new members denoted by a metaphor topic. Second, membership of a category is gradient rather than binary so that some metaphors can be more apt[①] than others in that some metaphor topics can serve as better members of the category denoted by a metaphor vehicle.

The prototype theory of category has been enjoying great popularity and acceptance in modern cognitive linguistics as this theory has been assumed to keep a great balance between two joint yet seemingly contradictory criteria of a sufficient theory of category and human cognition: structural stability and flexible adaptability(Wu and Chen, 1996, 2004). On the one hand, new entities and new experiences to various degrees can be readily associated to a prototype category, without necessarily causing fundamental reconstructing of the category. That is to say, categories have the tendency to maintain themselves as holistic entities, thus maintaining the overall structure of the category system. On the other hand, categories have dynamic ability to cope with changing conditions and new expressions in the ever-changing world. Thus, as Taylor(1995) points out, the prototype theory of category can better account for human cognition than the classical theory.

3. 1. 1. 3 Summary and comments

As reviewed above, disputes between the two category theories have deep philosophical bases: the classical theory on objectivism, and the prototype theory on subjectivism. What distinguishes the two from each other are different assumptions concerning the role of metaphor in category extension. According to the classical theory, imagery mechanisms such as metaphor, metonymy, and imagination are shut from mechanisms involved in human categorization. However, the prototype theory holds the opposite, regarding metaphor as one of the basic human cognitive

① The notion of aptness will be described in detail in Section 3. 2. 1. 2.

operations. The Classical Theory of category, which can be traced back to Aristotle, is mainly based on priori philosophical assumptions. Although the Prototype Theory, which comes together with what is titled "the second generation of cognitive linguistics", has a commitment to empirical evidence (Lakoff and Johnson, 1999: 79), it has also failed to provide strong empirical evidence to support their own assumptions so far.

In summary, despite their sharply different claims regarding the relation between metaphor and categorization, both sides still need more empirical evidence from psycholinguistic experiments before any disputes between the two approaches get settled.

3.1.2 A psycholinguistic perspective

Based on the widely recognized belief that language comprehension is a reliable reflection of language representation and human cognition, the present study will further review a number of metaphor comprehension models in psycholinguistic study with more weight on various assumptions held by these different models concerning the relation between metaphor and categorization. The analyses in this section hence serve as the very point for further digging the research questions.

3.1.2.1 The comparison model: metaphor as category deviation

The comparison model of metaphor comprehension, echoing with the classical Theory of category in the cognitive linguistic tradition (see 3.1.1.1), assumes that categories have clear-cut boundaries and that metaphors play no roles in category extension, thus metaphors entail a matter of category violation. The origin of the comparison model can be traced back to Aristotle who in his Poetics (1941) assumes that a metaphor such as "A lecture is a sermon." is an emphatic form of the comparison "A lecture is like a sermon." because the category named "sermon" does not conventionally include "lecture" as a member. Contemporary proponents of this view have argued that metaphors are processed in a sequential manner, that is, recognizing the comparison implied by the metaphor is the first step in metaphor comprehension (Malgady and Johnson, 1976; Miller, 1993; Ortony, 1993; Tversky,

1977; Verbrugge and McCarrell, 1977). Since a metaphor has the syntactic form of a literal category assertion, this recognition of the implied comparison coincides with a violation of semantic and syntactic rules (Kats, 1964; Kintsch, 1974) and conventional maxims of communication (Grice, 1975, 1978; Searle, 1979). In this sense, metaphor involves category mistake. Indeed, if taken literally, the statement that "A lecture is a sermon." is "defective" (Searle, 1979), i. e., it does not make sense. Once this category violation has been detected, an active search begins for an alternative, non-literal interpretation that is truthful and informative. A metaphor thus has to be processed in a three-stage process: (1) derive a literal interpretation of the statement; (2) assess the soundness of the literal interpretation given the context of the statement; (3) derive a metaphoric interpretation if the literal one is found to be anomalous or false.

Such indirect processing models of metaphor have largely fallen into huge disputes because a number of empirical studies have failed to support two key predictions of this deviance position. First, if literal interpretations have priority over metaphoric interpretations in terms of processing sequence, then metaphors should require additional processing time over literal statements. However, early studies on metaphor compression mainly found that metaphors often take no longer time to read than literals in sufficient context, (e. g., Inhoff, Lima, and Carroll, 1984; Ortony et al.1978; Shinjo and Myers, 1987). Second, if literal interpretations are obligatory, then metaphoric interpretations should only be sought when literal ones are defective. However, metaphoric meanings are often generated automatically and in parallel with literal meanings (e. g., Gildea and Glucksberg, 1983; Glucksberg, Gildea, and Bookin, 1982; Keysar, 1989).

Besides the sequence issue, the processing issue, i. e., how metaphoric mappings are established between different domains of knowledge is still at the center of many disputes. The Comparison View is that metaphors such as "Time is a river." are understood as implied comparison statements such as "Time is like a river.", which requires the hearer to seek for common properties of the target and the vehicle (e. g., Miller, 1979; Ortony, 1979; Tversky, 1977). The notion that metaphors establish similarity relations between ontologically distinct concepts is highly intuitive due to the facts that it can be traced back to Aristotle's philosophical position and that there is also some empirical support for this position. For example, the degree of similarity between the target and the vehicle has been found to be positively related to the aptness and interpretability of metaphors (Johnson and Malgady, 1979; Malgady and Johnson, 1976; Marschark, Katz, and Paivio, 1983) as well as to the speed of metaphor comprehension (Gentner and Wolff, 1997). The comparison view of metaphor comprehension postulates that metaphors are recognized as implicit similes and understood via a comparison process (Gentner, 1983; Gentner and Wolff, 1997; Miller, 1979; Ortony, 1979, 1993; Verbrugge and McCarrell, 1977). In the same vein with the comparison theory of metaphor, Tversky's contrast model (1977) of similarity judgment proposed a property-matching process: "In judgments of similarity one assumes a particular feature space...and assesses the quality of the match....In the interpretation of similes, one assumes a resemblances... and searches for an interpretation of the erasure space that would maximize the quality of the match."

This property-matching view has been criticized on several grounds. One major criticism concerns property selection. Although this model equates metaphoric meaning with sets of matched properties, not every matched property enters the interpretation of a metaphor. For example, in "A lawyer is a shark.", both "lawyer" and "shark" have the common property of being animate, both can breathe, move, etc., but none of the properties seems relevant to the understanding of the metaphor. A second criticism concerns the issue of asymmetry (directionality) in metaphor processing. That is, as we know, literal comparison is reversible in that the order of the two items should not influence the degree of their property overlapping (e. g. "A lemon is like an orange." →" An orange is like a lemon."). If metaphors are processed through property-matching as literal comparison, then reversed metaphors should also be acceptable. However, reversed metaphor either become nonsensical (e. g. "My lawyer is a shark."→"A shark is my lawyer.") or radically alter the original meaning (e. g. "A surgeon is a butcher."→"A butcher is a surgeon."). Consequently, this argument can only lead us to the conclusion that metaphors can not be the same as literal comparison in terms of processing mechanism.

In light of the criticisms concerning property selection and processing directionality in metaphor processing, Ortony(1979) proposed a salience imbalance mechanism to constrain property matching based on Tversky's(1977) contrast model of similarity. On this view, only common properties that are significantly more salient for the vehicle than for the topic will be recruited into the metaphoric meaning. So metaphor "A lawyer is a shark." only elicits the common properties "vicious" and "aggressive", etc., but not the common properties "animate" and "being able to breathe" because the former properties are of high salience for the vehicle and low salience for the topic, whereas the latter are of low salience for both the items.

Althoughin light of Ortony's salience imbalance hypothesis, there is still a challenge to the property comparison view, i. e., the phenomenon of new information induction. Consider the example "That film is a sermon.", for people who are not familiar with the film, there can not be a priori representation of the concept "that film" that includes properties such as "preachy" or "moralistic". Yet these are exactly the sorts of properties that come to mind upon reading the statement, even the film is not familiar to the reader. On this view, it is impossible to generate a metaphoric meaning by comparing existing properties. Actually, this is the point where a new property attribution account arises, which we will turn to in the following section.

3.1.2.2 The categorization model: metaphor as category retrieval

In view of the criticisms against the comparison view, glucksberg and colleagues (Glucksberg and keysar, 1990; glucksberg, McGlone, and Manfredi, 1997) propose that metaphors can not be processed as comparisons. Instead, they are understood as what they literally appear — category inclusion statements, with the metaphor vehicle serving as a name for the superordinate category to which the topic is assigned. Consequently, metaphors, just as literal category assertion, are processed in a direct manner through retrieving preexisting categorical senses. In the example "A lawyer is a shark.", the metaphor vehicle(shark) is used to refer to a superordinate category (predatory and vicious creatures) within which the metaphor topic (a lawyer) is included. The categorization model of metaphor comprehension echoes with the theory of ad hoc category(Barsalou, 1983), which asserts that the category exemplified by a metaphor vehicle has vague boundaries, and that metaphors are one major source of newly created categories.

An important aspect of the categorization model of metaphor is its supposition that the vehicle has dual reference at two levels of abstraction (Glucksberg, 2001: 64). In the "lawyer-shark" example, the vehicle term "shark" has dual reference, i. e., it can be used at the concrete literal level to denote the marine fish shark or at the abstract metaphorical level to denote the category of "predatory, ferocious creatures" exemplified by the literal term "shark". Dual reference is not unique to figurative language, but is instead a common communicative strategy. Virtually every concrete noun has at least two related meanings, one referring to an exemplar (e. g., "The dog barked at her boss.") or an individual referent, and one referring to a class or an generic referent (e. g., "A beagle is a dog.") (Murphy, 1997). Another striking example comes from words which represent brand names, for example, Jeep, a special design of one sort of vehicles, is commonly used to refer to a superordinate category, e. g., all vehicles that have similar design with Jeep products. The dual reference property is also especially useful in classifier languages, such as the American Sign Language which do not have names for superordinate categories, but have basic level names which can serve as prototypes of a category (Glucksberg, 2001). In such languages, the nameless superordinate category can still be referred to through a word used to represent the overall category. Even in English, not all categories have lexicalized names of their own, in which case a noun referring to a prototypical member of the class can be used to refer to the superordinate category as a whole (as in the Jeep example above). In Glucksberg and Keysar's another example "My job is a jail." (1990), the vehicle "jail" is considered to be a prototypical member of the class of "restrictive and unpleasant situations", and it can therefore be successfully employed to name the superordinate category of such confining places or circumstances to which the topic "job" belongs.

According to Glucksberg (2001), dual reference of a metaphor vehicle can be created on the fly, through ad hoc categorization. The analysis of ad hoc categories comes from the work of the cognitive psychologist Lawrence Barsalou (1983, 1987). Ad hoc categories like "things to sell at a garage sale" and "things to take on a camping trip" are spontaneously generated categories that are up to fulfill some goal.

On this view, ad hoc category is not the result of metaphor comprehension, but rather the starting point of it.

As for the processing mechanism, the categorization model, in contrast to the comparison model, asserts that metaphor comprehension involves property attribution (Glucksberg and Keysar, 1990; Glucksberg, McGlone, and Manfredi, 1997) rather than property matching. Two important criteria determine the attributing process (Glucksberg, 2001). One criterion is that there is a superordinate category specified by dual reference to which the vehicle term refers. The other criterion is the relevance of that superordinate category's prototypical properties to the topic, which is a function of the interaction between the vehicle attributes and the constraining topic dimensions. The second representational assumption assigns different roles to the vehicle and topic terms, with the vehicle yielding properties to be attributed to the topic and the topic yielding the relevant dimensions to receive these attributes. Again in the "lawyer-shark" metaphor, the topic "lawyers" provides different relevant dimensions such as competence, reputation and cost. The vehicle shark provides candidate properties such as vicious, predatory, which can be attributed to the topic. In this regard, it is the interaction between the topic and vehicle that determines the property attribution process.

The categorization model can explain some basic phenomena in metaphor comprehension which the comparison model fails to. First, for property selection, because the target concept is never actually compared with the literal base concept, there is no need to explain why not every property shared by the target and base is relevant to the meaning of the metaphor. Second, for the direction of paraphrasibility, it can explain why similes can be paraphrased as metaphors (e.g., "Some ideas are like diamonds." → "Some ideas are diamonds."), but literal comparisons cannot be paraphrased as category assertions (e.g., "Lemons are like oranges." →? "Lemons are oranges."). In literal comparisons, the two concepts are at the same level of abstractness and belong to the same category, e.g., both lemons and oranges are oranges. As the predicate term does not have any other level of abstraction beyond its literal referent, paraphrasing such a comparison as a categorization statement is not permissible. In metaphorical assertions, however, the vehicle refers to both the literal and the abstract referents, which allows for paraphrases of metaphors as similes and those of similes as metaphors. Third, irreversibility of metaphor can also be explained, as metaphor topic and vehicle are at the same level of abstractness, the relationship between the two is like that in literal class-inclusion relation, which, by definition, is not symmetrical. Fourth, new property attribution can be explained through the fact that properties of metaphor vehicles, as in literal category assertion, are automatically inherited by subordinate concepts.

Nevertheless, the categorization model also has some problems. Firstly, as Bowdle and Gentner (2005) claim, the categorization model seems to place unreasonable demands on a hearer's mental capacity. That is, many base concepts can suggest a potentially unlimited number of ad hoc categories. For example, in the metaphor "Youth is a snowflake.", the ad hoc categories that might reasonably be evoked by the concept "snowflake" would include not only "things that are unique" and "things that are ephemeral" but also "things that are delicate" "things that are white" "things that are wintry" "things that fall gently from the sky", and "things that accumulate to change the landscape". During comprehension, the hearer would have to generate and maintain all of these metaphoric categories (as well as the initial base concept) while the topic concept is scanned for dimensions of applicability. Once the relevant category has been selected, all competing categories would then have to be suppressed. In summary, most phenomena in metaphor comprehension can be explained in the framework of the categorization model, yet it seemingly puts unreasonably burden on human general cognition.

Secondly and more seriously, this ad hoc view of categorization in metaphor comprehension is at bigger risk of circular-reasoning in explaining the distinct roles played by the topic and the vehicle (Vega Moremo, 2007: 70): "metaphor interpretation begins and ends at the same point: with the metaphor topic and the dimensions provided by it. This leads to the conclusion that the processes of property selection, category construction and property attribution which form the basis of the class iInclusion model are ultimately dependent on the constraints imposed by the topic, that is, on the dimensions it provides and how relevant those dimensions are to interpretation."

Take "Youth is a snowflake." again as an example, as described above, there are an unlimited number of ad hoc categories that can be evoked in the vehicle, yet a trickier problem is the fact that there are also an unlimited number of so-called dimensions that can be simultaneously provided by the topic. The problem is how a listener can arrive at the proper one among all of these dimensions. In this regard, the categorization model seems to offer an account of the roles of the topic and the vehicle in a circular-determining fashion, i. e., the dimensions of the topic are determined by the vehicle, while the attributable properties are determined by the dimensions provided by the topic. This drawback has been attacked by many other scholars, which leads to the proposal of alternative models.

3. 1. 2. 3 The career model: a hybrid account

Basing their theoretical analyses on analogical reasoning, Bowdle and Gentner (2005) propose an evolutionary path in metaphor comprehension. This hypothesis — the career of metaphor postulates a shift in mode of mapping from comparison to categorization as metaphors are conventionalized. The career model hypothesis intends to offer a hybrid theoretical framework that can resolve the debates between the comparison and the categorization models of metaphor. This account posits whether metaphors are processed directly or indirectly and whether they operate at a literal, basic level or a superordinate category are constrained both by the vehicles' degree of conventionality and the linguistic form of the whole comparison. Degree of conventionality determines the semantic property of the metaphor vehicle. Metaphor vehicles can also have dual referents. Nevertheless, in contrast to the categorization model which assumes that dual reference is an innate property of metaphor vehicle, the career model posits that dual reference results from an evolutionary development of the metaphor vehicle — conventionalization, which is due to repeated use of the metaphor vehicle. Conventionalization as a process is shown in Figure 3. 1.

This hypothesis suggests that novel and conventional metaphors have computational distinctions in comprehension. Novel metaphors involve vehicle terms that refer to a domain-specific concept but have not yet acquired a domain-general, superordinate category. Novel metaphors thus are interpreted as comparisons, in which the target concept is structurally aligned with the literal base concept. In contrast,

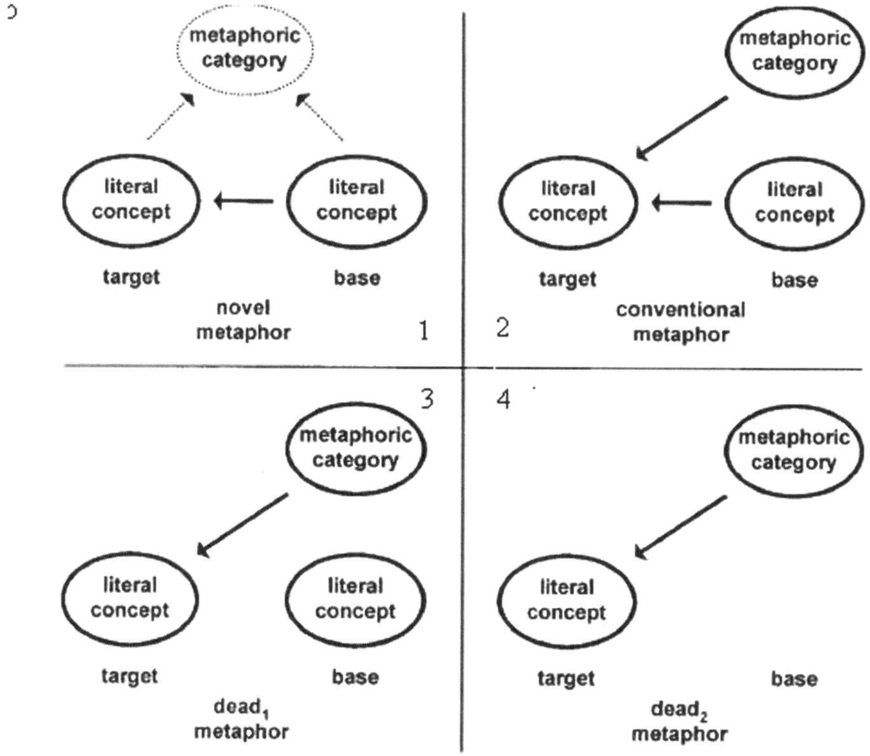

Figure 3.1 The career of metaphor(Taken from Bowdle and Gentner, 2005: 209. Numbers added by the author of the present book)

conventional metaphors involve base terms that refer both to a literal concept and to an associated metaphoric category. For example, the conventional base term "blueprint"(as in"A gene is a blueprint.") has two closely related senses:"a blue and white photographic print in showing an architect's plan" and "any thing that provides a plan". Conventional base terms thus are polysemous, with the literal and metaphoric meanings semantically linked because of their similarity. Conventional metaphors may therefore be interpreted either as comparisons, by matching the target concept with the literal base concept, or as categorizations, by seeing the target concept as a member of the superordinate metaphoric category named by the base term.

Consequently, the comprehending directness issue depends on both metaphor conventionality and linguistic from, which is referred by Gentner and Bowdle as

"Grammatical concordance"① in metaphor comprehension(2001:233).

Table 3. 1 effect of vehicle conventionality and grammatical form on processing mode: grammatical concordance

vehicle conventionality	*types of tropes*	*grammatical form*	*processing mode*
novel	metaphor	comparison	indirect
novel	simile	comparison	direct
conventional	metaphor	categorization	direct
conventional	simile	comparison	direct

As shown in Table 3. 1, novel figuratives, no matter in the metaphor form or the simile form, can only be interpreted as comparisons because novel base terms refer only to a domain-specific concept. Therefore, novel similes are comprehended directly because similes have the same form as literal comparisons which invite a comparison comprehension mechanism. However, novel metaphors are comprehended in an indirect manner because, with the same form as literal category assertion, they will invite a search for an established domain-general sense which does not yet exist. This will lead to a garden-path phenomenon in the hearer. As for conventional figuratives, they will always be comprehended directly, no matter in metaphor form or simile form. The reason is that as conventionalized, the metaphor vehicle has got dual reference. In a conventional metaphor, the domain-general sense is activated, while the literal domain-general sense is suppressed. However, the situation is the opposite in a conventional simile, with domain-general sense activated and literal domain-general sense suppressed.

Although the career model seems more powerful and comprehensive, it is not free from problems. Firstly, it only accounts for the categorization process in the

① grammatical concordance is referred to as the link between grammatical form and function in metaphor comprehension. More specifically, as metaphors are grammatically identical to literal categorization statements and similes are grammatically identical to literal comparison statements, based on the assumption that linguistic form typically follows function in language comprehension, metaphors and similes will promote different comprehension strategies. That is to say, metaphors should invite classifying the target as a member of the category named by the base term; whereas similes should invite comparing the target to the base.

vehicle, failing to explain the more basic categorization phenomenon in metaphor. That is, how the topic and the vehicle get categorically associated still remains a problem. The second problem is somewhat related to the first one: as the model merely focuses on the function of the vehicle in the categorical processing of metaphor, it ignores the role of the topic.

3.1.2.4 Summary and comments

From a review of major metaphor comprehension models, we can see that the comparison model and the categorization model do not take variation and diversity of metaphor into account, which is taken by the career model as the reasons for most experimental contradictory findings. Much empirical evidence has shown that metaphor comprehension can not be explained in a comprehensive manner merely through one single model.

The author assumes that in asserting metaphors are always comprehended through comparison, the comparison model fails to account for the semantic change phenomenon in metaphor use (Sweetser, 1990). Similarly, in asserting that the metaphors are always comprehended through categorization via the innate dual reference of the vehicle, the categorization model also fails to explain diachronical semantic change in metaphor on the one hand (ibid.), and more seriously, falls into circular reasoning in explaining the roles of the topic and the vehicle in metaphor comprehension on the other. Although the career model, which posits that the metaphor vehicle eventually undergoes a semantic change (conventionalization) through repeated use, seems to provide a solution to this problem, it neglects the interactive relation between the topic and vehicle. Given that conventionality merely denotes the vehicle and aptness denotes the relation between the topic and the vehicle, the author assumes that the career model neglects the role of the topic in explaining the categorical relation between the topic and the vehicle by asserting conventionality sufficiently determines metaphor comprehension. Most of the theoretical and methodological disputes arising out of related fields have been around these two factors — vehicle conventionality and metaphor aptness. Unfortunately, it was not until recent years that the two factors had drawn due attention in psycholinguistic studies, and what were brought by these studies were even more controversies rather than settled answers. Specifically, when experimentally developing the three major metaphor models we just discussed above, the researchers didn't take the two factors simultaneously into account. Those experiments manipulated neither of the two factors (Glucksberg and Keysar, 1990; Glucksberg et al., 1997) or just manipulated one factor without controlling the other (Bowdle and Gentner, 2005). In fact, Bowdle and Gentner discovered in a post-test that their conventional items were more apt than their novel items, thus indicating that they had inadvertently confounded conventionality and aptness (more detailed review will be presented in the following section). In light of all these controversies and disputes, the present study attempts to improve the relevant studies, and hopefully to get a more proper understanding of the relation between metaphor and category.

3.2 Studies on metaphorical categorization

As shown in Section 3.1, researchers have always been trying to explain category misjuxtaposition in metaphors through examining the relation between metaphor and category. This section is devoted to a review into previous studies on metaphorical categorization. More specifically, this section is organized as follows. Previous studies on the mediator of metaphorical categorization are clarified in Section 3.2.1. Then in Section 3.2.2 the author reviews previous empirical investigations into the measurement of the category inclusion relationship between the topic and the vehicle. The explorations into the categorizing process are provided in Section 3.2.3.

3.2.1 Mediator of metaphorical categorization

It is now commonly accepted that the syntactical acceptance of the category-inclusion form of "An x is a y." in a metaphor is the result of the process of metaphorical categorization whereby the topic and the vehicle undergo a recategorization process and join a parent superordinate category. In this view, constraints on the acceptability of the metaphor form versus the simile form of the topic and vehicle comparison can be considered as the mediators of metaphorical categorization. In fact, various metaphor models have proposed distinct constraints: vehicle conventionality, aptness and interpretive diversity. As these constraints in concern have distinct significantly theoretical implications to metaphorical categorization, it is necessary to have a closer look at both the theoretical and empirical studies in related fields.

3.2.1.1 Conventionality

As a general term in the literature of metaphor studies, "conventionality" is defined differently yet not contradictorily in cognitive linguistics and psycholinguistics. In cognitive linguistics literature, conventional metaphors are generally defined as phrases that exist at some point between literal and metaphorical uses. Conventionalization reflects a dynamical process whereby an expression that was originally metaphorical becomes established as literal within a language. As Lakoff and Turner (1989: 55) put it, a metaphor is conventionalized "to the extent that it is automatic, effortless, and generally established as a mode of thought among members of a linguistic community". These arguments have the following corollaries. Firstly, conventionality is obtained through a diachronic process. As Goatly (1997: 2) claims that conventionalization is a cyclical process through which active metaphors progressively become inactive and eventually die and become fossilized. Secondly, conventionality is a matter of continuum rather than a dichotomy. That is to say, a metaphor can be more or less conventional. On the scale of conventionality, Goatly (ibid: 31–35) distinguishes between dead metaphors (also termed homonyms), inactive metaphors (also termed polysemes) and active metaphors that use an unconventional vehicle. Apart from the terminology, Goatly's classification is no different from Black's classification in which metaphors are termed as extinct, dormant and active ones (Black, 1993). Thirdly, conventionality is closely related to the notion of metaphoricity. Based on the classifications put forward by the above-mentioned scholars, we can see that conventionalized metaphors can eventually "die" and become polysemous in nature. This means that conventionalization is usually applied to refer to reduction in metaphoricity of a metaphor. Fourthly, conventionality is related to cognitive effort in metaphor processing. It is generally accepted that conventionalization results in a reduction of semantic tension, and in turn, a reduction of cognitive effort in comprehension.

In psycholinguistic research field, conventionality is also taken as a central concept. As reviewed in Section 3. 1. 2. 3, the career model takes conventionality as the sufficient mediator for a shift in metaphor comprehending mechanism and the sufficient determinant of metaphor-simile distinction①. Conventionality is generally referred to as "the strength of association between a metaphor vehicle and its figurative meaning" (Bowdle and Gentner, 1997, 2005; Gentner and Wolff, 1997; Giora, 1997; Wolff and Gentner, 2000). Novel metaphors involve "vehicles that refer to domain-specific concepts, but are not (yet) associated with domain general categories". In contrast, conventional metaphors involve "vehicles that refer both to literal concepts and to associated metaphoric categories" (Gentner and Bowdle, 2001: 229). The more a term is used metaphorically, the more conventional it becomes. In this sense, vehicle conventionality results from repeated metaphorical usage with various topics.

The present study will generally follow the definition of vehicle conventionality in psycholinguistic literature of metaphor comprehension, i. e., "the strength of association between a metaphor vehicle and its figurative meaning or a domain general category". Besides the four conventionality-relevant notions proposed by cognitive linguistic approaches (see above), there is another important notion proposed by psycholinguistics, that is, vehicle conventionalization accompanies increase of abstractness of vehicle referent. As noted by Bowdle and Gentner (2005), conventionalization leads to an acquisition of "domain-general sense" or "abstract category" in the vehicle.

3. 2. 1. 2 Aptness

In cognitive linguistics literature, aptness of metaphors is generally referred to as how well a metaphor structures or reflects human embodied experience, as Lakoff (1999:72) points out: "The very notion of aptness of a metaphorical concept requires an embodied realism. Aptness depends on basic-level experience and upon a realistic body-based understanding of our environment."

In psycholinguistics literature, aptness is also a much studied concept. In

① A detailed description of related empirical studies can be found in Section 3. 2. 2

contrast to the career model which contends that conventionality is the sufficient determinant of metaphor-simile distinction, a number of research (Glucksberg, 2003; Jones and Estes, 2005, 2006) posit that aptness serves as the sufficient determinant of the categorical form of comparison①.

Aptness of a metaphor is generally defined as "the extent to which the metaphor statement captures important features of the topic" (Chiappe et al., 2003: 97), or "how well the metaphor expresses its specific nonliteral meaning" (Blasko and Connine, 1993: 297). Glucksberg (2001: 48) posits that apt metaphors are produced when prototypical members of metaphorical categories are used with appropriate topics. In defining "prototypicality" in metaphor vehicle, Glucksberg explains that the goal-directed ad hoc categories evoked by the vehicle term, as a special case of functional categories, have graded structure as well. That is, as ordinary categories, ad hoc categories also have prototypical effects. That is, members in ad hoc categories can also have different degrees of membership, and some members can be more typical than others. Take the example provided by Glucksberg (ibid, 48), "gold" is the prototypical member of the category of rare and valuable things, while "platinum", although more costly and even rarer than gold, is not a typical member of that category. Prototype effect of a metaphor vehicle in the corresponding ad hoc category can be a result of vehicle conventionalization. But it should be noted that a novel vehicle can also be the prototypical member of the category that has just been created de novo.

Following this argument, novel vehicles can also create apt metaphors. Take the metaphors "A library is a goldmine." and "A library is a platinum mine." for example, compared with "goldmine", the vehicle "platinum" is relatively newly created and used. Nevertheless, "platinum" can also aptly describe the important features of the topic "library".

As for how metaphor vehicles can be appropriate, Glucksberg explains that it depends on whether the metaphor describes the "good parts" of the topic, which, as Glucksberg points out, are functionally important to the topic. For example, the wing

① A detailed description of related empirical studies can be found in Section 3. 2. 2

is the good part for a plane; yet the floor is not. In summary, aptness thus differs from conventionality in that it takes both the vehicle and the topic into account; whereas conventionality pertains to the vehicle only.

According to Glucksberg(2003), for a metaphor to be apt, two conditions must be met. First, the vehicle term must have a salient property for attribution. This salience can result from either conventionalization or prototype effect. For a certain vehicle, that property is strongly associated with the term as the result of repeated use (i.e., the vehicle is conventional). But novel vehicles which are prototypical exemplar of the ad hoc category can also have salient property to attribute. The second condition of aptness is that the salient property of the vehicle must be relevant to the topic. Thus it is the interaction between topic and vehicle that is crucial for aptness, which is taken as the key factor distinguishing aptness from conventionality.

3.2.1.3 Interpretive diversity

Instead of conventionality and aptness, a more recent study (Utsumi, 2007) argued that interpretive diversity can better explain the categorical relation between the topic and the vehicle. According to Utsumi(idid: 292), interpretive diversity is referred to as "the semantic richness of the figurative interpretation of a topic-vehicle pair"and is determined by "both the number of features involved in the interpretation and the uniformity of salience distribution of those features". According to Utsumi's study, more interpretively diverse metaphoric topics and vehicle pairs were predicted to be more preferable to comprehend via a categorization process. Two experiments were conducted to test the hypothesis. It was revealed that interpretive diversity was correlated positively with metaphor preference(Experiment 1) and was also correlated positively with metaphor comprehensibility(Experiment 2).

Through explicitly asserting that it is interpretive diversity rather than aptness or conventionality that determines categorization in metaphor comprehension, Utsumi's study argues that interpretive diversity is a fully independent notion, having nothing to do with aptness or conventionality. We assume this argument gives rise to one serious drawback of the study: there was a big possibility that the interpretive diversity in concern has been confounded with the aptness concept in previous psycholinguistic studies. The point is, although the study, based on a series of very complex statistical processes including multiple regression analyses and a commonality analysis, finally successfully confirmed that interpretive diversity is more important in explaining metaphor preference than aptness and conventionality, it failed to draw a clear-cut conclusion concerning the relation among the three factors, i. e., interpretive diversity, aptness and conventionality. We believe that the suspected confounding of the three factors is a fatal problem. Firstly, the study failed to fully capture the most important aspect of the notion of aptness — the interaction between the topic and vehicle. In manipulating aptness based on rating, the subjects were just instructed to rate "how apt each metaphor or simile was" on a 7-point scale. We suspect that this instruction, whose generality and vagueness differ it from very specific ones in other previous studies on aptness (Chiappe and Kennedy, 1999; Chiappe, Kennedy and Chiappe, 2003; Jones and Estes, 2005, 2006), failed to arouse the subjects' attention on the core sense of aptness, i. e., explicitly taking both metaphor topic and vehicle into account. As Utsumi's study defined interpretive diversity of metaphor as "the semantic richness of the figurative interpretation of a topic-vehicle pair", it highly deserves suspicion that aptness and interpretive diversity may share the same essence of metaphor property, i. e., topic-vehicle interaction as a pair. Unfortunately, that study didn't take the notion of topic-vehicle pair into fully account in operationalizing this key aptness variable. As a result, the study could reach no more than a rather unsatisfactory, vague conclusion (ibid: 300): "vehicle conventionality does not lose its role as a supplementary source of metaphor preference; the conventionality view (the career of metaphor view) seems somewhat plausible. The aptness view is less plausible, but aptness functions as enhancement of diversity's or conventionality's effects on metaphor..."

It is assumed that such vagueness in this conclusion may result from several drawbacks apart from the technical failure in manipulating aptness. For one thing, it might be caused by one more serious theoretical drawback in that study — the research neither had a closer insight into the broader theoretical framework underlying the interpretive diversity nor made any attempt to integrate its findings with the two relatively well established models of metaphor comprehension. For another, as Utsumi himself pointed out, the study just took grammatical form preference and comprehensibility rating as its research paradigms, failing to capture the on-line information of metaphor comprehension. In fact the author admitted the weakness of these off-line measures of processing by asserting "the two experiments ...thus did not provide sufficient evidence for my argument about processing difference(ibid: 303)".

3.2.1.4 Comments and theoretical reflections

As discussed in this section, there have been a number of studies conducted to examine potential mediators which determine the juxtaposition of the metaphor topic and the vehicle in a categorizing form. Recall that juxtaposition of metaphor topic and vehicle in a categorization fashion reflects metaphorical categorization, it is of great theoretical significance to find out what exactly determines the categorical relation between the topic and the vehicle, i.e., what mediates metaphorical categorization, more operationally, what can serve as an explanation for the preference for metaphor form over simile form.

All the three factors reviewed previously are not theoretically adequate to capture the nature of the true mediator of metaphorical categorization. As for the notion of conventionality, there are several problems. First, we assume that conventionality of the vehicle can only be considered as an indicator of the association strength between the vehicle and the abstract categorical referent, rather than the motivator of this kind of association. Second, the argument that conventionality is created over time as a result of repeated use of the same vehicle paired with various topics gives rise to one problem: what motivates such repeated use? That is to say, there must be certain other underlying factor(s) that motivate the repeated use which leads to conventionalization(Zharikov and Gentner ,2002).

With regard to the argument that aptness sufficiently determines preference for metaphor form, we don't assume that it is exempt from the same pitfalls as those with the notion of conventionality. Aptness per se as a property of metaphor has a rather vague definition. Recalling that aptness is defined as "the extent to which the metaphor statement captures important features of the topic" (Chiappe, Kennedy and Chiappe, 2003: 97), a question arises here, i.e., what constitute(s) the important features of the topic? As any concept has countless properties, it seems that the notion of aptness can only become meaningful when we figure out what constitute(s) the important features, and how they are identified. In this line of argument, we conclude that aptness in its own right can not be taken as an irreducible, sufficient mediator of metaphorical categorization.

We assume that interpretive diversity is not free from problems either. Recall that interpretive diversity is referred to as "the semantic richness of the figurative interpretation of a topic-vehicle pair" and is determined by "both the number of features involved in the interpretation and the uniformity of salience distribution of those features"; it has the similar drawbacks as those with the notion of aptness. That is, it fails to account for what features are recruited for metaphor interpretation, and how they are identified.

In conclusion, all the three previously proposed factors can not be taken as the sufficient mediator of metaphorical categorization. First, the three notions are just superficial in that they can all be further reduced to other more deeply underlying factors. Second, although all the previously proposed factors unanimously rely on the notion "feature" for further definition, all the proponents of the three proposals did not depict what feature(s), among numerous others, can be recruited as the mediator of metaphorical categorization. Third, previous proposals have also failed to account for the underlying mechanism by which the critical features are identified and selected.

3.2.2 Measuring metaphorical categorization: experimental paradigms and major findings

So far there have been a considerable number of experimental studies on the extent to which a metaphor is comprehended through what a metaphor literally appears — category inclusion. The following is a review of major experimental paradigms and the corresponding findings in related studies. A critical evaluation is also provided.

3.2.2.1 Comprehension time recording and comprehensibility rating

Comprehension time and comprehensibility rating have been taken as indicators for a shift in metaphor comprehension in the psycholinguistic studies of metaphor comprehension. In one earlier study conducted to investigate the influence of conventionality on metaphor comprehension (Blank, 1988), subjects' comprehension time of high and low conventional metaphors were recorded and analyzed. The results indicated that conventional metaphors were comprehended faster than novel metaphors. Similar research and analysis methods were adopted in some recent studies (Gentner and Bowdle, 2001; Bowdle and Gentner, 2005) and similar results came out, further indicating that conventionality determines metaphor comprehension mode.

Similar research methods were adopted in a series of recent studies on aptness, but the results were at odds with the findings that conventionality mediates metaphor comprehension. In these studies, levels of aptness were controlled, and subjects were asked to interpret each metaphor and rate degree of comprehensibility. Results showed that apt metaphors were comprehended faster than unapt ones and that apt metaphors got higher comprehensibility rating scores (Chiappe, Kennedy and Chiappe, 2003; Gagne, 2002). In contrast to the studies on the influence of conventionality, these findings failed to support the career model which claims that it is conventionality that sufficiently determines metaphorical categorization.

To eliminate the possible confounding effect of conventionality and aptness in these early studies, a recent study (Jones and Estes, 2006) simultaneously manipulated these two factors. Researchers controlled conventionality by varying the vehicle concepts — some vehicles were novel and some were conventional, and manipulated aptness by varying the topic for each metaphor. Comprehension time and comprehensibility ratings were recorded. Researchers used a 2 (conventionality: conventional, novel) ×2 (aptness: high, low) ×2 (form: metaphor, simile) within-subjects design. As predicted by the notion of grammatical concordance (Bowdle and Gentner, 2005:202), conventional metaphors should be understood quickly and easily because conventional vehicles are processed categorically and metaphors have a categorical form. Novel similes should also be understood quickly and easily because novel vehicles induce comparison and similes have a comparative form. But for conventional similes and novel metaphors, their grammatical forms are contrary to their presumed processing tendency. That is, a conventional simile has the form of a comparative statement, but its conventionality evokes categorical processing (and vice versa for novel metaphors). Thus, the career model predicts an interaction between grammatical form and conventionality.

Alternatively, the categorization model (Glucksberg and McGlone, 1997, 1999) predicts that apt items should be comprehended faster and easier than unapt items, regardless of their conventionality and grammatical form (i. e., a main effect of aptness). Their experimental results showed that the prediction of the career model was unsupported, that is, conventionality did not mediate metaphorical processing. First, the interaction between conventionality and grammatical form was nonsignificant in both the comprehension time and comprehensibility analyses. Second, comprehension times were approximately equivalent for the conventional metaphors and the conventional similes. The main effect of conventionality was not significant in the ease ratings ($F_{p(1,59)} = 0.71$, $p = 0.40$ and $F_{i(1,124)} = 0.30$, $p = 0.58$), and in the comprehension times it was significant only in the participant analysis ($F_{p(1,59)} = 5.57$, $p < 0.05$ and $F_{i(1,124)} = 1.58$, $p = 0.21$). Given the importance of conventionality for the career model of metaphor, this grammatical concordance effect in the participant analysis was examined more closely. Conventional similes were comprehended faster than novel similes ($F_{p(1,59)} = 4.61$, $p < 0.05$), but conventional and novel metaphors were comprehended equally fast ($F_{p(1,59)} = 1.48$, $p = 0.23$). Thus, the effect of conventionality held only for the similes, only in comprehension times, and only in the participant analysis. Essentially, there was no evidence that conventionality predicts metaphor comprehension. This study failed to replicate the result of Bowdle and Gentner (2005), which showed a main effect of conventionality. Instead, this finding suggests that Bowdle and Gentner's result was more likely attributable to aptness than to conventionality. Stronger evidence supporting the categorization in the same experiment showed that aptness facilitated both the speed and the ease of comprehension. The main effect of aptness was highly significant in the analyses of both comprehension times ($F_{p(1,59)} = 77.05$, $p < 0.001$ and $F_{i(1,124)} = 34.88$, $p < 0.001$) and ease-of-interpretation ratings ($F_{p(1,59)} = 121.14$, $p < 0.001$ and $F_{i(1,124)} = 57.69$, $p < 0.001$). All in all, the results indicated that aptness mediated metaphor comprehension.

Although the studies reviewed above showed that metaphors vary in comprehension speed and comprehensibility, we can not draw any conclusion from all the above studies as to whether metaphors are comprehended through categorization per se due to the lack of evidence showing that categorization is really comprehended faster and more easily than comparison.

3. 2. 2. 2 Grammatical form preference rating

The experimental paradigm of grammatical form preference rating has been traditionally used in the psycholinguistic studies of metaphor-simile distinction. According to the notion grammatical concordance in figurative and literal language①, grammatical form typically follows function in both literal and figurative language, metaphors(having the same grammatical form as literal category assertion) and similes (having the same grammatical form as literal comparison assertion) may tend to promote different comprehension strategies. Specifically, metaphors invite classifying the target as a member of a category named by the base, whereas similes invite comparing the target to the base.

A number of experiments (Bowdle and Gentner, 2005; Gentner and Bowdle, 2001; Nakamoto and Kusumi, 2004; Zharikov and Gentner, 2002) tested this prediction by giving subjects novel and conventional figurative statements in the two grammatical forms and asking them to indicate which grammatical form they preferred for each statement. Results generally show the grammatical form preference ratings were higher for conventional figurative statements than for novel figurative statements. In other words, subjects found the metaphor form more acceptable for the conventional figuratives.

All the above studies released evidence supporting the career model which asserts that conventionality mediates metaphor comprehension. Yet other studies (ChiappeandKennedy, 1999; Chiappe, Kennedy, and Smykowski, 2003; Utsumi and Kuwabara, 2005) using the same experimental methods had contradictory findings, indicating that the grammatical form preference ratings were higher for apt figurative statements than for apt figurative statements.

A more recent study(Jones and Estes, 2006: Experiment 1) with conventionality

---

① Readers may refer back to 3. 1. 2. 3 where a detailed description of this notion is provided.

and aptness both manipulated and adopted this grammatical form preference paradigm to further clarify which factor was responsible for a mechanism shift in metaphor comprehension. The experiment yielded evidence showing that aptness mediates metaphor comprehension. Specifically, categorical preference was actually lower for the conventional items(M = 3.33, SE = 0.11) than the novel items(M = 3.51, SE = 0.12), $F_{p(1, 47)} = 12.61$, $p = 0.001$ and $F_{i(1, 124)} = 0.97$, $p = 0.33$. The result was therefore opposite to that of Bowdle and Gentner (2005, Experiment1), whose stimulus set confounded aptness with conventionality. In contrast, the results showed that metaphor preference was greater for high apt items(M = 3.57, SE = 0.12) than for low apt items(M = 3.27, SE = 0.13), $F_{p(1, 47)} = 13.07$, $p = 0.001$ and $F_{i(1, 124)} = 2.71$, $p = 0.10$. That is, aptness rather than conventionality predicted metaphor preference, so the career model was again unsupported.

3.2.2.3 Category membership rating

To directly test the career model, in a series of experiments, Jones and Estes (2005, 2006) initially introduced a category membership rating task to measure metaphorical processing. The logic is as follows: if metaphor comprehension does entail a categorization process, then the presence of the metaphorical prime (e.g., "The librarian is a mouse.") should increase the probability that the topic concept (i.e., librarian) is categorized as a member of the vehicle category(i.e., mouse). In addition, if the career model is right in that categorization results from conventionalization, then a conventional metaphor prime will result in higher rate for metaphor form than a novel metaphor prime. If the categorization model is right, which asserts that metaphors are always processed through categorization mechanism, then various levels of conventionality will not lead to different ratings.

In Experiment 2 in Jones and Estes's study (2005), participants were first exposed to either a literal or figurative prime, each having the same subject and predicate. The figurative primes were grouped into conventional metaphors and novel metaphors. For example, participants read either the metaphor prime "That librarian is a mouse." or the literal prime "That librarian saw a mouse.". Immediately following the prime, participants judged the extent to which the topic(e.g., that librarian) was a member of the vehicle category (e.g., mouse). A 3-alternative forced-choice methodology was used to assess class inclusion, in which "partial member" was included in addition to the "nonmember" and "full member" response options. The experiment used 16 high conventional and 16 low conventional (i. e., novel) metaphors taken from Gentner and Wolff's study (1997) as metaphorical primes. Results showed that the topic concept was reliably more likely to be judged as a member of the vehicle category following a metaphorical prime than following a literal prime, and both novel and conventional metaphors reliably induce categorization, but conventional metaphors reliably have higher rating than novel metaphors. These results could definitely speak for neither the career model nor the categorization model. One possible reason may be the fact that the experiment did not simultaneously manipulate the conventionality and aptness. The results could be confounded by the two factors.

In another experiment (Jones and Estes, 2005: Experiment 2), the same category membership rating task was adopted to determine whether the metaphor-induced categorization effect was truly due to metaphor comprehension (i. e., attributive categorization), or whether it extends to any prime with nominal structure (i. e., borderline literal) or to any nonsensical metaphorical prime (i. e., scrambled metaphor). The participants were randomly assigned to either a primed or an unprimed condition. In the primed condition, they read sentences containing the exemplar and category as the subject and predicate, respectively, before making the category judgment on a 7-point scale. This study yielded findings that replicated those of Experiment 1, indicating that the topic concepts were reliably more likely to be included in the vehicle categories when preceded by a metaphorical prime than when unprimed. This metaphor-induced categorization held for both conventional and novel metaphors and critically demonstrated that metaphor increases categorization. However, in a post test it was discovered that conventionality and aptness were confounded in that item set, then a re-analysis of the data was conducted with aptness as a covariate, and the effect of conventionality at that time disappeared. In contrast to Experiment 1 of Jones and Estes' study (2005), these findings seemed to support the categorization model.

In a third experiment having the same procedures as Experiment 2 of Jones and Estes' study (2005) with the exception that they manipulated aptness instead of conventionality, consistent evidence was again obtained: the topic concepts were reliably more likely to be included in the vehicle categories when preceded by a metaphorical prime than when unprimed. This metaphor-induced categorization held for both the apt and the unapt metaphors, and critically demonstrated that metaphor increases categorization for even the less apt metaphors (e. g., A forest is a harp.). However, aptness mediated the categorical processing of metaphors (Chiappe and Kennedy, 1999; Chiappe, Kennedy and Chiappe, 2003; Glucksberg, 2003), as this effect was reliably greater for the highly apt metaphors than for the less apt metaphors. The borderline literal primes (e. g., A jet ski is a boat.) again failed to increase category membership, once more demonstrating that the categorical structure of the prime sentences was insufficient by itself to induce categorization. The failure of the scrambled metaphor (e. g., An exam is a mouse.) primes for increasing class inclusion provides further evidence that the attributive categorization process is specific to sensible metaphors. In short, all the three experiments obtained a significant influence of aptness on metaphorical categorization, without supporting the career model.

A more resent experiment (Jones and Estes, 2006: Experiment 3) with a manipulation of both the two factors adopted the same category membership rating task to further investigate the potential mediator of categorization in metaphor comprehension. The experiment had a 2 (conventionality) × 2 (aptness) within-participant design. The results showed that category ratings were equivalent between the conventional ($M=2.98$, SE=0.19) and novel metaphors ($M=3.03$, SE=0.20), $F_{p(1,30)}=0.45$, $p=0.51$ and $F_{i(1,124)}=0.08$, $p=0.78$. The researchers concluded that conventionality exerted no effect on categorical processing, and hence the career of metaphor was not supported. On the other hand, category membership ratings were higher for the high apt ($M=3.63$, SE=0.20) than for the low apt metaphors ($M=2.38$, SE=0.19), $F_{p(1,30)}=133.69$, $p<0.001$ and $F_{i(1,124)}=55.86$, $p<0.001$. Furthermore, this effect of aptness was consistent across the novel and conventional metaphors, as evidenced by the lack of an interaction between conventionality and aptness, $F_{p(1,30)}=1.35$, $p=0.26$ and $F_{i(1,124)}=0.25$, $p=0.62$. Clearly, these results indicate that aptness rather than conventionality predicted categorical processing.

3.2.2.4 Comments and critiques

From the empirical studies reviewed above, we can see that the issue concerning the categorical relationship between the metaphor topic and the vehicle and the potential factors mediating it has attracted huge attention in related studies. Studies yielded mixed evidence as to the true mediator of the process of metaphorical categorization. The author assumes that most of the empirical controversies arise out of some drawbacks in terms of both theoretical and methodological concerns.

The first problem is related to the manipulation of linguistic materials. As reviewed above, earlier empirical studies on which the categorization model and the career model built their theoretical framework generally didn't simultaneously manipulate conventionality and aptness in terms of both theoretical assumptions and methodological designs. As a result, there have been huge disputes concerning which factor is the potential mediator of categorization in metaphor. So far, only one study (Jones and Estes, 2006) attempted to systematically control these two factors. Therefore, we can not reach any conclusions based on the studies due to the failure in manipulating conventionality and aptness simultaneously.

The second major weakness in available empirical evidence is the fact that the experimental tasks adopted have some disadvantages. In the first place, although several comprehension time studies yielded results showing that conventional metaphors were comprehended faster than novel metaphors, or apt metaphors were comprehended faster than less apt metaphors, these findings can only be taken as effective evidence for different processing mechanisms between comparison and categorization if one assumes that category statements are definitely comprehended faster and easier than comparison statements. As there has been no definite evidence so far showing that category statements are comprehended definitely faster and easier than comparison statements, findings from such experiments can not serve as evidence for a shift in comprehension mechanisms. More seriously, it is increasingly recognized that comprehension time itself is far from a sufficient measure of different processing mechanisms, as equivalent processing times do not necessarily indicate equivalent processing effort or mechanism because of possibly different amounts of cognitive resources allocated. Since studies on the impacts of metaphor aptness and conventionality are based on the underlying assumption that the two factors may lead to qualitatively different processing mechanisms, results concerning comprehension times can not serve as sufficient evidence. In the second place, the experimental task of category membership rating after reading a metaphor is merely an off-line judgment which does not directly reflect real-time categorization process, so the judgment can be affected by contaminations resulting from explicit consciousness of the category inclusion task rather than the implicit categorizing mechanism in metaphor comprehension itself. That is to say, this task may arouse the subjects' explicit consciousness of the task of "categorizing" the topic into the vehicle. Consequently, the subjects may be forced to have an explicit categorization process according to the experimental task requirement. For example, after reading a metaphor "A lawyer is a shark.", the subjects were asked to rate on a 7-point scale under the instruction "to what extent the topic lawyer is a member of the category named by the vehicle shark". We suspect that the explicit categorization instruction will undermine the validity of the task because, on the one hand, the subjects have no choice to show their preference for a comparison process even they have such comparison tendency; on the other hand, the subjects' judgments can be influenced by the explicit categorizing instructions rather than the real metaphor comprehension process.

The third threat to previous studies is their failure to provide direct evidence showing a real qualitative shift in metaphor comprehension mechanism — from comparison to categorization per se. In this sense, no direct evidence has showed that metaphor topic and vehicle are in a category inclusion relation. Firstly, it must be noted that, in grammatical form preference experiment (Jones and Estes, 2006: Exp 1), although the rating score for categorical form (i. e., metaphor) was indeed greater for highly apt statements than for less apt statements, it should be noted that even those highly apt statements were below the scalar midpoint of "4" ($M = 3.57$, $SE = 0.12$ on a 7-point scale, ranging from one extreme "1" representing comparison to another "7" representing categorization). In the same vein, in a category membership rating experiment (Jones and Estes, 2006: Exp 2), ratings were indeed higher for apt metaphors than for unapt metaphors, but again the highest ratings were below the scalar midpoint ($M = 3.63$, $SE = 0.20$). Thus, it can only be concluded from these experiments that there is just a tendency for categorization resulted from conventionalization and aptness, but not categorical processing per se. This suggests that, although certain kinds of metaphors are more likely to be processed through categorization than the other kinds, both groups of statements were actually more preferred in the comparative form(i. e., simile). Thus, this source of evidence can not be taken as fully supportive for the categorization shift in metaphor processing.

Furthermore, a couple of latest neuroimage studies on the impact of conventionality on metaphor comprehension (Coney and Lange, 2006; Arzouan, et al., 2007a, 2007b) showed that novel metaphors and conventional metaphors are processed differently in terms of component amplitudes and scalp distributions. However, these studies also suffered from some drawbacks. On the one hand, these studies may have confounded the two variables; on the other hand and more importantly, the experimental stimuli adopted in that study were, rather than metaphors in category form (i. e., An x is a y.), two-word expressions in the language of Hebrew denoting conventional metaphoric expressions (e. g., transparent intention), novel metaphors (e. g., ripe dream), semantically related words (e. g., burning fire), and unrelated words (e. g., wisdom wash). As a result, without an valid comparison between the two-word expressions and literal category statement, it is again impossible to reach a strong conclusion that metaphors are processed through categorization per se. In summary, whether there is a qualitative shift from comparative processing to categorical processing per se still remains an unsettled issue.

3.2.3 The process of metaphorical categorization: gestalt transformation

Recently, Xu (2008) proposed a mechanism termed gestalt transformation to account for how metaphor topic and metaphor vehicle get categorically associated.

As shown in Figure 3.2, according to Xu's proposal, metaphor topic x and vehicle y conventionally belong to two distinct categories respectively denoted by X and Y, and there is no conventional relation between x and y, so the juxtaposition of x

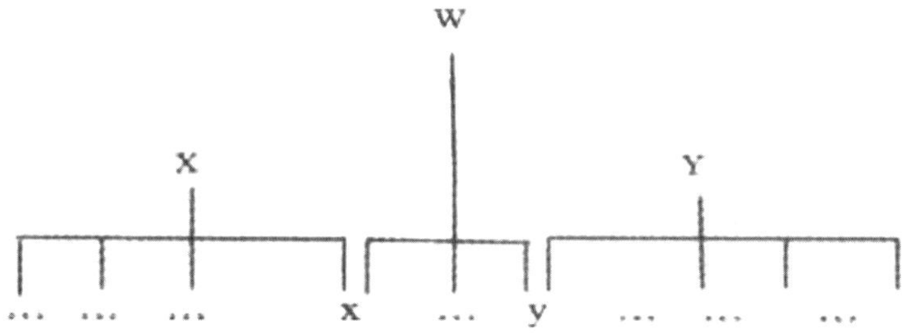

Figure 3.2 xu's account for metaphorical category(Xu,2008: 5)

and y via be in a category inclusion manner is conventionally regarded as a sort of category violation, which is considered to be the source of the "tension" in metaphor use. Yet, x and y can get categorically connected by a process termed gestalt transformation. When describing suchf kind of gestalt transformation more specifically, Xu takes the notion of abstract similarities between the topic and vehicle as the mediator of this transformation process. That is, x and y can leap over the conventional boundaries of the categories X and Y and get into a more abstract subordinate category W based on more abstract commonalities. Since both x and y become the subcategories of the same superordinate category W, they will both inherit the denotations and connotation of W. Henceforth, metaphorical "An x is y." can convey certain meanings.

Although Xu's theoretical exploration made significant contributions to our understanding of why metaphorical category inclusion statement is possible, it is not free from some drawbacks. As Xu himself pointed out (2008: 7), there are three problems remaining unsettled. First, how is it felicitous to juxtapose x and y in a categorical inclusion relation by using "be"? Second, what properties (commonalities or similarities) are identified in metaphor processing? Third, what is the relation between x and y? Besides the three problems, we argue that there is still another aspect that further studies should keep going on to explore. That is, the cognitive mechanism underlying the shared property identification should be more fully accounted for. Another problem with Xu's study is the fact that it is merely based on a theoretically introspective investigation without empirical verification. Consequently, the argued proposal still needs further empirical test.

3.3 Remaining problems

Based on the literature review, it is found that previous studies on metaphorical categorization leave one core question unsettled, i. e., how is it possible to put two concepts from distinct conventional categories in a categorical juxtaposition and still make sense? This question consists of five specific aspects:

The first aspect is concerned with what serves as the mediator of the categorical relation between the topic and the vehicle? Previous models have proposed various factors for this issue, including conventionality, aptness and interpretive diversity. We assume none of the three factors is of sufficient explanatory power in that they are all reducible to some other more deeply underlying factors. This study will take similarity as a fuller account(More detailed discussion is provided in Section 4.2.).

The second aspect and the third aspect are combinarily concerned with the core dynamic process of metaphorical categorization. That is, themechanism in which the metaphor topic and the vehicle get recruited in one superordinate category and the mechanism in which the vehicle become so abstract that it can include the topic as a category member. Existing competing models of metaphor are actually based on different assumptions concerning levels of abstractness of metaphor vehicle. The comparison model(Miller, 1979; Ortony, 1979; Tversky, 1977) argues that metaphor vehicles can not acquire abstract categorical reference, so they are always at the same abstractness level with the topics. In this view, metaphors can only be comprehended via comparison through the pragmatic three-stage processing. The categorization model (Glucksberg and Keysar, 1990), on the contrary, argues that metaphor vehicles inherently reach a higher abstractness level on the fly from the outset of metaphor processing, and that metaphors are processed via categorization—including the topic as a member of the ad hoc category denoted by the vehicle, so the properties of the subordinate category can be attributed to the topic. The career model(Gentner and Bowdle, 2001; Bowdle and Gentner, 2005) posits that the gaining of categorical reference in the vehicle is the result of conventionalization. The three models differ from each other with regard to the time-course of the categorization in the vehicle, yet no studies have so far offered on-line evidence as to the time-course of categorization in the vehicle. And more importantly, no studies have attempted to offer a unified account for the cognitive mechanism underlying the categorization of the vehicle. In this regard, the present study will rely on the notion of schema-induction for a better explanation (More details are offered in Section 4. 3.).

The fourth aspect is about potential constraints on the felicity of juxtaposing the topic and the vehicle in a categorizing fashion. As reviewed above, there could be some constraints on the categorical relation between the metaphor topic and the vehicle. Previous studies only showed that the category inclusion relation between the topic and the vehicle is just a matter of degree, and few studies investigated the potential constraints on the degree to which the topic is included in the vehicle.

Fifth, existing off-line evidence only shows that metaphor merely has the tendency to be comprehended via categorization, but not definitely through categorization per se. A comprehensive study on metaphorical categorization should investigate the potential differences between metaphorical categorization and conventional categorization.

In the following chapter, we will turn to the research framework of the present study in which the remaining problems are better outlined and the working hypothesis is proposed.

Chapter 4 Research framework

A detailed literature review and a summary of the major remaining problems in related research fields lead the study to its central research question, i. e., what is the cognitive mechanism underlying metaphorical categorization? More specifically, five aspects of this categorization process are to be investigated: (1) the mediator of the categorical relation between the topic and the vehicle; (2) the mechanism in which the topic and the vehicle get recruited into a common superordinate category; (3) the mechanism in which the vehicle obtains an abstract categorical referent; (4) The constraints on the justification of juxtaposing the metaphor topic and the vehicle in a categorical inclusion statement; and (5) the potential qualitative difference (s) between metaphorical categorization and conventional categorization.

More research is desirable to inquire into these five specific aspects of metaphorical categorization. For this purpose, a general research framework needs to be worked out. This chapter is intended to present such a framework. It embarks on five specific research questions (Section 4.1). Then it provides the theoretical framework in which the general hypothesis is put forward (Section 4.2). In Section 4.3, the working hypothesis is proposed. And finally in Section 4.4, the general empirical research design is depicted.

4.1 Research questions

In line with the remaining problems concerning metaphorical categorization discussed in the literature review section, five major research questions (henceforth referred to as "Q") are raised:

Q1: What serves as the mediator of metaphorical categorization?

Q2: How do the metaphor topic and the vehicle get categorically related?

Q3: How does the metaphor vehicle dynamically obtains an abstract categorical referent?

Q3 can be specified as two sub-questions:

Q3a: What is the characteristic of the time course in which the metaphor vehicle obtains an abstract categorical referent in the course of metaphor processing?

Q3b: What is the characteristic of the process in which the metaphor vehicle dynamically obtains an abstract categorical referent in a vitro diachronical setting?

Q4: What are the potential constraints on the category inclusion relation between the topic and the vehicle?

4.2 Theoretical framework

In order to seek answers to the five research questions, the author relys on the analogy theory as the general theoretical framework. More specifically, relational similarity theory and schema induction mechanism are taken as the theoretical analysis framework.

4.2.1 Mediator of metaphorical categorization: similarity

As reviewed in Section 3.2.1, conventionality, aptness and interpretive diversity all have some serious drawbacks in their explanatory power as the sufficient mediator of metaphorical categorization. All the three proposals failed to account for what features can be recruited as the mediator of the categorical relationship between the topic and the vehicle, and more importantly how. The anthor argues that a sufficient theory of metaphorical categorization has to give a fuller explanation in these two distinct yet related aspects.

In line with most cognitive approaches to categorization, we turn to the notion of similarity for better accounts. Similarity is an important construct in cognitive science. It has been recognized that similarity plays a central role in research on categorization (e.g., Medin and Schaffer, 1978; Nosofsky, 1986) and induction (e.g., Quine,

1981; Sloman, 1993; Xia, 2010). For instance, prototype theories of categorization posit that categorization decisions are made on the basis of the similarity of an entity to the prototypical member of that category(Rosch,1975).

Studies on similarity and categorization in the past few decades have yielded a series of significant findings pertaining to the cognitive mechanism which more comprehensively describes what similarity features are judged and more importantly how. These findings can actually account for the advantage in taking similarity as the mediator of metaphorical categorization over other mediators we have reviewed. For example, in his seminal work (Tversky, 1977), Tversky offered the contrast model, in which the process of similarity judgment is accounted for through a process of matching the features of the target and the vehicle. The comparison standard is taken to be based on the resulting number of individual shared and unshared features. Generally speaking, the more shared features and the fewer unshared features exist, the higher the judged similarity. Recall that in the field of metaphor study, this model has been adopted to explain metaphorical similarity(see section 3. 1. 2. 1). As the auther reviewed, due to its many drawbacks, this model has mainly fallen out of favor in the study of similarity.

More recent research move beyond the original focus on individual features and emphasize the importance of relational structures that hold between these features. The structure-mapping theory (Gentner, 1983; Gentner and Markman, 1997) and its computational model, SME (the structure-mapping engine) (Falkenhaine, Forbus, and Gentner, 1989; Forbus, Gentner, and Law, 1995) provide a more insightful theoretical framework in which the identification of structural similarity can be accounted for. This dessertation argues that these theories would better serve as the mediator of metaphorical categorization①.

The author posits that it is the nature of similarity that underlies the three previously proposed determinants of metaphorical categorization, i. e., conventionality, aptness and interpretive diversity. First, it can explain the motivation of the process of conventionalization, i. e., only those senses of the vehicles denoting

① A detailed argument for the validity of taking relational similarity as the mediator of metaphorical categorization is offered in Section 4. 2. 2.

relational similarity have the chance to be repeatedly used over time till get conventionalized. Second, aptness of a metaphor can rely on types of similarity between the topic and the vehicle. Recall that aptness is usually defined as "the extent to which the metaphor statement captures important features of the topic" (Chiappe et al., 2003:97). The important features of the topic, as Glucksberg(2001: 48) points out, are functionally important to the topic. According to Gentner's study, the function of a certain object naturally involves the relation between itself and other objects. Actually, it has been found that a major determinant of aptness in metaphor is the presence of a substantial relational match (Gentner and Clement, 1988; Clement and Gentner, 1991). In this line of argument, aptness of a metaphor can be accounted for by the mechanism in which structural similarity is detected. Third, as for the notion of interpretive diversity ,i. e., "the semantic richness of the figurative interpretation of a topic vehicle pair" as defined by Utsumi (2007), the author also posits that it can be accounted for by structural similarity theory. In fact, previous studies have indicated that types of similarity can determine the depth or richness of metaphor interpretation(Zharikov and Gentner, 2002). To sum up, the present study takes similarity as the mediator of metaphorical categorization.

4. 2. 2 Attributive similarity vs. relational similarity

Similarity is viewed as central to categorization, which includes metaphorical categorization with no exception. In general, similarity can be described in terms of two types of information: individual features and structural relations among these features. The literature of similarity is notoriously rich with terminology pertaining to these two various types of similarity, and there is even lack of consistency in the use of terminology by the same researchers across various publications in the same period of their research career[①]. The present study, following the tradition held by the study of categorization in cognitive science, adopts the most commonly used terminology "attributive similarity" vs. "relational similarity".

Of the two proposals concerning types of similarity, perceptual or attributive features make more intuitive contribution. That is, the more independent features two things share in common, the more similar they are usually considered. This intuition is initially theoretically formalized in the contrast model of similarity(Tversky, 1977; also see Section 3. 1. 2. 1), which construes the similarity of two concepts as a function of their common features weighed against their distinctive features. Similarity increases as the number of commonalities increases or the number of differences decreases. Actually, the comparison model of metaphor comprehension (found in Section 3. 1. 2. 1) echoes with this account. However, a number of important studies have discovered that perceptual features alone are not sufficient for determining similarity and that human's sense of similarity is more influenced by common relational structure held between features rather than mere perceptual features.

In contrast to the notion that similarity merely resides in perceptual commonality, it is increasingly recognized that "abstract relation(s)" take(s) the upper hand in determining similarity and thus categorization. Generally, the abstract relation has two layers of meanings. Firstly, identifying similarity or the categorizing process depends on the abstract relation between certain "internal" individual features. This notion can be demonstrated directly and explicitly by some classic empirical studies. For example, consider the pairs of geometric forms taken from one prior experiment done by scholars in 1978(Holyoak, Gentner, and Kokinov, 2001:3).(see Figure 4. 1)

---

① For example, among many others, there are overall, concrete or object similarity vs. relational similarity by Loewenstein and Gentner (2005); surface, literal similarity vs. deep, relational similarity by Gentner and Kurts(2001); intrinsic similarity vs. extrinsic similarity by Barr and Caplan(1987); direct or element similarity vs. structure similarity by Holyoak(2004); and structural vs. superficial similarity by Blanchette and Dunbar(2000).

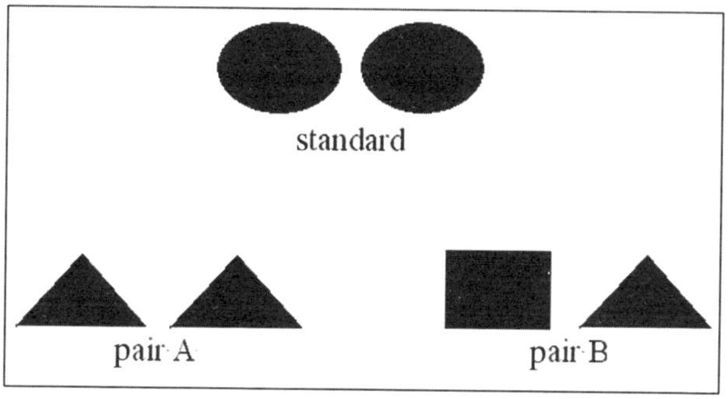

Figure 4. 1 relational similarity illustrated by premack
(cited from Holyoak, Gentner and Kokinov, 2001: 3)

As shown in Figure 4. 1, it is obvious that pair A is similar to the standard pair in a way in which pair B is not. In fact, pair A is judged to be more similar to the standard rather than to pair B. This phenomenon can not be explained through the feature-based notion of similarity because pair A at least has a shared perceptual feature, i. e., a triangle, with pair B, while having no identical features with the standard at all. That is to say, if similarity merely resides in perceptual features, then pair A and B should be considered to be more similar than pair A and the standard. However, the experiment findings showed that pair A and the standard are considered to be in the same category.

A serious theoretical question arises here: what is the similarity that mediates pair A and the standard pair? It does not reside in the physical, perceptual forms, which do not overlap at all. Rather, it abstractly resides in the relation between the two triangles in pair A and the relation between the two circles in the standard. That is, both the two pairs contain the same abstract relation "sameness of shapes".

A second account of the abstract relational similarity relies on the abstract relation between a certain object and certain "external" objects. This notion can be illustrated by Goswami's study(1995).(see Figure 4.2)

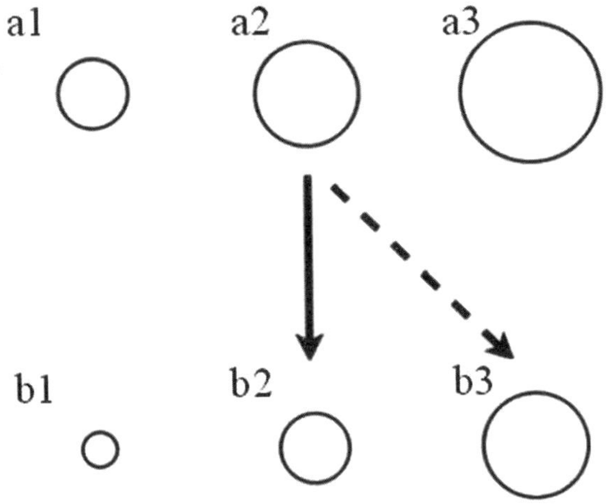

Figure 4. 2 relational similarity illustrated by Goswami(1995)

As shown in Figure 4. 2, the circle in the middle of the top row (a2) is considered to be equally similar to two of the circles(b2 and b3) in the lower row as indicated by the arrows. On the one hand, the dashed arrow shows a literal similarity mapping where a2 is mapped onto b3 merely based on the perceptual feature of "size". On the other hand, the full arrow shows that the relational cross-mapping where object perceptual identity is ignored and the similarity are based on the "relational" size of the objects. In the same vein, when categorizing, the subjects tend to take a1 and b1, a3 and b3 as three categories respectively. Goswami's study empirically demonstrated that the perception of the "relational" size tacitly weighs over the mere perceptual size even for 4-year-olds.

In light of the drawbacks of the feature-based similarity theory, the structural relation model(Bassok and Holyoak, 1989; Gentner and Markman, 1997; Haun and Call, 2009; Leech, Mareschal and Richard, 2008) posits that concepts are structured representations that encode features as well as the relations among the features(i. e., structural relations). A striking notion of structural relation model which differs it from feature matching comparison theories is that the key similarities tacitly reside in the relations that hold within two conceptual domains rather than concrete features held within individual objects.

4. 2. 3 Schema induction as categorization

As to the nature of the dynamic process of categorization in metaphor, the present study attributes it to the process of schema induction in analogical reasoning which is mainly based on the mapping of relational similarity between the topic and the vehicle.

Schema has been an important notion in cognitive linguistics. Johnson(1987:29) defines schema as follows: "A schema consists of a small number of parts and relations, by virtue of which it can structure infinitely many perceptions, images, and events. In sum, image schemata operate at a level of mental organization that falls between abstract propositional structures on the one side and particular concrete images on the other."

A schema is a recurrent representative pattern, shape and regularity of the ongoing experiences in life. To understand the notion of schema, several points should be borne in mind.First, schemas are dynamic rather than static in nature. Second, schemas have the gestalt properties. That is, although they may contain components and relations among components, their meanings could only be interpreted at the level of the whole. Third, as Lakoff(1987:456) proposes, schemas are the basis for abstract reasoning and the mechanism in which abstract concepts are represented. Categorization is often interpreted as an abstract representation that captures what the instances have in common. This study refers to such abstract representation as schema. A schema might specify the number of exemplars. Once a schema has been acquired, it can support several kinds of inferences. A schema can be used to make predictions about hidden aspects of the examples already observed.

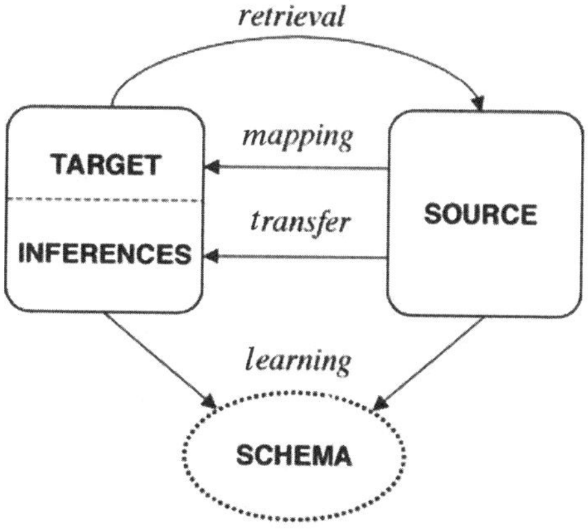

Figure 4. 3 schema inductions in analogical reasoning

As for the induction process of a schema in metaphor processing, This study mainly relys on Holyoak's argument for the schematic learning in comparison (2004). (see Figure 4.3)

As depicted in the diagram above, in acomparison(e. g., man-wolf), the target analog(e. g., man) initially provides certain meaningful retrieval cue for a potential source analog (e. g., wolf), then a structure mapping or a set of systematic correspondences that serve to align the elements of the source and target is established. On the basis of the mapping between structural relations, new inferences about the target could be developed, by which the whole analogical reasoning convey some new information. What is of more significance for human cognition is the fact that based on such analogical reasoning about a pair of analogs, some form of relational generalization may take place, yielding a more abstract schema for a category of situations, in which the source and the target are both included. This induction of the abstract representations paves the way for the schema, which can be applied for incoming new experiences in life. This process has been mainly regarded as the basic mechanism of learning.

As to the schema induction in comparison, there have developed two proposals at two levels, i. e., a macro-level which addresses the whole shared relation and a micro-level which addresses individual arguments involved in the relation. First, according to earlier studies on schema induction in analogy (Gick and Holyoak, 1983), at the macro-level, schematic category relations will be formed between whole systems that contain similar relations, rather than the component terms. Take the analogy cub: bear; kitten: cat as an example, the macro-category addresses the broader structural relation animal development, as cub to bear and kitten to cat both exemplify the relation animal development. Consequently, this level describes categorization of the whole systems (e. g., the cub-bear system and the kitten-cat system) rather than categorization of the individual component terms (e. g., cub and kitten) that make up these systems.

At the micro-level, a distinct yet non con icting hypothesis proposed recently is that, in addition to occurring at the macro-level of structural relations, schema induction also occurs at the micro-level within the individual arguments involved in the common relations (Green et al., 2006a, 2006b, 2008). The micro-level account is so termed because it addresses the small-scale abstraction of individual components or argument terms or elements within the larger-scale aligned relational schemas in the process of analogical mapping. A series of empirical studies (ibid) have indicated that category relations between aligned terms that play similar roles become spontaneously activated during analofgical mapping. Also borrow the analogy cub: bear; kitten: cat as an example, the micro-level category addresses the individual elements involved in the structure alignment. As a result, though cub and kitten can also be defined in numerous other categories, in the current structural alignment animal development, they will be definitely defined in the ad hoc category young animal in a de novo fashion.

It is vitally noteworthy to point out that, according to Green et al. (2008), the micro-level account does not argue against the macro-level account. Rather, it introduces an additional level of induction into the analogy process. In asserting the relation between the two categorizations, Green et al. (ibid) posit that any completely serial account, in which micro-categorization is completed before macro-level categorization begins, is overtly simplistic. It is more likely that there is a feed-back, feed-forward relationship between the two processes of categorization at the micro- and macro-levels during the analogy process.

4.3 Working hypotheses

4.3.1 An analogical approach to metaphor categorization

As discussed above, this study hypothetically takes an analogical approach to metaphorical categorization. For the sake of a better presentation, the author would like to develop the theoretical framework in a flowchart as shown in Figure 4.4.

As shown in Figure 4.4, the relation between metaphor and categorization is shown in the upper part of the flowchart. Metaphor comprehension begins as category violation since metaphor topic and vehicle conventionally belong to two distinct categories (as shown on the upper left corner), which serves as the source of the tension in metaphor comprehension, i. e., metaphoricity. Nevertheless, such categorical misjuxtaposition conveyed by metaphor can still make sense based on the

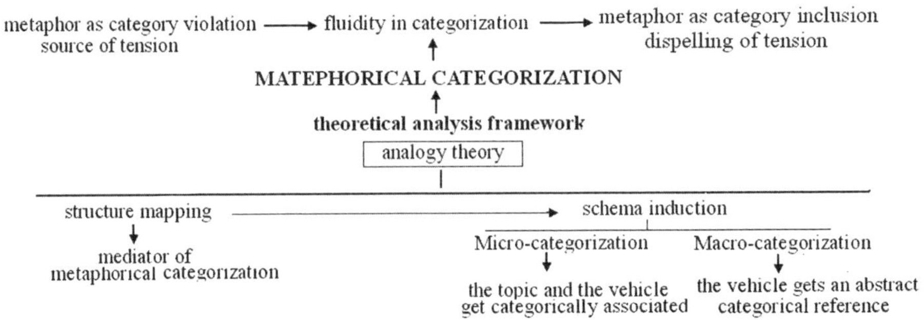

Figure 4.4 Theoretical analysis framework of the present book

dispelling of the tension (as shown on the upper right corner). The author assumes that the dispelling process can be accounted for through fluidity of categorization (as shown in the middle of the upper flow).

The account for fluidity in categorization leads to the core concept of the present study, that is, metaphorical categorization (as shown by the bold capitalized words in the center of the flowchart). Based on this argument, metaphorical categorization can serve as an explanation for two significant theoretical issues. On the one hand, why metaphors are possible can be better accounted for; on the other hand, the fluid nature of categorization can be better explained.

As shown in the center of the flowchart, the present study takes analogy theory as the major theoretical analysis framework (as shown in the rectangle right below the core concept metaphorical categorization). More specifically, analogy theory consists of two aspects (as indicated by the thick line in the middle). In the first place, analogy between the metaphor topic and the vehicle is based on structure mapping. Thus it is structural relational similarity that mediates the categorical relation between the topic and the vehicle. In the second place, the structure mapping between the topic and the vehicle gives rise to the induction of two abstract schemas, which accounts for the core dynamic process of metaphorical categorization.

In sum, as to the issue of the identification of categorization mediator, the author relys on the relational similarity between the topic and the vehicle. Such identification process is based on the mechanism of structure mapping between the topic and vehicle. As to the categorization process per se, the author relys on the mechanism of schema induction.

4.3.2 The dual-categorization account of metaphor

As discussed above, since metaphor can be justifiably studied in the framework of analogical reasoning, the present study attempts to adopt a combined approach to metaphorical categorization which is based on schema induction. As discussed in 4.2.3, schema induction in analogy is processed at two layers. Thus we also take this approach to account for metaphorical categorization. Hopefully, two aspects of schema induction (i.e., categorization) in metaphor can be better explained in such a hybrid account of categorization. This framework, tentatively entitled as "the dual-categorization account of metaphor", is depicted diagrammatically in Figure 4.5:

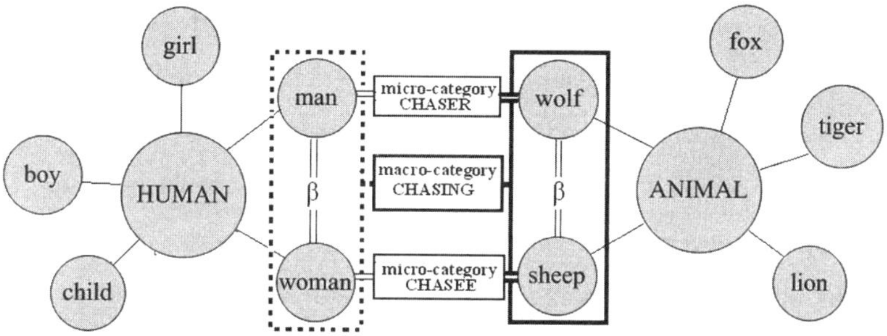

Figure 4.5 The dual-categorization account of metaphor

Specifically, such a dual account has the following central ideas.

On the one hand, as to metaphoricity which is generally considered to be the result of the tension in metaphorical category juxtaposition, it is assumed to be due to the fact that the metaphor topic and vehicle conventionally belong to two distinct categories. As shown in Figure 4.5, for the famous metaphor "A man is a wolf.", "man" and "wolf" are respectively included in two distinct conventional superordinate categories, i.e., human and animal as denoted in the two biggest circles in the diagram.

On the other hand, as to the dispelling of the tension arising from the misjuxtaposition of category, it is assumed to be the result of a recategorization which the topic and the vehicle undergo in the course of metaphor processing. That is, as shown in the diagram, the topic (e. g., "man") and the vehicle (e. g., "wolf") undergo a metaphorical categorization and leap over the boundaries of the conventional categories human and animal) and are included in one shared superordinate category (CHASER). Specifically, echoing with the five research questions raised for the present study (see 4.2), the author develops the following four sub-hypotheses (henceforth referred to as "Sub-H").

Sub-H1 (echoing with Q1): Identification of the mediator of the recategorization relies on structure-mapping between the topic and the vehicle. Thus, the similarity between the topic and vehicle resides in the relations in which the topic and the vehicle are connected with objects other than themselves, as indicated by the two βs in the two rectangles, rather than the perceptual features. In the man-wolf example, "man" and "wolf" are not similar in a perceptual way, but they have similar structural relations with other objects, namely, "woman" and "sheep", that is, in the analogy man: woman; wolf: sheep, man chases woman as wolf chases sheep.

Sub-H2 (echoing with Q2 and Q3): With regard to the recategorization process per se, the author argues that it is the by-product of the schema induction based on structure-mapping between the topic and the vehicle. Schemas are formed at two levels. At the micro level, echoing with Q2, the individual arguments involved in the matched relations which play similar roles form categories. As demonstrated in the micro-category in the diagram, "man" and "wolf" will form the category CHASER, while "woman" and "sheep" form CHASEE. The capitalized letters denoting the category names indicate that the categories are more abstract and may have not lexicalized yet. At the macro level, echoing with Q3, a schema denoting the abstract shared relation is induced, as indicated by the rectangle denoting the macro-category in the middle of the diagram. That is, the relation between "man" and "woman" and the relation between "wolf" and "sheep" can be included in the same category CHASING. As the vehicle is used as the predicate in metaphor language, the vehicle will get associated with the abstract relation, thus giving rise to the abstraction of the vehicle(as indicated by the bold rectangle)[①]. It should be noted here that the capitalized letters indicate that the category may have not been lexicalized.

As to the schema induction which is proposed as the basic mechanism concerning the categorical relationship establishment, the author argues that the essential characteristic of this process is dynamicity.

Sub-H3(echoing with Q4): As the category association occurs at two levels, there should be two potential constraints on the category inclusion relation between the topic and the vehicle. On the one hand, the category relation at the micro-level should be strong enough, i.e., the strength of the categorical relation between the topic and the vehicle should reach a certain level. On the other hand, the category relation at the macro-level should be strong enough, i.e., the strength of the relation between the vehicle and the relational category should also reach a certain level. The present dissertation operationally defines the category relations at the two levels as metaphor aptness and vehicle conventionality respectively, thus these two factors would combinarily influence the category inclusion relation between the topic and the vehicle.

Sub-H4(echoing with Q5): There should be difference(s) between conventional category relation and metaphorical category relation. That is to say, the topic(e.g., "man") and the vehicle(e.g., "woman") conventionally belong to two distinct categories, i.e., human and animal respectively. When they are juxtaposed in a category inclusion fashion(as in a metaphor), there arises metaphoricity or tension of metaphor interpretation. It is assumed assume that such tension could be accounted for by the processing difference(s) (either quantitatively or qualitatively, or both) between conventional categorization and metaphorical categorization.

Besides the four sub-hypotheses, it is still vital to point out that in actual metaphor use and interpretation, the recruitment of particular individual participants in a common relation is open-ended. That is, in the man-wolf example, besides the man: woman; wolf: sheep analysis, it is also possible to recruit among numerous

① In contrast, the dashed rectangle on the left indicates that the macro-category does not usually get associated with the topic(e.g., man) in that the topic serves as the subject in a metaphor and does not provide new information.

other potential interpretations (e. g., man: money; wolf: prey) due to differences in cultural background or encyclopedic knowledge, etc. What is emphasized here is the point that it is certain shared relation that determines the nature of the similarity between the topic and the vehicle.

The author argues arguethat this hypothetical account has relatively larger explanatory power concerning several aspects of metaphorical categorization: firstly, the mediator of recategorization is better accounted for; secondly, the mechanism underlying the categorization process per se is more comprehensively depicted; thirdly, the dynamicity of metaphorical categorization is more fully accounted for.

4.4 Empirical research design

In this section we turn to the empirical research design of the present study. As discussed in 4.3, this study adopts analogy theory as the general hypothesis for metaphorical categorization.

In the general theoretical framework, four sub-hypotheses are developed to seek the answers to the five research questions. For the sake of a better presentation, we put forward the empirical research design in the flowchart shown in Figuare 4.6.

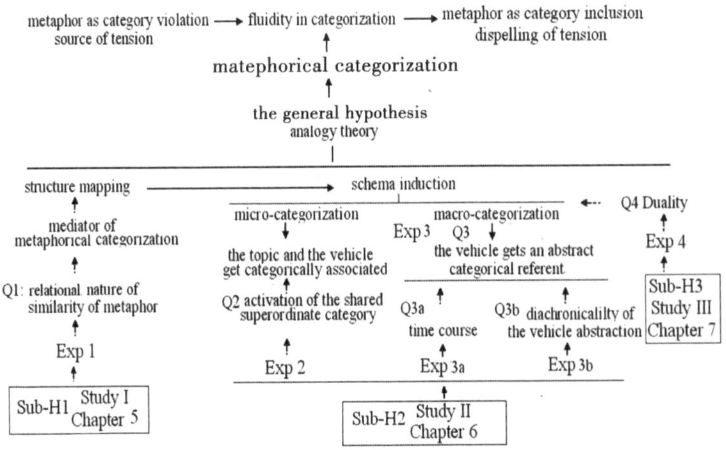

Figure 4.6 The framework of the empirical studies

As indicated in Figure 4.6, based on the theoretical framework of analogy, we get to the core research question of the present study: what is the nature of metaphorical categorization? Or in other words, how is it possible to put two concepts from two distinct conventional categories in a categorical juxtaposition and still make sense? This core question can be specifically investigated through looking at the five research questions. As the research design of the present study is based on the research questions and the corresponding hypotheses, a review of the empirical research questions is necessary.

The first research question (Q1 as shown in Figure 4.6), echoing with Sub-hypothesis 1 (Sub-H1 as shown in Figure 4.6), is about the mechanism in which the mediator of the categorical relation between the topic and the vehicle is identified. Sub-H1 is that metaphorical categorization is based on structure mapping and that the mediator of metaphorical categorization is relational similarity.

Q 2 and 3, echoing with Sub-hypothesis 2 (Sub-H2), are centered on the core dynamic process of metaphorical categorization. More specifically, Q2 is concerned with the micro-categorization process, i. e., the mechanism in which the vehicle gets categorically associated with the topic. Q3 is concerned with the micro-categorization process, i. e., the mechanism in which the vehicle dynamically gets associated with an abstract categorical referent. This question can be investigated through looking into two specific sub-questions which are Q3a concerning the time course of the gaining of the abstract referent in the vehicle and Q3b concerning the abstract schema induction in the vehicle.

Q4, echoing with Sub-hypothesis 3 (Sub-H3), is focused on the potential constraints on the category inclusion relation between the topic and the vehicle to investigate the duality of metaphorical categorization.

In line with the five specific research questions and the four specific sub-hypotheses, the following independent albeit related empirical studies were designed.

Study I (delivered in Chapter 5), consisting of one survey study, is designed to seek the answer to research Q1which is raised in Sub-H1. More specifically, it is designed to explore the structure mapping nature of metaphorical categorization. Empirically, this study operationalizes the notion of structure mapping as the relational similarity between the topic and the vehicle and seeks the correlation between the nature of similarity and the grammatical form preference of figurative language.

Study II(Chapter 6) is intended to provide the answers to research Q 2andQ 3 raised in Sub-H2 concerning the core dynamic process of metaphorical categorization. Thus, Study II is comprised of two experiments. Exp 2 is designed to answer research Q 2, i. e., the micro-categorization process. More specifically, Exp 2 takes a look into the mechanism in which the topic and the vehicle get categorically related and recruited in a shared superordinate category. Exp 3 is concerned with Q 3, with Exp 3a and Exp 3b designed to investigate Q 3a and Q 3b respectively. That is to say, Exp 3a is intended to see the time course of the dynamic abstraction of the vehicle in the course of metaphor comprehension, and Exp 3b is concerned with the historical gaining of the abstract categorical referent in the vehicle.

Study III(Chapter 7) is intended to provide the answers to research Q 4 raised in Sub-H3, which is concerned with the duality of the potential constraints on the category inclusion relation between the topic and the vehicle.

The present dissertation is generally data-driven. That is to say, the theoretical interpretations and conclusions in the present study mainly depend on empirical data statistic analyses. Specifically, in linguistic data sampling, questionnaire surveys and subjective ratings were adopted to manipulate the variables explored in the study. In Study I, ratings and scorings were recorded in Exp 1 to investigate the mediator of metaphor categorization. All the experiments in Study II and III were run by E-prime programs in the psycholinguistics lab. In these two studies, traditional psycholinguistic research paradigms were adopted to collect behavioral data such as the reaction time(RT) and the accuracy rate .

Chapter 5 Study I: the mediator of metaphorical categorization

5.1 Introduction

As discussed in Section 4.3, the present dissertation takes the dual-categorization account of metaphor as its general hypothesis. Such a general hypothesis can be more specifically divided into four sub-hypotheses. The present chapter will seek the answer to research Q1 through examining the first sub-hypothesis (Sub-H1), i.e., the mediator of metaphorical categorization. According to Sub-H1, metaphorical categorization, like conventional categorization, also takes similarity as the mediator. That is to say, the metaphor topic and vehicle can only be categorically associated as far as they have something in common. A comprehensive theory of metaphorical categorization must provide explanations as to what is the nature of the similarity and how it is identified. As the dual-categorization account of metaphor proposed in the present study holds that the categorization process is based on structure-mapping which takes relational similarity between the topic and vehicle as the mediator, this chapter, consisting of Exp 1, is intended to test this hypothesis by investigating the correlation between types of similarity and preference for different grammatical forms in expressing the relation between the topic and the vehicle.

5.2 Exp 1: the correlation between relational similarity and grammatical preference

5.2.1 Research aim

The research aim of the present experiment is to examine research Q 1, i.e., what serves as the mediator of metaphorical categorization. As discussed in Section 4.1.2, there are two most widely recognized types of similarity involved in comparison and categorization, namely, attributive similarity and relational similarity. According to the hypothesis of this present study, relational similarity plays a dominant role in determining metaphorical categorization. Experiment 1 adopted the technique of metaphor grammatical form preference rating based on the notion of grammatical concordance in metaphor① to test the central prediction of this dissertation concerning the mediator by which the topic and vehicle get categorically associated.

5.2.2 Hypothesis

According to the dual-categorization account of metaphor proposed in the present study, justification of juxtaposing two concepts from two conventionally distinct categories in a metaphor (literally having the category inclusion form) relies on the process of metaphorical categorization, which takes relational similarity between the topic and vehicle as the mediator.

Technically, the independent variable involved in the present experiment is the type of similarity conveyed by the topic-vehicle pairs, and the dependent variable is the score in the grammatical form preference rating task. Based on these analyses, the following hypothesis can be derived: If metaphorical categorization takes relational similarity between the topic and the vehicle as its mediator, then topic-vehicle pairs with relational similarity (e.g., history-mirror) should have the tendency to be juxtaposed in metaphors which have the identical grammatical form of literal categorization statement (e.g., History is a mirror); whereas topic-vehicle pairs with attributive similarity (e.g., lake-mirror) should

① Readers may see Section 3.2.2.2 for a detailed description of this notion.

have the tendency to be juxtaposed in similes which have the same grammatical form of literal comparison statement (e. g., The lake is like a mirror.). We predicted that those topic-vehicle pairs (e. g., lake-mirror) that convey attributive similarity (e. g., being flat) would get lower scores, whereas those pairs (e. g., history-mirror) that convey relational similarity (e. g., being reflective) would get higher scores. In other words, there would be a correlation between similarity type and rating scores.

5.2.3 Method

Participants: 33 participants were recruited (8 male, 25 female) from the population of postgraduate students at School of Foreign Studies, South China Normal University. The ages of these participants ranged from 24 to 29, with a mean of 25.5 (SD = 1.6). Participants spoke Chinese as the first language, and had normal or corrected-to-normal vision.

Design: A single factor (similarity types are attributive and relational) within-subject design was adopted. Similarity types between the topic and the vehicle were manipulated as the independent variable, and the scores in the grammatical preference rating task were recorded as the dependent variable.

Material development: Material development is composed of three steps which are operationalizing different kinds of similarity, rating and statistical analysis.

(1) Operationalizing attributive and relational similarity

The present experiment followed Gentner and Clement (1988) in operationally describing the distinction between attributive and relational similarity. According to Gentner and Clement (ibid), attributive similarity involves predicates which involve "one-place (argument)" predicates, and structural similarity involves "n-place (argument)" predicates. In fact, the number of argument (s) in a predicate reflects the number of participants involved in the logic relation denoted by the predicate. Based on this analysis, this study operationally defined distinct kinds of similarity between metaphor topic and vehicle depending on the following dimension: "the extent to which the similarity between the topic and vehicle involves things (or objects) other than themselves."

More specifically, attributive similarity does not involve abstract relations with other objects. As in the topic-vehicle pair "moon-plate", the similarity only relies on the commonality that they are both perceptually round, which is visually sensed and has nothing to do with other objects; whereas in the topic-vehicle pair "boss-shark", the similarity between the two concepts obviously does not reside in their perceptual properties, but in some abstract analogical relations with other objects, that is, "boss" to "employees" is like "shark" to "small marine creatures".

(2) Rating

A sample of 50 attributively similar topic and vehicle pairs (e. g., lake surface, mirror) and 50 relationally similar pairs (e. g., history, mirror) mainly from previous metaphor or analogy literature were initially translated into Chinese, and then subjected to several stimulus norming pre-tests. An independent panel consisted of 30 judges who satisfied the same inclusion criteria but did not participate in the formal experiment were recruited for the similarity-property norming task at their full leisure.

We defined the property of similarity as a function of the strength of the association between the topic-vehicle pair and object(s) other than themselves. The participants were assigned to rate on a 7-point scale as to "the extent to which the similarity between the two words involve thing(s) other than themselves". The scale ranged from 1 denoting "very closely associated" to 7 denoting "not associated at all". The orders of the points are counterbalanced between participants. Half the scores with 1 denoting "not associated at all" and 7 denoting "very closely associated" were reversely scored. The pairs scored lower than 3 were recruited as ones with attributive similarity, and the ones scored higher than 5 were taken as structural similarity. The complete version of the questionnaire is presented in Appendix I.

(3) Statistic analysis

An independent t-test was adopted to see whether the two groups of topic-vehicle pairs intended to be of distinct types of similarity nature were actually significantly different in terms of the rating scores. The difference between the two groups reached significant level in the rating scores, $t_{(1, 62)} = -28.950$, $p<0$. The mean score in Group 2(e. g., boss-shark) ($M = 5.28$, SD = 0.36) which were taken to have relational similarity was significantly higher than that in Group 1(e. g., moon-banana) ($M=2.96$, SD=0.27) which were taken to have attributive similarity. Thus the two groups of materials have significantly different properties of similarity. A complete list of recruited stimuli and their scores is presented in Appendix II.

Procedure: All the 64 topic-vehicle pairs derived from the material development section were used for grammatical preference norming. On each trial, the metaphorical form and the simile form of a pair appeared on the two opposite extremes of a 7-point scale. The left-right location of metaphors and similes was counterbalanced across lists. The number 1 was presented directly below the statement on the left of the display, and the number 7 was presented below the statement on the right of the display, with numbers 2 through 6 evenly spaced between. Participants were asked to indicate their form preference for each figurative statement by ticking the number (from 1 to 7) that corresponded with their preferred form. Specifically, they were instructed to indicate "which form sounded more natural". They were further informed that the stronger their preference for the statement on the left side, the closer their answer should be to 1, and the stronger their preference for the statement on the right side, the closer their answer should be to 7. The orders of the points were counterbalanced between two halves of the participants to ensure that 7 always denoted the metaphor form and 1 the simile form. Here we take the "moon-banana" pair as an example for a better presentation (The entire questionnaire is presented in Appendix III.):

月亮像香蕉	1	2	3	4	5	6	7	月亮是香蕉
	非常倾向用“像”连接	倾向用“像”连接	有点倾向用“像”连接	说不清	有点倾向用“是”连接	倾向用“是”连接	非常倾向用“是”连接	

5.2.4 Results

When collecting the data, half of the lists in which the metaphor form was indicated by the number 1 were reversely scored to ensure that higher numbers always indicated greater metaphor form preference. A full list of the scores in the grammatical preference rating is presented in Appendix IV. Data were analyzed via an independent t-test. Form preference scores were taken as the dependent variable. Mean categorical preference ratings are shown in Table 5.1 and Figure 5.1.

Table 5.1 Mean categorical preference rating scores in Exp1(SD in the parentheses)

similarity type	attributitve similarity	relational similarity
N	31	33
mean score	3.42(0.94)	5.66(1.07)

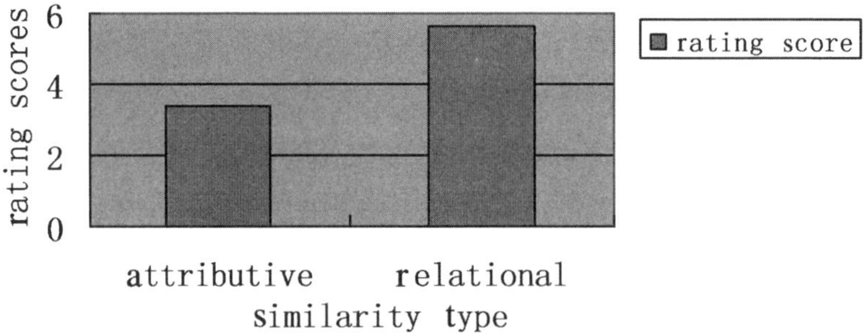

Figure 5.1 Mean scores in grammatical form preference rating in Exp 1

As shown in Table 5.1 and Figure 5.1, the relational similarity group(e.g., boss-shark) got a mean score of 5.67 which was 1.67 above the middle point 4 in the 7-point scale, showing that the topic-vehicle pairs which convey relational similarity had the tendency to be judged as more natural in the metaphor form. On the other side, the attributive similarity group(e.g., moon-silver plate) got a mean score of 3.43 which was 0.57 below the middle point 4 in the 7-point scale, showing that the topic-vehicle pairs which convey attributive similarity were more likely to be judged as more natural in the simile form.

The t-test between the two groups data indicated that the difference between the two groups reached a significant level in the grammatical preference rating scores, $t_{(1, 62)} = -8.752$, $p<0$; the mean score in the relational similarity group(e.g., boss-shark)($M=5.67$) was significantly higher than that in the attributive similarity group(e.g., moon-silver plate)($M=3.43$) which were taken to have attributive similarity(see Table 5.2).

Table 5.2 The correlation between the similarity rating scores and the grammatical reference scores in Exp 1

			a	r
		correlation coefficient	0.645″	1.000
Spearman's rho	r	sig.(2-tailed)	0	
		N	64	64

As shown in Table 5.2, Spearman correlation test revealed that the correlation coefficient between similarity rating scores and the grammatical reference scores reached significance, $r = 0.645, p < 0$

5.2.5 Discussion

The primary objective of Exp 1 was to test Sub-H1 through seeking the answer to research Q 1, i.e., what serves as the mediator of metaphorical categorization? Operationally, this objective was examined through exploring the correlation of similarity type and the scores of grammatical form preference rating. Two general findings emerged from the present survey. Firstly, the mean score in the relational similarity group (e.g., boss-shark) was significantly higher than that in the attributive similarity group (e.g., moon-silver plate), which showed that the relational similarity group had the tendency to be judged as metaphor form, while the attributive similarity group had the tendency to be judged as simile form. Secondly, there was a correlation between types of similarity and grammatical preference. Thus the prediction of the hypothesis and the first research question for this survey were generally confirmed. That is, the schematic categorical relation between the topic and the vehicle is given rise to by the structure mapping between two concepts. The justification of juxtaposing the two concepts conventionally from two distinct categories relies on the identification of the relational similarity rather than individual features between them, thus metaphorical categorization takes relational similarity as its mediator.

Empirically, the results of the present study echoed with two existing relevant studies (Chiappe and Kennedy, 1999; Jones and Estes, 2006), in which the paradigm of grammatical preference rating was also adopted to examine the true determinant of the use of the categorizing form or the comparison form. In their studies, it was found that aptness determined the preference for metaphor form. That is, lowly apt pairs of topic and vehicle tended to be used in the comparing form, i. e., simile; whereas highly apt ones in the categorizing form, i. e., metaphor. The author assumes that, if analyzed from the perspective of the nature of similarity, this finding could also alternatively serves as evidence for the hypothesis put forward for the present survey. Recall that in Section 3.2.1, the author argued that the nature of aptness is inherently determined by the relational nature of similarity between the topic and the vehicle. As Glucksberg(2001:21) points out, aptness of a metaphor depends on the extent to which the metaphor describes the "good parts" of the topic which are functionally important. As we know, the function of an object definitely more abstractly involves the relation between two arguments (participants) in a certain predicate. For example, the concept "bridge." has numerous dimensions of features. In terms of the shape, it can be arched or flat; in terms of the material, it can be made of iron, or cement, or wood, etc. However, in the metaphor "Friendship is a bridge.", the features that weigh over others and are recruited in the appropriate interpretation are related to its function rather than its perceptual appearance. That is, "friendship" functionally "connects" people as "bridge" functionally "connects" the two banks of a river.

Moreover, our suspicion concerning the potential confounding effect of levels of aptness and types of similarity was validated by some further analyses on the experimental materials used in Chiappe and Kennedy's study(1999). For example, in their study, the metaphorical pair "cigarettes-bombs" was rated as highly apt and thus was preferred as metaphors; whereas "highways-snakes" was rated lower in aptness and thus was preferred as similes. This study assumes that the nature of aptness actually resides in the nature of similarity if analyzed in the framework offered by the present study. That is, "Cigarettes are time bombs." is highly apt in that the similarity between the topic and the vehicle involves other object(s), resulting in an n-place predicate, that is, "cigarettes" cause unexpected harm as "time bombs" cause unexpected harm. Nevertheless, "highways-snakes" is low in aptness in that no other object(s) enter(s) the similarity between the topic and the vehicle, resulting in a one-place predicate. That is, this metaphor only conveys certain perceptual similarity: both highways and snakes are winding in their shapes. In fact, to test our conjecture, we recruited the two metaphors in our rating section of the present survey. The results showed that the similarity nature rating scores confirmed the hypothesized correlation between similarity nature and aptness. The highly apt metaphor "Cigarettes are time bombs." got a mean score of 5.13 in the similarity rating, which indicated a high involvement with other object(s) and hence relational similarity; whereas the lowly apt one "Highways are snakes." got 2.54, indicating attributive similarity. In sum, if analyzed in the framework of relational similarity, the grammatical preference evidence gained in previous studies on aptness could speak very well for our hypothesis that relational similarity serves as the mediator of metaphorical categorization.

Theoretically and more importantly, the result of the present survey seemed to have provided cognitively motivated evidence for the qualitatively nonequivalent view of metaphor and simile, which sheds significant light on our basic hypothesis concerning the notion of metaphorical categorization. The relation between metaphor and simile can never be overstated as perplexing. There have been two major views on this relation: the equivalent view and the nonequivalent view. For a long history in both linguistics and philosophy, leading theorists, following the Aristotelian tradition, have regarded the two tropes as equivalent. The highly influential conceptual metaphor theory proposed more currently by Lakoff and Johnson (1980) also followed this equivalent view. In this approach, the weight is put on conceptual phenomena rather than on linguistic forms. Despite its huge influence, many psycholinguistic studies have challenged this equivalent view. For example, some scholars revealed that metaphors sound stronger than similes (Chiappe and Kennedy, 1999), and that there is a trend from simile to metaphor in child cognition and language development (Reynold and Ortony, 1980). Challenges have also been raised by some philosophers who argue that the equivalent view is at odd with the economical principal of human language, as put by Chiappe and Kennedy (1999:250): "If metaphor and simile convey exactly the same meaning, why not simplify our language and eliminate one?"

Although it is rather empirically convincing and obvious that metaphors are distinct from similes, people are still puzzled by such a question: where does the relative strength and depth in metaphor stem from? As demonstrated by the current experiment, since similarity is taken as the ground for the two tropes, it can also be theoretically taken as the digging point for the solution to this question. Basically and traditionally, there have been two approaches to this question. First, "the quantity approach" assumes that the distinction between metaphor and simile resides in the "amount" of similarity shared by the topic and the vehicle. As metaphor has the identical linguistic form of categorization which denotes attribution of "all" properties, it may be connected to greater similarity; whereas the simile form, which has the literal form of comparison, is associated with fewer similarity. Although this approach highly appeals to our intuition, it fails to capture the basic definition of similarity or to operationalize it. More importantly, it fails to explain the fact that there can be certain "underlying" or "hidden" properties recruited in metaphor interpretation other than the superficial perceptual similarities (Liu, 2001; Li and Liu, 2003; Liu and Gu, 2005; Li, 2007; Wang, 2006).

The second major approach, echoing with the result of the present experiment, is "quality" oriented. In this account, figurative claims are also modeled on literal forms of expression, and metaphors and similes are considered be to qualitatively distinct. That is, metaphor is a statement of categorization and simile a statement of comparison. Recall that in Section 4.1.2, we reviewed the notion that relational similarity is qualitatively distinct from superficial perceptual similarity, and that the former tacitly weighs over the latter in determining categorization. These tacit preferences would contribute to theory (rule)-based biases in categorization. In light of the result of the present survey, we can reach the conclusion that the theory of relational similarity in determining categorization speaks very well for our findings. That is, the categorical relationship between the topic and the vehicle in a metaphor is cognitively motivated by the relational similarity between the two concepts.

Another contribution of this experiment is more empirically oriented. Through adopting a rating task on "the degree of the involvement with other object(s)", the present experiment offered a relatively more operational technique to measure the so-called "underlying" "deep" abstract similarity in metaphor comprehension, which definitely shed new light on the nature of the "abstract" similarity in metaphor.

Despite its important findings and contributions, the present experiment only provided the metalinguistic judgment rating over the grammatical form, failing to provide solid on-line evidence concerning the dynamic process of metaphorical categorization. This limitation motivates further on-line studies which are presented in the following chapters.

5.3 Summary

The findings from the present experiment provided answers to research Q1 through confirming Sub-H1 that metaphorical categorization is based on structure mapping between the topic and vehicle, thus it is relational similarity that mediates metaphorical categorization. Besides this major finding, this experiment also provided a more operational definition of "abstract" similarity in terms of "n-place" argument rating, which contributed significantly to the theories of both metaphor and categorization.

Nevertheless, the present study can merely serve as a source of off-line evidence concerning the correlation between types of similarity nature and trope grammatical preference. Since one of the major hypotheses of this study is that metaphorical categorization is based on schema induction resulting from structure-mapping between the topic and the vehicle, an adequate theory of metaphorical categorization has to provide evidence concerning the dynamic aspect of the schema induction process. To look into this aspect, the author conducted three independent albeit related experiments which are presented in the following chapter.

Chapter 6 Study Ⅱ: the core process of metaphorical categorization

6.1 Introduction

This chapter centers on research questions 2 and 3(Q2andQ3) through examining Sub-H2 which concerns the core dynamic process of metaphorical categorization. Theoretically, the two research questions are raised to look into the schema induction mechanism in metaphorical categorization. According to our general hypothesis(see Section 4.3), schema induction(metaphorical categorization) involves two layers — the micro-categorization process and the macro-categorization process. This chapter will cover three separate yet related experiments to investigate the two layers respectively.

More specifically, Exp 2(delivered in Section 6.2) sets out to address Q2 concerning the micro-categorization of metaphorical categorization, i.e., the mechanism in which the topic and the vehicle get categorically associated. As to this aspect, according to the general hypothesis developed in Section 4.3, the author argues that the activation of the shared superordinate category in which both the topic and the vehicle are included is based on the structural mapping process between the two terms.

Exp 3(delivered in Section 6.3) is concerned with research Q3, i.e., the macro-categorization process of metaphorical categorization. This process is investigated through looking into its two aspects, thus Exp 3 is further specified as Exp 3a and Exp 3b. Exp 3a takes a look into the time course of the rise of abstractness in the vehicle in the course of metaphor processing. Exp 3b explores the gaining process of the abstract categorical reference in the vehicle in an experimentally diachronical context.

6.2 Exp 2: the micro-categorization process

6.2.1 Research aim

Exp 2 seeks the answer to Q 2, i. e., how do the topic and the vehicle get recruited in a parent subordinate category? This research question is concerned with the micro-categorization process of metaphor categorization.

6.2.2 Design logic and hypothesis

According to the theoretical framework of metaphorical categorization developed for the present study, the mapping or alignment between the relational structures between the topic and the vehicle is believed to be the basis for the micro-categorization, i. e., the activation of the superordinate category which includes both the topic and the vehicle as co-members (see Section 4. 1. 3). Our hypothesis is that the recruitment of the topic and the vehicle into a parent category depends on the alignment of the structure mapping between the two terms. That is to say, once the structures get matched, the individual items involved in the structures will also get categorically matched. If this hypothesis is on the right track, then it could be operationally predicted that the activation of the superordinate category can be a function of ways in which the semantics of the topic and the vehicle are explicitly processed. More specifically, the following two hypotheses can be formulated for Exp 2.

H1: The matching of the relational structures denoted by the topic and the vehicle will activate the categorical relation between the two terms. Operationally, the term denoting the category in which both the topic and the vehicle are included should spontaneously become active during structural-mapping between the topic and the vehicle even when the subjects are not explicitly instructed to identify the category relation. It can be technically predicted that there will be shorter response time for category-referent target words when they are preceded by four-word sets processed in a structure-mapping task than when they are preceded by the same four-word sets yet in a simple semantic associating task.

H2: Priming effect of category-referent words should be detected both when they were preceded by four-word sets processed in a structure-mapping task and in an explicit categorizing task. Operationally, reaction time to the category target words will be faster in both the structure-mapping task and the categorizing task than in the mere semantic processing task.

6.2.3 Method

Participants: 90 participants, comprising 26 males and 64 females, were recruited from the population of undergraduate students at South China Normal University (44 freshmen and 46 sophomores). The ages of these participants ranged from 18 to 23, with a mean of 20.5 (SD = 2.4). Participants spoke Chinese as their first language, and had normal or corrected-to-normal vision.

Material development:

(1) Metaphorical four-word set generation

A sample of 50 metaphors were taken from previous research or created by the author of the present dissertation. An independent group of 30 subjects were assigned to a task of four-word set generation in a pen-and-paper based questionnaire, in which each metaphor was schematically presented in the manner shown below:

The instruction for the task went as follows: "Please read each metaphor carefully, and write down one or two corresponding words associated with the topic and the vehicle respectively which first come into your minds." This task has no time limitation, and the subjects can take the questionnaires to their dormitories and finish them at their full leisure. The questionnaire is fully presented in Appendix V.

Based on the generation task, for each topic and vehicle in a set the words which were most frequently generated were chosen for the four-word set. For example, for the metaphor "A man is a wolf.", a four-word set like "man: woman; wolf: sheep" was generated. Only those sets which got agreements level above 80 % among the total 50 metaphors were selected for the formal experiment, thus resulting in a pool of experimental stimuli of 20 valid sets. The full list of the recruited sets is presented in Appendix VIII.

(2) Target word generation

Each four-word set obtained in step a was further subjected to a probe word generation task in which two distinct kinds of probe words were generated. For the target to be used as the categorizing target, the subjects were instructed to write down two nouns denoting two common categories which could respectively include the top and bottom word-pairs as two members. As the subordinate category created on the fly of metaphor comprehension may have not been lexicalized, the subjects were particularly informed that they were allowed to creatively coin the subordinate category referent by combining a verb with the Chinese character "者", which has similar meaning and grammatical function as the suffix "er" in English language. Thus, for each set (*e.g.*, "*man*: *woman*; *wolf*: *sheep*"), a three-character Chinese noun (e.g., "追逐者" meaning "chaser") was generated to denote the category in which man and wolf were both included. The full questionnaire and the recruited targets are presented in Appendix VI and Appendix VIII respectively. For the sake of a better explanation, each set was schematically presented in the manner shown below.

For the targets to be used in both the SEM (semantic processing) task and MAP (structure mapping) task①, the subjects were instructed to "write down a verb denoting the two semantic relations between the two words in the left and right word-pairs". The set was schematically presented in the manner shown below.

For each set (e.g., "man: woman; wolf: sheep"), a two-character Chinese phrase (e.g., "追逐" meaning "chase") was generated to describe the semantic relations in both the "man to woman" and the "wolf" to "sheep" systems. In order to keep the numbers of characters balanced across different types of target words, the Chinese character "着" was added to each of these two-character verbs. Thus the resulting three-character word denotes a Chinese progressive construction as the English corresponding form "be + V-ing" without altering the basic semantic meaning. The choice of the character "着" is also based on the consideration that the two Chinese characters "者" and "着" have very close topographical shapes and

① Detailed description of the tasks is provided in the Procedure session of the present experiment.

pronunciations. The questionnaire used is fully presented in Appendix VII and the recruited targets are presented in Appendix VIII.

Based on the target word generation task described above, for each target word, the most frequently generated ones were chosen for further use in the formal experiment. Thus, 20 critical metaphorical four-word sets were created. Due to the relatively small number of the critical sets, all these 20 sets were used across all the three processing tasks. Besides the 20 critical sets in each list, for each processing task group, another 10 semi-scrambled sets and 10 fully scrambled sets were generated as response counterbalancing fillers. As shown in Figure 6. 1, in the semi-scrambled sets, one of the two critical relations is not formed. That is, for the semantic semi-scrambled set, semantic relation exists in either the left pair or the right pair, but not both. For example, semantic relation is found in "man-woman" pair, yet not in the "elephant-scarf" pair. For the category semi-scrambled set, category relation exists in either the above pair or the below pair, but not both. For example, category relation is found in "man-wolf"pair, yet not in the "woman-eraser" pair. For the mapping semi-scrambled set, semantic relations exist in both the left and right pairs, as "man-woman"and "sky-plane", yet these two semantic relations have no way to be mapped. The 10 fully scrambled sets were used across all the three tasks. The materials are shown in Figure 6. 1:

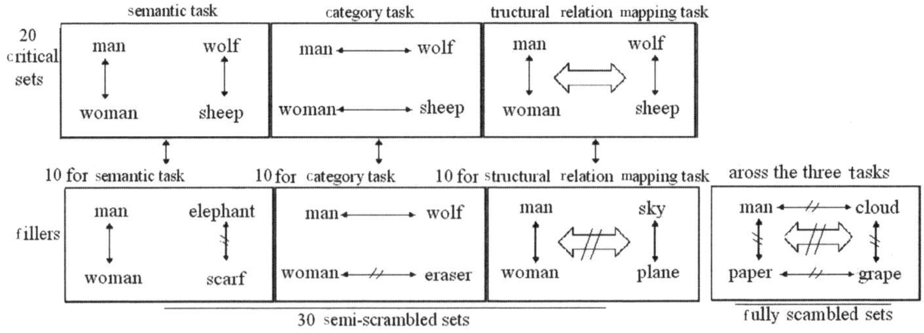

Figure 6. 1　Examples of each trial type in Exp 2

A full list of the experimental word sets and their corresponding target words is presented in Appendix VIII.

Design: A 3(word set processing task: pure semantic task, categorizing task, structural relation mapping task) × 3 (probe word type: semantic relation target, categorical relation target, unrelated target) mixed design was adopted. Word set semantic processing task types were manipulated between subjects while target word types were manipulated within subjects.

Procedure: The experiment paradigm adopted in this experiment was mainly inspired by Green et al. (2008). In this experiment, participants were randomly assigned to either the semantic associating task condition (SEM for short) ($N = 30$), the structural mapping task condition (MAP) ($N = 30$), or the categorizing task condition (CAT) ($N = 30$). For all the three tasks, trials began with the presentation of a four-word set. In the semantic associating task (SEM), participants were instructed to judge whether the four-word set included two conventional semantic relations simultaneously (one in the left word-pair and the other in the right word-pair). A conventional semantic relation was defined as "when there is a common sense way in which two things often do, or easily could, have to do with each other". For example, for the word set "man: woman; wolf: sheep", the semantic associating task (SEM) is shown diagrammatically as follows.

In the structural relation mapping task (MAP), participants judged whether the left word-pair and the right word-pair constituted a match in that the two semantic relations respectively denoted by the two pairs have certain commonality. For example, again in the four-word set "man: woman; wolf: sheep", participants judged whether the two word-pairs on the left and right represented the analogical abstract relation. This task was explained to the subjects diagrammatically as follows.

In the categorizing task (CAT), participants judged whether the top and bottom word-pairs respectively constituted words that were "both members of a more abstract common category". Again given the four-word set "man: woman; wolf: sheep", participants judged that both "man" and "wolf" could be included in the more abstract superordinate category "CHASER", and that both "woman" and "sheep" could be included in the more abstract superordinate category "CHASEE".

More importantly, the participants were further informed that the category might have not been lexicalized, or in other words, the parent category may not have a particular name. In this regard, as the experiment was performed in Chinese, the participants were informed that the category could be denoted by an unlexicalized noun which consisted of a verb and a suffixing morpheme "者", which has quite the similar meaning and function as the suffix "er" in English. The stimuli were identical across the three processing tasks, and the instruction given to participants was the only difference manipulated across the tasks.

In each trial, the four-word set was presented until participants made a key press response with the key "F" denoting true and "J" denoting false. Participants were instructed that a four-word set was true if and only if all the relations delineated in the instructions were present in the four-word set; otherwise the four-word set was false. Immediately upon the participants' response, the four-word set disappeared and a single target word appeared at the center of the screen. This target word remained on the screen until the participants performed a lexical decision task through making a button press. The participants were instructed to press "F" if the target was a word, and to press "J" if the target was not a word. Thus, each trial involved two separate stages: silent evaluation of a four-word set and a lexical decision. Response time for word-set processing task and the lexical decision button press were both recorded. The latter were recorded as the critical dependent variable and were subjected to statistical analysis. The procedure is shown in Figure 6.2.

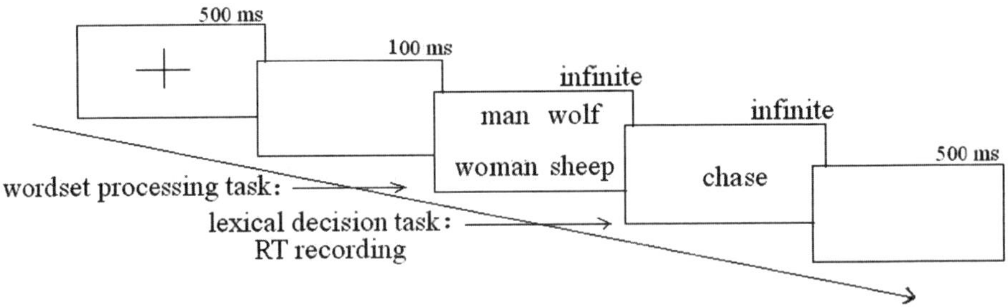

Figure 6.2 The experimental procedure of Exp 2

6.2.4 Results

Only correct responses were recruited for further analysis. The data from 3 subjects who got accuracy rate less than 80 % were removed. Response time beyond 2.5 standard deviations were considered outliers and removed prior to analyses, resulting in an elimination of 4.7 % of all the correct responses. The descriptive statistics for the mean response times and accuracy rates are shown in Table 6.1 and Table 6.2

Table 6.1 Mean lexical decision RTs(in ms) and ACC(%) in Exp 2

word set processing task type	target type semantical related	categorical related	tnrelated	*N*
semantic associating(SEM)	669(95.3)	698(93.4)	711(92.4)	29
categorical associating(CAT)	691(93.4)	656(97.2)	720(91.2)	29
relational mapping(MAP)	657(95.8)	659(94.6)	713(92.4)	29

Table 6.2 Results for the mixed anova in Exp 2

source	type III sum of squares	df	mean square	*F*	sig.
within-subjects targe	106 417.870	2	53 208.935	23.297	0.000
target * task	38 429.004	4	8 607.251	4.206	0.003
error(target)	383 706.460	168	2 283.967		
between-subjects					
task	12 524.421	2	6 262.211	0.524	0.594
error	1 003 643.885	84	11 948.141		

As shown in Table 6.2, a 3×3 mixed anova (word set processing task type: SEM, CAT, MAP) ×(target type: semantic, category, unrelated) was performed. This anova indicated a significant main effect of target type, $F_{(2,168)} = 23.297$, MSE = 53208.935, $p<0$. Collapsing across word set processing task types, subjects were significantly faster in the semantic target condition ($M = 673$ ms) (the mean of 669, 691 and 657 ms) and the category target condition ($M = 672$ ms) (the mean of 698, 656 and 659 ms) than in the unrelated target condition ($M = 715$ ms) (the mean of 711, 720 and 713 ms). The main effect of task type did not approach significance, $F_{(2, 84)} = 0.524$, MSE = 6262.211, $p = 0.594$. Collapsing across target types, the three means of the three tasks didn't vary significantly, with the SEM task having a mean of 692 ms (the mean of 669, 698 and 711 ms), the CAT task having a mean of 689ms (the mean of 691, 656 and 720 ms), and the MAP task having a mean of 677ms (the mean of 657, 659 and 713 ms). More importantly, the interaction between word set processing task type and target type was significant, $F_{(4,168)} = 4.206$, MSE = 9 607.251, $p = 0.003$; the pattern of the prime of different targets (especially in the semantic and category target types) varied across three word set processing tasks.

The anova on the accuracy (ACC) rate yielded a significant main effect in target type, $F_{(1, 84)} = 10.386$, MSE = 0.036, $p = 0.002$. However, neither the main effect of word set processing task nor the target type by word set processing task interaction approached significant level, $F_{(2, 84)} = 0.107$, MSE = 0.001, $p = 0.899$, and $F_{(2, 84)} = 0.154$, MSE = 0.001, $p = 0.858$ respectively.

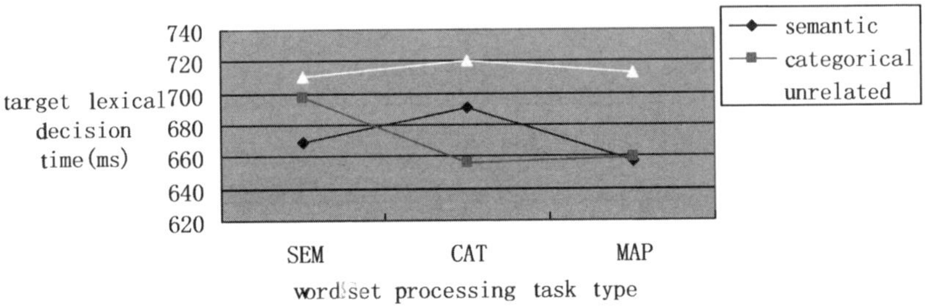

Figure 6.3 Lexical decision mean times in Exp 2

In order to further detect sources of the observed variances in each processing task, several planned comparisons were performed. These took the form of paired-sample t-tests at each level of processing task. Two paired t-tests revealed that in the MAP task condition, mean reaction time for the category target words ($M = 659.1$ ms) was significantly faster than that for the unrelated target words ($M = 713.6$ ms), $t_{(28)} = -3.553$, SE = 14.933, $P < 0.001$, and that in the CAT task condition, mean reaction time for the category target words ($M = 656.5$ ms) was significantly faster than that for the unrelated target words ($M = 720.0$ ms), $t_{(28)} = -4.474$, SE = 14.206, $P < 0.000$. These comparisons verified the priming effect of category relations both in the CAT task and the MAP task. Furthermore, an independent sample t-test showed that the reaction time for the category-related target words was as fast as in the CAT task ($M = 656.5$ ms) and the MAP task ($M = 659.1$ ms), $t_{(58)} = -0.168$, SE = 15.435, $P < 0.868$, indicating that priming of category relations in the MAP task was as strong as in the CAT task.

In the SEM task, paired sample t-test indicated that mean reaction time for the category target words (M = 698. 6ms) was not significantly faster than that for the unrelated target words (M = 711. 1ms), $t_{(28)}$ = − 1. 112, SE = 11. 259, P = 0. 276, showing that there was no priming effect of the category relation in the SEM task. Moreover, independent sample t-tests revealed that the reaction time for the category target words(M=656. 5 ms) in the CAT task condition was significantly faster than that for the category target words (M = 698. 6ms) in the SEM task condition, $t_{(56)}$ = 2. 356, SE = 17. 886, p = 0. 02, and that the reaction time for the category target words(M=659. 1 ms) in the MAP task condition was marginally significantly faster than that for the category target words (M = 698. 6ms) in the SEM task condition, $t_{(56)}$ = 1. 921, SE = 20. 590, p = 0. 06.

As for the priming effect for the semantically related target words in the three tasks, paired sample t-tests showed that in the SEM task, response time for the semantically related target words(669. 1) were significantly faster than those for the unrelated target words(711. 1), $t_{(28)}$ = −3. 861, SE = 10. 896, p = 0. 001. In the CAT task, response time for the semantic target words(691. 7) were also significantly faster than that for the unrelated target words (720. 0), $t_{(28)}$ = − 2. 476, SE = 11. 435, p = 0. 02. In the MAP task, response time for the semantic target words(657. 8) were also significantly faster than that for the unrelated target words(713), $t_{(28)}$ = −4. 216, SE = 13. 258, p<0. Moreover, response time for semantically related target words did not differ significantly between the CAT task (M = 691. 7 ms) and the SEM task (M=669. 1 ms), $t_{(56)}$ = −1. 166, SE = 19. 433, p = 0. 249, or between the MAP task (M=657. 7 ms) and the SEM task (M = 669. 1 ms), $t_{(56)}$ = 0. 742, SE = 15. 283, P = 0. 461. However, between the CAT task (M = 691. 7 ms) and the MAP task (M=657. 7 ms), the difference reached marginal significance, $t_{(56)}$ = 1. 875, SE = 18. 133, p = 0. 066, which indicates that the priming effect for the semantically related target words in the MAP task was significantly greater than that in the CAT task.

6. 2. 5 Discussion

Experimental results were obtained concerning two central predictions of the hypothesized relation between structure mapping and metaphorical categorization.

Firstly, in the MAP task, even though the participants were not explicitly instructed to identify the category relations, decreased response time for the category target words indicated that category relations were activated in this task. In fact, our experimental data showed that the MAP task had the equal priming effect on category relations as the CAT task in which the category relation was explicitly instructed to be identified. Secondly, the priming effect of category relation was separated from that of the semantic association in the present experiment. Recall that in this research, the three processing tasks involved identical word sets and identical target words, thus identical semantic associations were therefore equated across various tasks. Consequently, the observed different levels of effects for the category target words could only be attributed to different word set processing tasks. If the observed priming effect had been the result of simple semantic association, priming for the category target words in the SEM task would have been equal to the priming for the category target words in the MAP task and the CAT task. However, compared to the CAT task in which the category relation was explicitly activated, the MAP task had the equal priming for category target words, yet this prime effect was not detected in the SEM task. Note that only the MAP task rather than the SEM task involved structure mapping of analogical relations between the topic and the vehicle, thus these experimental results could be interpreted as evidence for this study's central hypothesis that the activation of the category relation between the topic and the vehicle during metaphor processing results from the relational mapping mechanism and can not be explained by simple semantic association between the target words and the words in the word sets.

These results combinarily lend support to our hypothesis that the categorical relation between the topic and the vehicle get established through the alignment between the two analogical relations are denoted by the topic and the vehicle. Such a finding significantly extends our understanding concerning metaphorical categorization, i. e., the process in which the metaphor topic (e. g. man) and the vehicle (e. g. wolf) are recruited in a shared category on the fly. To our best knowledge, although several other researchers have theoretically suggested that metaphors and categories may be importantly related (Bowdle and Gentner, 2005; Xu, 2008), no existing empirical studies prior to the present one has systematically examined the mechanism underlying this process. The priming effect for the category target words(e. g. chaser) in the MAP task demonstrates that the metaphor topic(e. g. man) and the vehicle(e. g. wolf) are recruited in the same unconventional category because the two concepts share similar structural relations (chasing) with other concepts (e. g., woman and sheep correspondingly).

Previous studies generally agreed that similarity is central to categorization, and we assume that there is no exception in metaphorical categorization. However, this general similarity-based account has been criticized recently on the ground that they failed to capture the role of theory(or rule)-based knowledge in category formation (Murphy and Medin, 1985; Murphy and Allopenna, 1994; Wisniewski, 1995), especially between the metaphor topic and the vehicle which usually have no commonality in their perceptual appearances. To solve this problem, Exp 1 in this dissertation discovered that it is relational similarity rather than perceptual similarity that serves as the basis for metaphorical categorization, yet the mechanism underlying the relation between abstracting this kind of relational similarity and the induction of the common superordinate category still remains unsolved. In this regard, the present experiment provides important implications as to how relational similarity is detected and how categorical relation forms between the metaphor topic and vehicle.

These results concerning the priming effect for the category target words in various tasks cohere with, and more importantly, extent Green et al.'s study(2008) in which only so-called within-domain analogies (e. g., gun: bullet; bow: arrow) were investigated. Within-domain analogies(e. g., gun: bullet; bow: arrow), terms playing the same roles in the analogical relations are included in a conventional category, that is, "gun" and "bow" are conventional comembers of a superordinate category "weapon". According to Green et al's study (ibid), in within-domain analogies, overtly instructing to process the common relation(e. g., shoot) held by the two word pairs(gun to bullet and bow to arrow) led to a significant priming of the conventional common superordinate category(e. g., weapon). The same pattern of priming effect was also detected in the task that the common superordinate category was explicitly instructed to be delineated. Based on this important finding, the researchers concluded that analogical reasoning entailed a categorizing process in which the individual terms involved in the shared analogical relation were identified as comembers of a certain category. It is worthwhile to note that our study can be considered as a significant extension on this previous study concerning the relation between analogy and categorization. The point is, in our study, although the word sets (e. g., man: woman; wolf: sheep) based on metaphors can also be legally treated as analogy, the terms playing the same role in the analogical relation can not be included in the same conventional category. The author tentatively terms such relation as "cross-domain" analogy. As described in Chapter One, metaphoricity (the quality of being a metaphor) resides in the tension between processing as category violation and as category inclusion (or in other words, the quality of being included in cross-domain categories).

Regarding the nature of metaphorical cross-domain category processing, the present experiment releases two significant findings. Firstly, the experimental results indicate that cross-domain structure-mapping involves more cognitive effort. Recall that with regard to the priming effect for the semantic target words, there was naturally a significant priming effect for the semantic target words in the SEM task in which the semantic association was explicitly instructed to be identified. In the same vein, in the MAP task, as semantic association is necessary for relational mapping, there was also a significant priming effect for the semantically related target words. However, it is worthwhile to note that in the CAT task, although semantic association was not explicitly instructed to be identified, there was also a significant priming effect for the semantic target words. This finding can be interpreted as evidence for the assumption that processing metaphorical relation between the topic and the vehicle (e. g., man: wolf) involves processing the analogical semantic relations held by the two terms. Actually, this conclusion is based on the comparison between the present experiment and Green et al.'s (2008) study which focused on within-domain categories (e. g., gun: bow). According to Green's study, the priming for the semantically related target word (shoot) was not activated in the CAT task in which only the categorical relation was overtly delineated. Combined with Green et al.'s (2008) study, conclusion can be drawn that metaphorical (cross-domain) categorization involves more cognitive effort in processing analogical semantic relations held by the topic and the vehicle, yet this type of processing can not be detected in conventional categorization.

Secondly, the analogical semantic relations (e.g., structure-mapping) in metaphorical categorization are automatically processed. Recall that in the present experiment, the CAT task did not delineate the semantic relation at all, yet the priming effect for the semantic target words reached significance. This finding can only be accounted for through the assumption that the semantic processing is unconscious in the process of categorization. The author believes that this finding can also speak very well for our basic hypothesis. That is, the categorization of the individual terms is determined by the common structures shared by both the two items. If this hypothesis is on the right track, the categorizing task definitely involves the processing of the structures denoted by the two terms. As the structural mapping depends on the semantic processing, the categorizing task will unconsciously activate the semantic information.

6.2.6 Summary

Through adopting a word-set processing task and a primed lexical decision task, this section centers on research Q2 raised by Sub-H2, i.e., the mechanism underlying the induction of the superordinate category in which the topic and the vehicle are included.

Generally, our hypothesis concerning the relation between structure-mapping and metaphorical categorization was conformed. That is, the unconscious structure mapping between the analogical relations held by the topic and the vehicle terms leads to the induction of the categorical relation between the topic and the vehicle. This conclusion is mainly based on one major finding released by the present experiment, i.e., the priming effect for the category target words reached significance in the MAP task wherein the subjects were merely instructed to process the mapping between the structural relations held by the topic and the vehicle, yet without being explicitly instructed to process the category relation.

Except for these conclusions, there is yet an interesting pattern of priming effect observed in the data for the semantically related target words in the CAT task, which can only be interpreted as evidence showing that overtly categorizing two concepts belonging to two distinct conventional categories entails processing relational semantic information in the two terms. This point is distinct from the finding in Green's study which showed that, for conventional categories, the CAT task did not prime the semantically related target words. Combining the results of the present experiment and Green's study, it could be at least tentatively concluded that metaphorical categorization differs from conventional categorization in that the former involves activation of the relational information held by the two concepts being processed while the later does not.

To conclude, on the one hand, these findings cohere with Exp 1 in that metaphorical categorization also takes relatiofnal similarity as the basis; on the other hand, metaphorical categorization as a dynamic process involves structure mapping of the analogical relations held by the topic and the vehicle.

Findings of Exp 2 could only be interpreted as evidence concerning the micro-categorization, i. e., the relation between structure-mapping and the induction of the shared category in which both the topic and the vehicle are included. Research Q3 raised by Sub-H2, however, still remains unsolved. That is, what is the mechanism of macro-categorization, i. e., how does the vehicle gain an abstract categorical referent? In the following section, we will turn to Exp 3 through which research Q3 is explored.

6.3 Exp 3: the macro-categorization process

Exp 3 is concerned with research Q3 concerning the macro-categorization process of metaphorical categorization (see Figure 4.6), i. e., how do the topic and the vehicle get categorically associated? According to the general hypothesis put forward for the present study, the categorical relation between the vehicle and the abstract referent is established through the dynamic schema induction of the matched structures denoted by the topic and the vehicle. Recall that in Section 4.3.2, such process of schema induction is termed as macro-categorization in that it accounts for the general relational structures (e. g., chasing) rather than the individual items involved in the structures(e. g., chasers or chasees).

According to the dual-categorization account of metaphor proposed for the present dissertation, the induction of the abstract referent in the vehicle (or the macro-categorization) depends on a dynamic process. On the one hand, in the process of metaphor understanding, the vehicle undergoes an increase in the level of its referent abstractness as the vehicle gets associated with the relational category which is termed as macro-category in our dual-categorization account. On the other hand, from a long-term perspective, repeated activation of the relational category will diachronically result in an establishment of the abstract referent in the vehicle. A comprehensive understanding of the mechanism in which the vehicle gets categorically related with the abstract referent should definitely involve the two aspects.

In this regard, Exp 3 was divided into two independent albeit related sub-experiments, i. e., Exp 3a and Exp 3b to respectively look into the two aspects of macro-categorization in metaphorical categorization. More specifically, Exp 3a was intended to examine the induction of the abstract referent in the vehicle in metaphor processing through a look into the time course of metaphorical processing from a short-term perspective. Exp 3b was conducted to investigate the induction of the abstract reference in the vehicle in a vitro(i. e., experimental) diachronical setting.

6. 3. 1 Exp 3a: the gaining of the abstract referent in the vehicle: a time course study

6. 3. 1. 1 Research aim

As the central goal of Exp 3 is to reveal the underlying dynamic aspect of metaphorical categorization at the macro-level, a clear investigation into levels of abstraction of metaphor vehicle at various stages of this process is indispensable. Exp 3a takes a further insight into Q3a, i. e., what is the characteristic of the time course of the abstract schema induction in the vehicle in the course of metaphorical processing(also see Figure 4. 6).

6. 3. 1. 2 design logic and hypotheses

The design logic of this experiment can be depicted by describing the theoretical background against which the experiment hypothesis is raised.

Different theories have different predictions concerning the time course of the rise of the level of categorical referent abstractness in the vehicle. According to the Comparison Model(see Section 3. 1. 2. 1), at the outset of metaphor comprehension, metaphor vehicles do not get their categorical referents, and metaphor topic and vehicle are at the same level of abstractness. Metaphors are processed through a comparison mechanism by evaluating the degree of the overlapping of the concrete features shared by the two terms. Thus, the comprehension process will initially be thwarted because the metaphor(with the same grammatical form as category inclusion statement) in its linguistic nature invites categorization. On this view, metaphors are processed indirectly, i. e., in a sequential manner: they are initially recognized as anomalous as category mistake, then comprehended through property-matching (Tversky, 1977). On this account, metaphors are processed via retrieving and matching the concrete literal meanings of the topic and the vehicle. Throughout the time course of metaphor processing, there is an even activation of the literal meanings in the vehicle.

According to the categorization model (see Section 3. 1. 2. 2), metaphor comprehension begins with a directional property attribution, with the vehicle providing abstract properties from an ad hoc category and the topic providing dimension (s) to receive the property attribution. On this categorization view, metaphor-related abstract features in the vehicle are initially activated, and metaphor-unrelated concrete features are actively suppressed (Gensbacher, Keysar, and Robertson, 2001). Throughout the time course of metaphor comprehension, there is always an activation of the abstract referent and a suppression of the concrete literal meaning in the vehicle. Moreover, similar to the categorization model, the comparison model also fails to take into account the role of the topic, i. e., the type of the similarity between the topic and the vehicle, that is, the role of the metaphor topic in constraining the induction of the abstract referent in the vehicle is not specified.

According to the hypothesized dual-categorization model proposed for the present dissertation, if an abstract superordinate category is created on the fly as the by-product of schema induction based on structure-mapping between the topic and the vehicle, as structure-mapping process entails the property of first-matching-later-mapping in the time course, then metaphorical categorization will occur at later stage in the time course of metaphor processing. Operationally, this tendency can be detected through testing priming effects of various metaphors with distinct types of similarity on various targets at different stages of metaphor processing. More specifically, there will be a positive priming effect for concrete target at an early stage of metaphor processing(e. g.,375 ms SOA①) and increasingly positive priming effects for abstract categorical target at later stages(e. g., 750 ms SOA and 1 500 ms SOA). The choice of these three SOAs is based on the consideration that they respectively stand for three qualitatively distinct phases in the course of language processing. More specifically, 375 ms represents the opportunity to assess automatic processing of simple linguistic information, such as basic conventional semantic features, etc. 1 500 ms was long enough to permit attentional processing of complex linguistic information, such as syntactical reconstruction and sentence-level reanalysis, etc. And 750 ms constituted an intermediate, transitional stage between these two extremes (Neely, 1991).The author assumes that with hypothetical propose, if metaphor is processed through structure-mapping and schema induction mechanism, then the initial stage of concrete feature alignment can be tentatively detected by investigating the activation of various semantic features at the 375 ms SOA, and the induction of abstract features which are crucial for metaphor understanding in terms of abstract attributes projection at the 1 500 ms SOA. And the intermediate stage at the 750 ms SOA may reflect a transition between the two stages. Moreover, since the present study hypothesizes that metaphorical categorization takes structure mapping as the basis, the nature of the similarity between the topic and the vehicle should exert influence on the induction of the relational referent in the vehicle.

Based on the above theoretical analyses, two hypotheses can be explicitly

① SOA is the abbreviation for stimulus onset asynchrony, referring to the interval between the onsets of the prime and the target.

derived concerning the pattern of the time-course of metaphorical categorization:

H1: If metaphorical categorization results from abstract schema induction which is based on structure mapping between the topic and the vehicle, as structure-mapping and schema induction has a characteristic of first-alignment-later-projection in the processing time course, there will be an early-concrete-late-abstract tendency in priming effect in metaphor processing. Operationally, this tendency can be detected through testing the priming effects of metaphor vehicles on various targets with different levels of abstractness throughout the time course. More specifically, there will be a positive priming effect for the concrete literal target at an early stage of metaphor processing (375 ms SOA) and increasingly positive priming effect for the abstract categorical target at later stages (750 ms SOA and 1 500 ms SOA).

H2: If metaphorical categorization relies on structure mapping between the topic and the vehicle, then it could be predicted that only those that convey structural similarity have the pattern of priming effect described in H1. For those conveying attributive similarities①, throughout the time course, only concrete meanings in the vehicle will be evenly activated, which will be reflected through an even priming effect for the literal senses in the vehicle. Accordingly, there should be no priming effect for the abstract senses throughout the time course.

6.3.1.3 Method

Participants: 96 participants were recruited from the population of English undergraduate majors from SCNU. Data from 96 participants comprising 26 males and 68 females were initially collected. The ages of these participants ranged from 18 to 24, with a mean of 21.5 (SD = 1.2). Participants spoke Chinese as their first language, and had normal or corrected-to-normal vision.

Design: A2 (priming metaphor type: attributive metaphor; relational metaphor) × 3 (target type: abstract, concrete, unrelated) × 3 (SOA: 375 ms, 750 ms, 1 500 ms) mixed design was adopted. SOAs were manipulated between subjects while priming

---

① Metaphors conveying attributive similarities and those conveying relational similarities are abbreviatively termed as "attributive metaphors" and "relational metaphors" respectively in the rest of the dissertation.

metaphor type and target type were manipulated within subjects.

Material development: Material development was conducted through two steps which were manipulating the similarity property of the priming metaphors that were used in the formal experiment and manipulating the target words.

(1) Priming metaphor similarity manipulation

A sample of 30 pairs of metaphors was taken from previous research or generated by the author. Each pair was designed to have the same vehicle yet different topics e. g., "湖面 — 镜子"(lake surface- mirror) and "历史 — 镜子"(history- mirror). It was intended that in each pair, one metaphor has attributive similarity between the topic and vehicle(e. g., lake surface- mirror) while the other had relational similarity (e. g., history-mirror).

Following the same rating method for material development for Exp2 described in 6. 2. 3, the original 30 pairs were subjected to a similarity rating conducted by an independent group of 32 subjects. Following the definition depicted in 6. 2. 3, the type of similarity is also defined based on "the extent to which the similarity between the topic and vehicle involves object (s) or thing (s) other than themselves". Operationally, attributive similarity involves predicates which are "one-place (argument)", and structural similarity involves "n-place (argument)" predicates. For the sake of space saving, readers may turn to Section 6. 2. 3 for a detailed description of the design of the questionnaire.

The two sets of rating scores for the pairs intended to be attributively similar and those to be structurally similar were subjected to an independent t-test. The result showed that there is a significant difference between the attributive metaphors (M=3. 19) and the corresponding relational metaphors (M=5. 75) in each pair (t=−11. 734, P<0), indicating that the similarity type in each pair was effectively controlled. A full list of the metaphor pairs and their mean similarity rating scores is presented in Appendix IX.

(2) Target words manipulation

The target words for each pair were generated through four steps as follows. First, 20 undergraduates participated in a property generation task, the aim of which was to identify the two target words that are most commonly semantically associated with each vehicle. Both the two metaphors in a pair were presented simultaneously, and each participant generated two words(no constraints on word class) which were most closely related to the two metaphors respectively and first came into his or her mind(e. g., “湖面 — 镜子 — 平静” lake surface — mirror — flat and “历史 — 镜子 — 反思” history — mirror — reflective).The task was conducted at their full leisure. Second, all the words generated in the first step were subjected to a frequency statistics analysis. For each metaphor, the most frequently created word was chosen as the target word. The words for the attributively similar metaphors were taken as the concrete literal targets, and the ones for the structurally similar metaphors were taken as the abstract metaphorical targets. Third, the unrelated target for each metaphor pair was initially created by the author herself, and then subjected to a 7-point scale rating with 1 denoting “not related at all” and 7 denoting “ very closely related”. 20 independent subjects participated in the rating task. The result showed that the intended unrelated words got a meaning of 2. 3. Fourth, the nonword filler targets were generated by the author.

In order to control the frequency of the target words, all of them were further subjected to a 7-point scale frequency rating with 1 denoting “not frequently encountered at all” and 7 denoting “very frequently encountered”. The scores of the three critical conditions of target words were subjected to a one-way anovo test, and the results showed that there were no significant difference among the three critical groups of target words($F=0.330$, $p=0.720$), with the means as 5. 44, 5. 46 and 5. 56 respectively.

Based on the manipulating processes described above, 30 pairs of metaphors were finally recruited as the experimental stimuli. Owing to the difficulty in finding metaphor pairs which have the same vehicles yet distinct topics denoting distinct types of similarity, each subject encountered each of the vehicles six times in the whole experiment. Of the six times, three times were with the topic providing attributive similarity, and three times were with the topic providing relational similarity. Although six times of repetition for each vehicle would lead to the problem of memory effect, as all the trials were randomly presented in the order, the potential effect of memory could be maximally eliminated by counterbalancing across trials and subjects.

For each critical experimental pair, there were three types of targets, thus yielding 180 trials in total. All the nonword targets were paired with the filler metaphors which were an independent group of 90 metaphors presented twice. So there were totally 180 trials in the formal experiment. A sample of the stimuli is presented in Table 6. 3.

Table 6. 3 composition of the stimuli used in Exp 2A

priming metaphorical pairs	target word types		
30 attributive metaphorical pairs (e. g.,湖面 — 镜子 lake surface — mirror)	literal	abstract	unrelated
30 relational metaphorical pairs; (e. g.,历史 — 镜子 history — mirror)	concrete (e. g.,光滑 smooth)	metaphorlcal (e. g.,反思 reflective)	word (e. g.,旋律 melody)
90 fillers (e. g.,爱情 — 游戏 love — game)		nonword	

As the nonword filler targets were not subjected to further statistical analysis, only the critical metaphor pairs and their corresponding targets are presented in Appendix X.

Design: A2(metaphor prime type: attributive metaphor prime, structural metaphor prime)×3(target type: concrete literal, abstract categorical, unrelated)×3(target SOA: 375 ms,750 ms,1 500 ms)mixed design was employed. Metaphorical pair type and target type were manipulated within subjects, and SOAs were between subjects.

Procedure: Subjects were instructed to comprehend a metaphor presented visually on the computer screen and then to fulfill a lexical decision task. The procedure was run by E-prime software. A red fixation "+" was initially presented for 500 ms, then a stimulus metaphor was presented sequentially. That is, a metaphor topic(e. g., "男人") was presented for 500 ms, and then the copula verb(e. g., "是") was presented for 200 ms. Following this, the vehicle(e. g., "狼") was presented for 375 ms, 750 ms or 1 500 ms respectively within subjects as manipulation of target SOAs. Upon the offset of the vehicle, a target(e. g., "尖牙") was presented for 2 000 ms. The participants were instructed to carefully read and figure out the similarity conveyed by the topic and vehicle pair, and make a key press as quickly and accurately as possible as to whether the target word was a meaningful Chinese word or not. The reaction time between the onset of the target and the key press was recorded as the dependent variable. Reaction time longer than 2 000 ms were regarded as invalid responses. After the key press, a 1-second blank was presented as trial interval. The participants were informed that one cloze test related to the experimental stimuli would be conducted to guarantee that they were fully attended to the experiment tasks. The procedure is presented diagrammatically in Figure 6. 4.

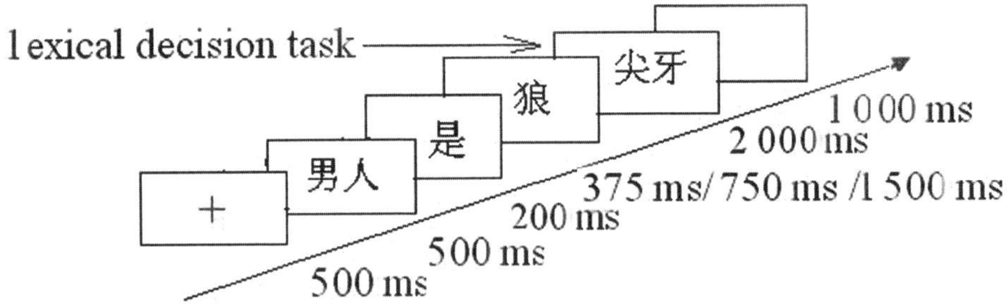

Figure 6. 4 The experimental procedure of Exp 3a

6. 3. 1. 4 Results

The data from 8 subjects were excluded from further analyses due to their failure to reach an accuracy rate of 80 %. Only correct responses were recruited for further statistics. On each condition, reaction times falling out of 2. 5 standard deviations were considered as outliers and excluded from further analyses, resulting in a rejection of 4. 08 % of all responses. Missing response time were randomly distributed across subjects and conditions and were not replaced. The data from the remaining 88 subjects, 30 in the 375 ms SOA condition, 31 in 750 ms SOA and 27 in 1 500 ms SOA, were included in the following analyses. All the data were analyzed through SPSS16. 0.

Firstly, the descriptive data of mean response times and mean accuracy rate for each condition are presented in Table 6. 4 and Table 5.

Table 6. 4 Mean lexical decision RT(in ms) and ACC(%) in Exp 3a

metaphor similarity type	attributive	relational	*N*
target type	literal metaphorical unrelated	literal metaphorical unrelated	
375 ms SOA	544(95. 7)563(95. 4)560(95. 2)	539(95. 7)557(94. 2)563(94. 3)	30
750 ms SOA	546(95. 3)578(93. 4)563(93. 4)	588(90. 7)545(95. 6)573(93. 7)	31
1 500 ms SOA	520(93. 3)542(96. 3)545(95. 4)	541(92. 4)521(96. 1)541(95. 2)	27

Table 6. 5 Results for the mixed-design ANOVO in Exp 3a

source	type III sum of squares	df	mean square	F	Sig.
within-subjects					
metaphor similarity type	82.716	1	82.716	0.085	0.771
metaphor similarity type * SOA	2 026.208	2	1 013.104	1.042	0.357
error	82 622.875	85	972.034		
target type	10 834.371	2	5 417.185	3.709	0.027
target type * SOA	10 120.059	4	2 530.015	1.732	0.145
error	248 315.665	170	1 460.680		
metaphor similarity type * target type	34 575.707	2	17 287.853	17.868	0
metaphor similarity type * target type * SOA	21 462.369	4	5 365.592	5.546	0
error	164 476.059	170	967.506		
betwwen-subjects					
SOA	81 140.016	2	40 570.008	4.171	0.019
error	826 703.226	85	9 725.920		

The overall results from the three-factor analysis of variance (metaphor prime type, target type, and SOA) using subjects as a random factor are reported first. There was no significant main effect of metaphor similarity type on target lexical decision time, $F_{(1,\ 85)} = 0.085$, MSE = 82.716, $p = 0.771$. Collapsing across all conditions of target types and SOAs, subjects were equally fast in the attributive similarity condition (M=552 ms) (the mean of 544, 563, 560, 546, 578, 563, 520, 542 and 545) as in the relational similarity condition (M=553 ms) (the mean of 539, 557, 563, 588, 545, 573, 541, 521 and 541). The main effect of target type reached significance, $F_{(2,\ 170)} = 3.709$, MSE = 5 417.185, $p = 0.027$. Collapsing across conditions of metaphor similarity type and SOAs, responses were equally fast in the concrete target condition (M = 546 ms) and the abstract target condition (M=551 ms); and the two in turn were significantly faster than in the unrelated target condition (M=558 ms). The main effect of SOA was also significant, $F_{(2,\ 85)} = 4.171$, MSE=40 570.008, $p = 0.019$. Responses were faster when targets were presented at 1 500 ms (M=535 ms), and were slower at the 375 ms SOA (M=554 ms) and 750 ms SOA (M=566 ms). The interaction between metaphor similarity type and SOA was not significant, $F_{(2,\ 85)} = 1.042$, MSE = 1 013.104, $p = 0.357$. The interaction between target type and SOA was not significant either, $F_{(4,\ 170)} = 1.732$, MSE = 2 530.015, $p = 0.145$. More importantly, the interaction between metaphor prime type and target type was significant, $F_{(2,\ 170)} = 0.17.868$, MSE = 17 287.853, $p<0$. Collapsing across three SOAs, when primed by the metaphors with attributive similarity, the concrete targets were responded faster than the unrelated control targets, ($M = 537$ ms and $M = 556$ ms respectively). Whereas the responses for the abstract target words were slower than the unrelated control targets, ($M = 561$ ms and $M = 556$ ms respectively). However, for the abstract target words, when primed by the metaphors with relational similarity, the priming pattern got reversed. That is, the abstract target words were faster than the unrelated control targets, ($M = 541$ ms and $M = 559$ ms respectively), yet the concrete target words were not significantly slower than the unrelated control targets ($M = 556$ ms and $M = 559$ ms respectively). The three-way interaction with SOA also reached significance, $F_{(4,\ 170)} = 5.546$, MSE = 5 365.592, $p < 0$, and indicated that the pattern of the interaction between metaphorical similarity and the target words altered across the three levels of SOAs.

The anova on the ACC rate yielded a significant main effect in target word type, $F_{(2,\ 170)} = 3.728$, MSE = 0.008, $p = 0.026$, and a marginally significant main effect in SOAs, $F_{(2,\ 85)} = 2.761$, MSE = 0.01, $p = 0.069$. The two-way interaction effect between the target word type and the SOA, and the three-way interaction effect between metaphor similarity type, target word type and the SOA both reached significance, $F_{(4,\ 170)} = 3.605$, MSE = 0.007, $p = 0.008$ and $F_{(4,\ 170)} = 3.273$, MSE = 0.007, $p = 0.013$ respectively.

To test the predicted effects of metaphor similarity on different targets at the three SOAs, several planned comparisons were conducted. Figure 6.5 shows the mean target decision times at the 375 SOA condition.

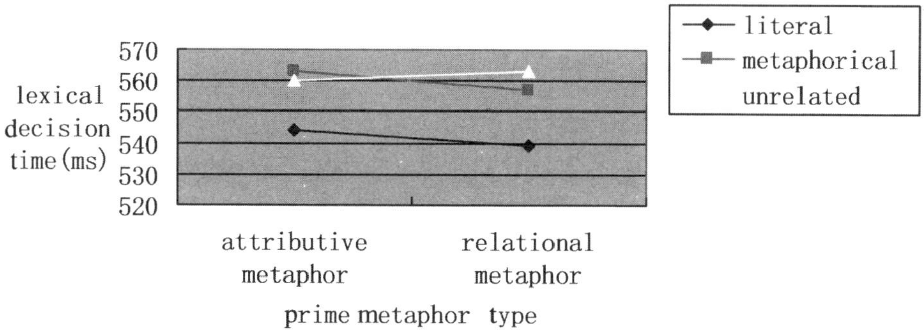

Figure 6.5 Lexical decision times in Exp 3a when SOA = 375 ms

When presented at the shortest SOA (375 ms) and primed by metaphors with attributive similarities, subjects responded to concrete literal targets ($M = 544$ ms) marginally significantly faster than to the unrelated control targets ($M = 560$ ms), $t_{(29)} = -1.894$, $p = 0.068$; subjects responded to abstract targets ($M = 563$ ms) as fast as to the unrelated control targets ($M = 560$ ms), $t_{(29)} = 0.549$, $p = 0.587$. A similar pattern of priming effect was detected when primed by metaphors with relational similarities, subjects responded to concrete literal targets ($M = 539$ ms) significantly faster than the unrelated control targets ($M = 563$ ms), $t_{(29)} = -3.514$, $p = 0.001$. Although the mean reaction times for the abstract metaphorical targets ($M = 557$ ms) was faster than the unrelated control targets ($M = 563$ ms), the difference didn't reach statistical significance level, $t_{(29)} = -1.193$, $p = 0.242$. This pattern of data showed that at an early stage of metaphor processing, no matter whether the metaphor had attributive similarity or relational similarity, there were similar patterns of priming effect for both the concrete literal target words and the abstract metaphorical target words. That is, at the outset of metaphor processing, the concrete features of the vehicle were always activated, yet the same pattern of activation did not occur to the abstract metaphorical target words. This is unsurprising for the metaphors with attributive similarity. However, for metaphors with relational similarity, this finding is of more significance. This finding seemed somewhat counter-intuitive in that the initial retrieval of lexical knowledge also involves concrete literal features even for relational metaphors which have abstract ultimate interpretations.

These findings also have important implications for the nature of structure mapping, as we described above, structure mapping is assumed to have the characteristic of first-matching-later-projecting in terms of the time course of processing. The nature of this processing still remains unraveled. In this sense, this study can be of greater theoretical enlightenment. Recall that 375 ms SOA is generally considered as a stage at which automatic processing of simple semantic information occurs, we can then tentatively conclude that the initial stage based on concrete semantic feature matching in metaphor processing is automatically processed (see Figure 6.6).

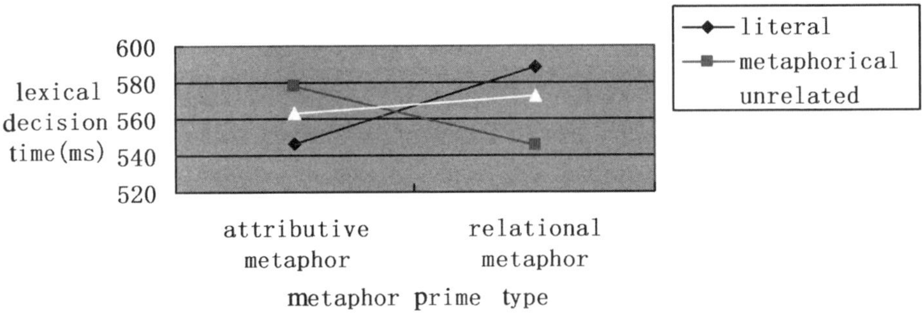

Figure 6.6 Lexical decision times in Exp 2a when SOA = 750 ms

Figure 6.6 presents the mean target decision time from the 750 ms SOA. The pattern of response time in this longer delay decision condition is quite different from that in the 375 ms SOA. When primed by attributive metaphors, subjects responded to concrete literal targets ($M = 546$ ms) marginally significantly faster than the unrelated control targets ($M = 563$ ms), $t_{(30)} = -1.378$, $p = 0.078$; different from the 375 ms SOA condition, subjects responded to abstract metaphorical targets ($M = 578$ ms) more slowly than to the unrelated control targets ($M = 563$ ms), $t_{(30)} = 1.733$, $p = 0.093$. These results indicate that when primed by attributive metaphors, the concrete literal features remain activated till 750 ms SOA. Contrary to the 375 ms SOA in which the abstract target words were not significantly faster to respond despite that the mean response time was slower than the unrelated control target words, the abstract lexical features become actively suppressed at this stage of processing. The pattern of priming effect was roughly in an opposite direction for metaphors with relational similarity. Although the concrete literal targets ($M = 588$ ms) had a slower mean response time than the unrelated control condition (M = 573 ms), the difference did not reach significance $t_{(30)} = -2.651$, $p = 0.13$, indicating that the relational metaphors exerted no priming effect for the concrete target words at the intermediate 750ms SOA. In contrast, the abstract targets(M = 545 ms) were significantly faster to respond to than the unrelated control target(M = 573 ms), (M = 563 ms), $t_{(30)} = -3.694$, $p < 0.001$, indicating a strong priming effect on the abstract targets in this condition(See Figure 6.7).

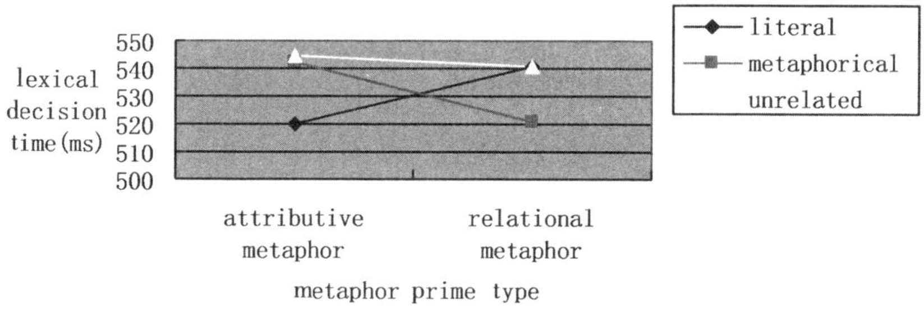

Figure 6.7 Lexical decision times in Exp 2a when SOA = 1 500 ms

Figure 6.7 presents the mean target decision time in the 1 500 ms SOA. In the condition of attributive metaphor, subjects responded to concreteliteral targets (M = 520 ms) faster than to the unrelated control targets (M = 545 ms), $t_{(26)} = -2.335$, $p = 0.028$; yet the difference between the abstract target words and the unrelated control targets did not reach significance(M = 542 ms and M = 545 ms respectively), $t_{(26)} = -0.357$, $p = 0.724$. When primed by relational metaphors, there was not a significant priming effect for the concrete targets(M = 541 ms) in comparison with the unrelated control condition(M = 542 ms), $t_{(26)} = -0.0267$, $p = 0.979$; yet the priming effect for the relational target words (M = 521ms) was marginally significant, $t_{(26)} = -1.900$, $p = 0.069$. These results indicate that at the later stage of metaphor processing, only the senses related to the final interpretation of the metaphor are activated, and those that are irrelevant to the final interpretation are not activated. However, different from the 750 SOA condition in which the irrelevant senses are actively suppressed, the irrelevant senses are merely not activated, not actively suppressed.

Further t-tests indicated that when primed by attributive metaphors, response time for concrete literal targets in the 375 ms SOAwere as fast as those in the 750 ms SOA(M=544 ms and M=546 ms respectively), $t_{(59)} = -0.147$, $p = 0.884$, and they were both slower than those in the 1500 SOA (M = 520 ms), $t_{(26)} = -0.0267$, $p = 0.979$, $t_{(55)} = 2.506$, $p = 0.015$ and $t_{(56)} = 2.117$, $p = 0.039$ respectively. This result indicated that when primed by attributive metaphors, the prime effects for the concrete literal targets maintained to be evenly strong in both the 375 and the 750 ms SOAs, and got greater in the longest SOA. Response time for abstract target words were as fast in the 375 ms SOA as in the 750 ms SOA(M=563 ms and M=578 ms respectively), $t_{(59)} = 1.292$, $p = 0.201$. The difference between the response time for abstract target words in the 375 ms SOA and in the 1 500 ms SOA did not reach significance either, (M = 563 ms and M = 542 ms respectively), $t_{(55)} = 1.421$, $p = 0.161$, indicating that throughout the time course, the abstract targets were not significantly primed in the attributive metaphor condition. It should be noted that although the response time for the abstract target words were faster in the 1 500 ms SOA than in the 750 ms SOA, (M = 542 ms and M = 578 ms respectively), $t_{(56)} = 2.273$, $p = 0.027$, which seemingly indicated a significant priming effect for the abstract metaphorical target words at later stages of the processing course of metaphors with attributive similarity, a deeper look into the data at the 1 500 ms SOA would restrain us from such a conclusion. That is, as shown in the above result analysis, at the 1 500 ms SOA, response times for the abstract metaphorical targets were not significantly faster than those for the unrelated control(M=542 ms and M=545 ms respectively), $t_{(26)} = 2.273$, $p = 0.724$)

When primed by relational metaphors, the priming effect for the concrete literal target words was different from when primed by attributive metaphors. Response times for the concrete literal target words in the 375 ms SOA(M=539 ms) was significantly faster than that in the 750 ms SOA(M=588 ms), $t_{(59)} = -4.128$, $p<0$, and as fast as that in the 1 500 ms SOA(M=541 ms), $t_{(59)} = -0.174$, $p = 0.863$. These results demonstrate that for metaphors with relational similarity, the concrete meaning of the vehicle is immediately activated at an early stage of processing and get suppressed at later stages. As the 375 ms in the time course of metaphor processing generally involves an automatic processing, it could be tentatively concluded that the activation of the attributive feature in metaphor is automatically motivated. And as the hypothetical structure-mapping initially entails processings which are based on feature alignment, the auther assumes these experimental results speak strongly for this hypothesis.

With regard to the response time for the abstract metaphorical target words primed by relational metaphors across different SOAs, the findings were quite different. Subjects responded to the abstract metaphorical target words in the 375 ms SOA (M = 557 ms) as fast as in the 750 ms SOA (M = 545 ms), $t_{(59)} = 0.940$, $p = 0.351$. And both the response time for the abstract metaphorical targets in the two SOAs were significantly slower than those in the 1 500 ms SOA (M = 521 ms) $t_{(55)} = 3.335$, $p = 0.002$ and $t_{(56)} = 1.960$, $p = 0.055$. These results indicated that when primed by relational metaphors, abstract metaphorical targets were evenly activated at relatively early stages of processing, and were most robustly activated at the latest stage of processing. As 370 ms is presumably considered as a stage at which lexical information is automatically processed in the time course of comprehension, it could then be assumed that the early stage of structure-mapping, i.e., the stage of feature alignment involves an automatic retrieval of abstract metaphorical senses. It is interesting to note that at the 1 500 ms SOA, all response time become significantly shorter, indicating lighter cognitive load under this condition. This finding could be explained through the assumption that at the 1 500 ms SOA, the subjects were under lighter time limitation pressure when performing the lexical decision task.

6.3.1.5 Discussion

The primary objective of Experiment 3a is to explore the dynamic aspect of metaphorical categorization, i.e., the time course of the induction of abstract categorical referent in the vehicle. Operationally, this experiment explores the effects of similarity type of the topic and vehicle pair on metaphor processing through investigating the priming effect of the metaphors on the lexical decision times of various target words throughout the time course.

Two relevant interesting findings emerged from this study: (1) It was revealed that metaphor similarity type had significant influence on the priming pattern of various targets words; (2) For different types of metaphors with different natures of similarity, there were very different patterns of activation over time for concrete literal andabstract metaphorical target words.

These findings provide crucial support to the basic hypotheses derived for the present experiment. More specifically, on the one hand, as to the foundation of metaphorical categorization, the present experiment hypothetically took structure-mapping between the topic and the vehicle as the basis for the abstract schema induction which is taken as the basis for metaphorical categorization. In this respect, the first major finding reported above shows that only those metaphors which are of relational similarity exerted priming effect on the abstract target words, indicating that the induction of the abstract schematic referents in the vehicle can be attributed to the structure mapping between the analogical relations held by the topic and the vehicle. Recall that in the present experiment, when primed by attributive metaphors, the concrete literal target words were consistently primed to greater degree across the time course, yet the abstract target words were not activated throughout the time course. It is worthwhile to note that at the stage of 750 ms SOA, the abstract target words were even significantly slower than the unrelated control target, indicating an active suppression of the abstract sense retrieval in metaphor comprehension.

What are of more interest and significance are the findings in the relational metaphors condition. When primed by this type of metaphors, the concrete literal target words were initially activated at an early stage of comprehension (375 ms SOA), yet the activation fades as time passes by, and in a few milliseconds till 750 ms SOA, the activation for the concrete target words disappears. In the latest stage of processing (1 500 ms SOA), the concrete target words still remain suppressed. Contrary to the concrete literal targets, the abstract metaphorical target words were not primed at an early stage of processing, however, in no more than four hundred milliseconds and at 750 ms SOA they were significantly activated, and the activation remains till the later stage of processing (1 500 ms SOA). The author assumes that these patterns of priming cohere with our hypothesis concerning the time course of the induction of the abstract categorical representation. Recall that in describing the theoretical framework for the present experiment in Section 4. 3, we recognize schema induction as the basis for metaphorical categorization. Schema induction is assumed to have the time course of first-matching-later-projecting (Gentner and Markman, 1997). That is, comparisons (even those with relational similarity) at the initial stage of processing involve the emergence of the concrete literal meanings. At later stage, the alignment of these concrete literal senses will lead to the induction of a more abstract representation which can include both the topic and the vehicle as its co-members.

For a comprehensive theoretical interpretation, these supportive findings are to be discussed in three related theoretical frameworks. First, we will discuss the findings in different models of metaphor comprehension in terms of the relation between metaphor and category; second, the implications on the time course of metaphor comprehension will be discussed; and third, the results will be discussed in the framework of the mechanism of enhancement and suppression in language processing.

Firstly, these results shed new light on our understanding of the relation between metaphor and category. In this regard, these findings in the relational metaphor condition can be explained through analyzing the phenomenon of "metaphoricity" which, as we described in Section 3. 1. 2, presumably arises from the tension between category inclusion and category violation in metaphor comprehension and has been regarded as one essence for an assertion to be a metaphor. In this respect, the present experiment generally provides contradictory evidence to two metaphor comprehension models, i. e., the comparison model and the categorization model. Second, The comparison model together with its corresponding similarity theoretical foundation, i. e., the contrast model of similarity (Tversky, 1977) posits that metaphor comprehension only involves the matching of concrete features and that the outcome of metaphor comprehension depends on the overlapping of the literal features that get matched. According to this view, metaphor interpretation does not lead to the emergency of any abstract properties, so a metaphor is always considered as "category violation". As described in the literature review chapter, one criticism against the comparison theory is that it can not account for the phenomenon of abstract property emergence and attribution in metaphor comprehension. In light of the empirical findings released by the present experiment, we can at least assume that the comparison view is not comprehensive in that it can only serve as the theoretical explanation for the topic and vehicle pairs with attributive similarity. In a similar vein, the contrast model (Tversky, 1977) of similarity can also merely speak for metaphors with attributive similarities.

The results of this present study are also to some extent at odds with the categorization theory which posits that metaphor understanding is as natural as the understanding of literal category inclusion assertions. According to this model, metaphor comprehension starts with the retrieval and projection of the abstract representation in an existing category which is denoted by the vehicle. Readers do not encounter an anomaly when they read a metaphor sentence because the vehicle stands for the superordinate ad hoc category; and the sentence is understood as a normal category statement. One fatal criticism against this model is also the problem pertaining to the source of "metaphoricity". The logic is, if metaphor is totally the same as a literal category inclusion assertion, then what makes a metaphorical category inclusion assertion a metaphor rather than a literal categorical assertion?

In this regard, the present study lends some special evidence to the notion that metaphor is based on category construction. Recall that in the experiment, even when primed by relational metaphors, the concrete literal meaning of the vehicle was initially primed at an early stage of processing, indicating an early activation of the attributive property in the vehicle. Actually, this finding can better explain the source of the "metaphoricity" in metaphor processing which has been always considered as a pitfall for the categorization view. That is, if metaphors, as the categorization model claims, are processed directly through projecting abstract properties from the vehicle to the topic, then the metaphorical category-inclusion will not be recognized as different from literal category-inclusion assertion. Our tentative account for "metaphoricity" is as follows. As literal meanings would not lead to legitimate understanding in metaphor reading, they would result in what is termed as "semantically defection" arising from an initial aberration (Searle, 1979). This will tax the listeners' cognitive resource to actively search for a sound candidate interpretation of the metaphor based on the world knowledge. The realization of "metaphoricity" in a metaphor can be accounted for by the tension arising from the extra cognitive burden in competitively suppressing the literal concrete senses which were initially automatically activated and effortfully searching for an alternative metaphorical reading at later stages.

Besides the issue of metaphoricity which arises from the tension between category aberration and category construction, a second crucial problem is the time course of the category construction process per se. In this respect, the findings in the present study can also shed significant light on the process of metaphorical categorization in terms of its time course. Although several previous studies have initially explored the mechanism underlying categorization in metaphor processing (Gentner and Bowdle, 2001; Bowdle and Gentner, 2005), those studies were mainly theoretically oriented and did not empirically investigated the dynamic aspect of this process, especially its time course. Actually, only the very initial stage of the metaphor comprehension has been examined by two empirical studies, leaving the later stages of the processing still a moot point. Wolff and Gentner (2000), through using a priming paradigm, explored the initial stage of metaphor processing in terms of metaphorical categorization in the theoretical framework of structure-mapping. In that study, the metaphors were preceded by the base term, the target term, or nothing. Subjects' latencies to interpret the metaphors were recorded in three experiments. The research rationale was as follows. First, interpretations should be faster with advanced terms than without, simply because of advanced encoding. Second, matching-first models predict no difference in interpretation time between base and target priming in that both the two terms play equal roles in metaphor processing. In contrast, mapping-first models predict a bigger priming effect for base priming than target priming in that metaphor processing begins with retrieval of the related senses in the base. Their experimental results generally supported matching-first models. Unfortunately, they did not explore the later stages of metaphor comprehension. This present experiment, on the one hand, coheres with Wolff and Gentner' study regarding the initial stage of the metaphor processing; on the other hand, this study also further looks into later stages of the process. Besides the time course, this study also complements previous studies in that the author manipulated the similarity type of the metaphors used in the study.

The third piece of enlightenment shed by the present experimentis concerned with the nature of metaphorical categorization when the time course is analyzed in the framework of enhancement and suppression mechanism of general language processing. Several studies (Gernsbacher, 1989, 1997; Gernsbacher and Jescheniak, 1995; Gernsbacher and Shroyer, 1989) have shown that language comprehension is enabled by modulating two mechanisms, i. e., enhancement and suppression. Enhancement is the increase in activation of memory nodes that represent information central to the on-going comprehension. Suppression is the active reduction in activation of the memory nodes that represent information potentially confusing or irrelevant for understanding. One more recent study specifically focuses on metaphor processing (Gernsbacher, Kayser, and Roberston, 2001) suggests that metaphor comprehension also unexceptionally entails these two mechanisms. Based on a series of priming experiments, their study concluded that suppression plays a crucial role in arriving at an ultimate intended meaning of metaphors. That is, the readers can infer a metaphorical intended meaning in context by actively suppressing a literal meaning.

It is noteworthy that. Gernsbacher et al.'s study (ibid) demonstrated that the literal meaning of the metaphor is "actively" suppressed, which implies that the literal meaning is to some extent activated so that it is cognitively taxing to get actively suppressed. Indeed, Blasko and Connine (1993) provide evidence for the activation of the literal meaning of metaphor vehicles as people hear metaphorical sentences. Using a cross-modal priming paradigm, they demonstrated that immediately following the vehicle of the metaphor (e. g., "Hard work is a ladder.") the concept "rungs" was activated. Blasko and Connine's (ibid) finding suggested that the literal meaning of ladder was available for the readers during comprehension. In contrast to Blasko and Connine's study, some other studies strongly claimed that metaphor comprehension merely involves the activation of the abstract superordinate meaning of the metaphor (Glucksberg and Keysar, 1990; also see Section 3. 1. 2. 2). Combining these two contradictory findings concerning the activation of the literal meaning in previous studies with the findings of the present experiment, we can reasonably suspect that these contradictory findings were due to the failures in manipulating the latency of the priming effect on the one hand and in manipulating the similarity nature of the topic and vehicle on the other.

Specifically, in Glucksberg and Keysar' studies (1990), although not reported, the priming effect for the literal meaning might have been detected at later stages of processing, so their results showed that only the abstract superordinate meanings of the vehicle were activated. In contrast, Blasko and Connine's study might have been detected at an initial stage of processing, thus their result showed a priming effect for the literal meanings. All the contradictory results revealed by the present study against previous studies can be tentatively attributable to the fact that previous studies did not manipulate the types of similarity of the topic-vehicle pairs or the SOAs. In this regard, the present experiment, via manipulating SOAs of priming, can serve as a more comprehensive study on various priming effects for various target words at different stages of processing.

Generally, the results of this study showed that in attributive metaphors, only literal meanings of the vehicle were activated, and the activation maintains throughout the entire time course. That is, the abstract meanings which were irrelevant to ultimate metaphor understanding were suppressed from the beginning to the end. However, for relational metaphors, although the literal meanings of the vehicle were irrelevant to the ultimate interpretation, they were still activated at the outset of processing (375 ms), after a delay of approximate 300 ms, these activations would get actively suppressed, and the suppression maintain till the later stage of processing.

In conclusion, metaphors (especially those with relational similarity) have a first-matching-later-projecting processing time course, which can be generally interpreted in the framework of structure-mapping theory.

6.3.1.6 Summary

In this section, we empirically examined research Q3a through testing one aspect of Sub-H2 concerning the dynamic aspect of metaphorical categorization at the macro level through employing a priming paradigm. We proposed that it is structure-mapping and schema induction that underlie the mechanism of metaphorical categorization. Specifically, two major hypotheses have been generally confirmed.

Firstly, it was revealed that metaphors conveying relational similarity resulted in a priming effect for the abstract target words, yet the same priming effect was not discovered in metaphors conveying attributive similarity. This finding can be interpreted as evidence showing that metaphorical categorization takes structure-mapping based on abstract relational structures as its foundation.

Secondly, the findings pertaining to the time course of the priming effect on various types of target words indicate that, as predicted by the structure-mapping and schema induction theory, there is a first-matching-later-projecting feature in the time course of the induction of the abstract schematic meanings in the vehicle.

Findings of Exp 3a could only be interpreted as evidence concerning the dynamic induction of the abstract category from the angle of the time course of the processing. Exp 3b sets out to examine the mechanism wherein the vehicle gets a categorical referent in the long run.

6.3.2 Exp 3b: abstract schema induction in the vehicle: a vitro study

6.3.2.1 Research aim

Exp 3b continues to explore the macro-categorization in metaphorical categorization, i. e., the mechanism in which the vehicle gets an abstract categorical referent. Being complementary to Exp 3a which looked into the time course of the abstraction of the vehicle, Exp 3b adopted a vitro-diachronical paradigm (diachronial in an experimental context) to investigate the dynamic process in which the metaphor vehicle gains the abstract categorical referent which is presumably based on the abstract schema induction from structure mapping between the topic and the vehicle. The following research question echoes with Q 3b (see Figure 4.6). Firstly, is the gaining of the abstract categorical referent in the vehicle the by-product of the structure mapping between the topic and the vehicle? Secondly, is the abstraction of the vehicle based on repeated induction of the structures shared by the topic and the vehicle, or merely on the repeated memorization of the same schema?

6.3.2.2 Design logic and hypothesis

Before proceeding to describe the design logic for this experiment, it is necessary to have a look at previous empirical studies which investigated the diachronical process in which the vehicle gets abstract categorical referents.

The hypothesized categorization process in the vehicle was assessed most directly in Bowdle and Gentner's study (2005) that attempted to stimulate the process of metaphor conventionalization in vitro. In that study, participants were exposed to sets of novel similes with the same vehicle, e. g., "An acrobat is like a butterfly." relative to the simile form, e. g., "A figure skater is like a butterfly.". Then they were asked to generate a topic for the statement "________ is like a butterfly." such that it expresses the same meaning as in the previous two similes. The test phase measured participants' expressed preference for the metaphor form, e. g., "A ballerina is a butterfly.", relative to the simile form, e. g., "A ballerina is like a butterfly.". Metaphor preference was greater when participants had been exposed to the vehicle concept than when they had not. Assuming that the repeated exposure to the same vehicle simulated the diachronical conventionalization of metaphors, the results were taken as support evidence for a dynamic shift from comparison to categorization in metaphor comprehension.

The author thinks that the experiment reviewed above has several serious drawbacks. Firstly, the experiment merely manipulated conventionality level of the vehicle yet without controlling the topic. Although this experiment paired the same vehicles with various topics, the nature of the similarity between the topic and the vehicle were not manipulated. Thus, a further comprehensive investigation into the role of metaphor similarity in vehicle categorization is still needed. Secondly, as pointed out in Section 3. 2. 2. 4, the grammatical preference rating adopted in the testing phase was not adequate to reflect the on-line processing of metaphor.

Contrary to the career model, the dual-categorization model proposed by the present study asserts that the process by which the metaphor vehicle gets associated with the macro-category denoting the abstract structural schema is diachronical. The basic tenet concerning this diachronical process is that the induction of the macro-category in the vehicle is the by-product of the structure-mapping between the topic and the vehicle. Following this are several corollaries. First, with regard to the similarity nature, this study assumes that only those topic-vehicle pairs with structural similarity can give rise to abstraction in the vehicle. Second, the abstraction of the vehicle results from the activation of the relational schema which is based on the structure-mapping between the same vehicle with various topics across historical use, rather than repeated memorization of a certain fixed topic-vehicle pair.

Given these considerations, the present experiment was intended, on the one hand, to further look into the potential role of similarity in vehicle categorization, and on the other, to test whether the association between the macro-category and the vehicle is the result of merely repeated memorizing or of an induction process based on repeated activation of the same schema arising between the same vehicle and various topics, which usually happens in natural metaphor use. Consequently, two variables were manipulated in the present experiment, i. e., the similarity nature of the topic-vehicle pair and the type of learning experience. Based on the proposed dual-categorization account of metaphorical categorization for the present study, we can derive the following hypotheses concerning the macro-categorization process in the vehicle.

H1: Comparing topic and vehicle pairs which denote relational similarity can lead to categorization in the vehicles; whereas comparing topic and vehicle pairs which denote attributive similarity can not. This will be operationally reflected by the various priming effects of the vehicle on different types of target words at different levels of abstraction in the testing phase of the present experiment. More specifically, a significant priming effect for the abstract categorical targets can only be detected in the conditions wherein the subjects undergo the comparison between topic and vehicle pairs denoting relational similarity.

H2: Categorization in the vehicle will be more facilitated when the same vehicle is repeatedly used with variant topics over time than repeatedly with the same single topic. This hypothesis will be operationally reflected by various priming effects of the vehicle on different target words at different levels of abstractness. More specifically, a significantly greater priming effect for the abstract categorical targets would be detected in the variant-topic condition than in the repeated-topic condition.

6.3.2.3 Method

Participants: 120 participants, including 39 males and 81 females, were recruited from the population of undergraduate students at SCNU. Participants speak Chinese as their first language and have normal or corrected-to-normal visions.

Material development:

Topic and vehicle pairs: The 30 vehicles used in Exp 3b were the same as those used in Exp 3a. So for each vehicle(e. g., mirror), two types of topics were generated based on the criterion that one type denotes attributive similarity(e. g., lake surface—mirror) and the other denotes structural similarity(e. g., history—mirror). In order to prepare sufficient variant topics for the learning phase, three separate topics with the same property of similarity were generated for each vehicle. For example, for the vehicle mirror, three pairs with attributive similarity and another three pairs with structural similarity were generated respectively, as shown in Table 6.6:

Table 6.6 Examples of the stimuli used in the learning phase of Exp 3b

pairs with attributive similarity	e. g.,湖面(humian,lake surface) — 镜子(jingzi,mirror); e. g.,湖面(humian,lake surface) — 镜子(jingzi,mirror); e. g.,湖面(humian,lake surface) — 镜子(jingzi,mirror)
pairs with structural similarity	e. g.,历史(lishi,history) — 镜子(jingzi,mirror); e. g.,朋友(pengyou,friend) — 镜子(jingzi,mirror); e. g.,评论(pinglun,comment) — 镜子(jingzi,mirror)

To guarantee the validity of the similarity manipulation, the similarity property rating procedure(the involvement of the number of arguments) which had been used in Exp 2 was adopted in the present similarity manipulation(See Section 6.2.3 for a detailed description). Across the three variant topics for the same vehicle in each group, one-way anovas showed that no significant difference appeared among the three topics either in the attributive similarity group or in the relational similarity group $F_{(2, 87)} = 0.861$, $P = 0.426$, and $F_{(2, 87)} = 0.085$, $P = 0.919$ respectively. An independent t-test between the mean scores of the two groups showed that there was a significant difference between these two types of topic-vehicle pairs with means as 3.49 and 5.54 respectively, $t_{(58)} = -8.208.$, $P<0$, indicating that the two types of materials were qualitatively different from each other in terms of their similarity nature. Thus, six topics were created for each vehicle, resulting in 180 topics for 30 vehicles in total. A complete list of the materials is presented in Appendix XI.

Design: A 2(similarity of word pair: attributive similar, structural similar)×2 (learning type: repeated topic, variant topic)×3(probe type: abstract categorical, concrete literal , unrelated control)mixed design was adopted. Similarity of word pair and learning type were manipulated between subjects while probe word type was varied within subjects.

Procedure: The whole experiment consisted of two phases which are a learning phase and a testing phase. The learning phase was taken as the manipulation of the diachronical process of the categorization in the vehicle, and the test phase in which a semantic priming paradigm was adopted was taken as the investigation into the abstraction level of the vehicle. The whole general procedure is presented in the Figure 6.8:

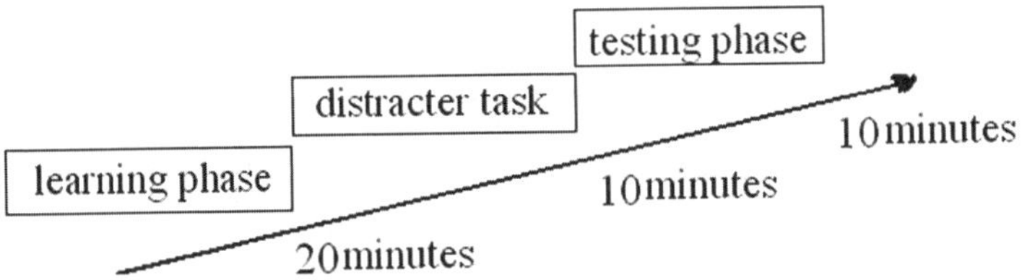

Figure 6.8 The experimental procedure of Exp 3b

The learning phase: Different from other studies in which the learning phase was conducted on a paper-and-pen basis, the learning phase in the current experiment was carried out through an E-prime procedure on computer screen. There were four different conditions according to the 2 (similarity of word pair: attributive similar, structural similar) ×2 (learning type: repeated topic, variant topic) design. That is to say, each vehicle underwent four types of learning experience. The 120 subjects were randomly and evenly assigned to one of the four tasks, resulting in 30 in each condition.

During the learning phase, the types of learning experience were determined by the fashion of pairing the vehicle with various topics. The subjects encountered a specific vehicle word paired with its three corresponding topic words and were instructed to explicitly figure out the similarity conveyed by each pair. In order to guarantee that the subjects carefully imagine the similarity, the subjects were instructed to "to judge the degree of the similarity conveyed by a pair after reading it, and correspondingly press the number buttons 1, 2, 3, or 4 to indicate the degrees of the similarity". For half of the subjects, the numbers from 1 to 4 were assigned to increasing degrees of similarity, sequently from "no similarity conveyed at all" "a little similarity conveyed" "some similarity conveyed", to "much similarity conveyed". For another half, the order was reversed. The subjects were also confirmed that the major aim of the learning phase was to interpret and memorize the similarity conveyed by each pair without pressure of time limitation or accuracy rate, and there would be a test of similarity word recording following the similarity judging task.

Also different from both Bowdle and Gentner's (2005) and Mckay's (2004) studies in which the presentation of the pairs were in a fixed consecutive order, the present experiment presented the three pairs with the same vehicle in a random order on the ground that the random occurrence was more like the natural situation of language occurrence. For the variant-topic condition, alternative topics were selected that shared the same salient figurative meaning. Taking the vehicle word "mirror" as a case, the four conditions of learning are as follows:

Condition 1(attributive similar, repetition):

1st presentation: lake surface — mirror

2nd presentation: lake surface — mirror

3rd presentation: lake surface — mirror

Condition 2(attributive similar, variant topic):

1st presentation: lake surface — mirror

2nd presentation: floor — mirror

3rd presentation: sky — mirror

Condition 3(structural similar, repetition):

1st presentation: history — mirror

2nd presentation: history — mirror

3rd presentation: history — mirror

Condition 4 :(structural similar, variant topic):

1st presentation: history — mirror

2nd presentation: friend — mirror

3rd presentation: comment — mirror

The learning procedure was run by the E-prime software on computer screen. On each trial, a red fixation "+" was initially presented for 500 ms to remind the subjects to get ready for the forthcoming stimuli, then a blank remained on the screen for 500 ms. After the blank, a topic-vehicle pair was presented for 4 000 ms. The subjects were instructed to interpret the degree of the similarity conveyed by the pair and judge the degree by pressing 1, 2, 3 or 4. For half of the subjects, they were informed that the bigger the similarity was, the bigger the number would be; and for another half the assignment of the keys was reversed. To guarantee that the subjects carefully derived the similarity, they were informed that there would be no recording of the response time and that there was no right or wrong response either. They were also informed that after the learning task, there would be a test to examine how efficiently they had processed and memorized the similarity. We assume that these instructions could direct the attention of the subjects to the task of similarity per se without time pressure. The word pair disappeared upon the number press. Upon the offset of the word pair, an inter-trial interval lasted for 1 000 ms before another "+" appeared for the following trial. The e-prime procedure of the learning task is presented schematically as follows (see Figure 6.9).

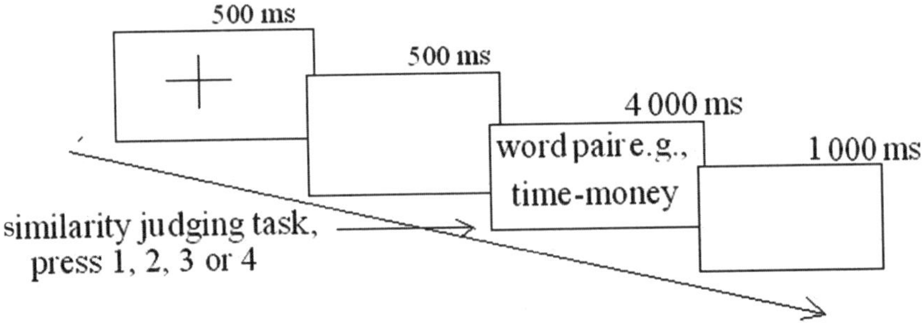

Figure 6.9 The E-prime experimental procedure in the learning phase of Exp 3b

The four lists created respectively for the four conditions are presented in Appendix XII.

Distracter task: After the learning task, the subjects took part in a 10-minute break as a distracting task.

Testing phase: Immediately after the 10 minutes' relaxation, participants began the test phase of the experiment. The author constructed 30 metaphor vehicles as the experimental priming items. 90 words were chosen as lexical decision targets. Of the 90 target words, 30 were related to the abstract categorical meaning of the vehicles, 30 were related to the concrete literal meaning of the vehicles, and 30 were unrelated control targets. Besides these critical experimental items, another 30 nouns were included as filler primes. For each filler trial, one nonword was created as a filler target. The 30 critical experimental metaphor vehicles and their corresponding 90 target words are shown in Appendix XIII.

To avoid repetition effect of materials within participants, three lists of prime vehicle-and-target pairs were constructed. The 30 prime vehicles were rotated across the three lists in a Latin-square design so that a vehicle appeared in any given list no more than once. In addition, each list contained 30 filler prime vehicles that were followed by 30 non-words. The same list of filler primes and their corresponding nonword targets were used cross different lists. The mean frequency of the filler metaphors and their nonword targets was comparable to that of the experimental materials. A sample of the materials used in one list is presented in Table 6. 7.

Table 6. 7 A sample of the materials used in one list in Exp3b

critical experimental materials	10 prime vehicles	10 concrete literal targets
	10 prime vehicles	10 abstract categorical targets
	10 prime vehicles	10 unrelated targets
filler materials	30 prime nouns	30 nonwords

The testing procedure was run by E-prime software on computer screen. On each trial, a red fixation "+" was initially presented for 500 ms to instruct the subjects to get ready for the forthcoming stimuli, then followed by a blank remained for 100 ms. After the blank, a prime vehicle was presented for 500 ms. The subjects were instructed to figure out the meaning of the prime vehicle word. Following that, a blank lasting for 100 ms was presented. Upon the offset of the blank, a target word was presented for 1 500 ms. The participants were instructed to carefully read and comprehend the target word, and make a key press as quickly and accurately as possible as to whether the two characters constituted a legal Chinese word or not[①].

① In Chinese, it is rather difficult to define what constitutes a word. Traditionally, a word is usually considered as the minimal linguistic unit which carries a meaning. In Chinese, one character (e. g., 人) can be a word, and two characters(e. g., 蝴蝶) or more(e. g. 兴高采烈) can also serve as a word. Sometimes, two separate one-character words can be combined to form another word (e. g., 麦+田 — 麦田). The present experiment did not distinguish these two types of two-character words. That is to say, the two characters appearing in the two-character word can either have their independent meanings(e. g., 麦+田 — 麦田) or do not(e. g., 蝴蝶). As the two conditions were used randomly, their effects were assumed to have been counterbalanced.

The reaction time between the onset of the target and the key press was recorded as the dependent variable. After the key press, a 500 ms blank was presented as a trial interval. To guarantee that the subjects pay full attention to and understand the prime vehicles, the subjects were informed that there would be a memory test on the vocabulary which had presented in the priming experiment. The procedure for each trial is shown in Figure 6.10.

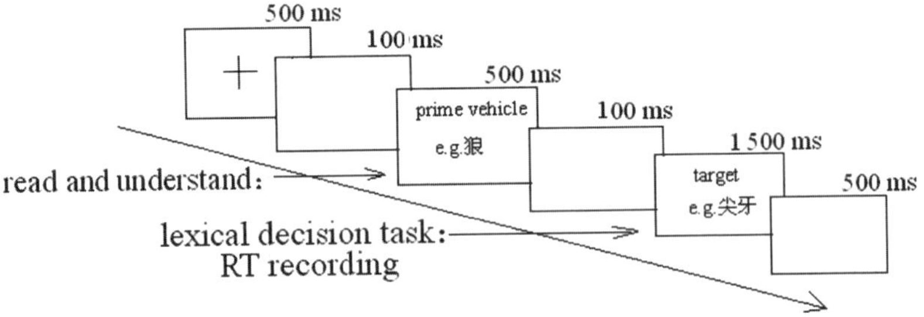

Figure 6. 10 The experimental procedure in the testing phase of Exp 3b

6. 3. 2. 4 Results

The results from the two sections of the experiment are reported separately. The results gained in the learning phase are reported first, and then followed by the results in the testing phase.

6. 3. 2. 4. 1 Results in the learning phase

In the similarity judgment task, the subjects were instructed to interpret the similarity between the two words in a pair and were informed that there was no right or wrong response distinction or time limitation. All the RTs and the similarity judgment scores were recruited for further analyses. The descriptive statistics for the mean response time and the similarity judgments are shown in Table 6. 8.

Table 6. 8 Descriptive data gained in the similarity Judgment task in the learning phase of Exp 3b

	attributive similarity			relational similarity		
	latency time	score	N	latency time	score	N
repetition	1 524(355)	2. 33(0. 38)	30	1 599(266)	2. 63(0. 46)	30
variant topic	2 050(530)	2. 33(0. 32)	30	1 960(451)	2. 49(0. 36)	30

* SD indicated in the parentheses

More descriptive statistics concerning mean latencies and mean rating scores in the similarity judgement task in the learning phase of Exp 3b can bee seen in Figure 6. 11 and Figure 6. 12.

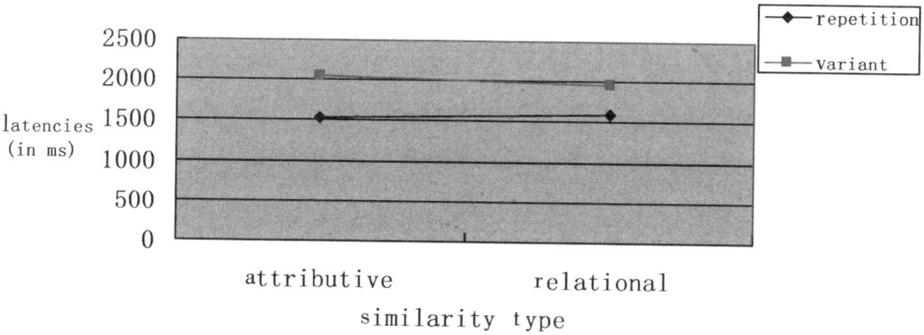

Figure 6. 11 Mean latencies in the similarity judgment task in the learning phase of Exp 3b

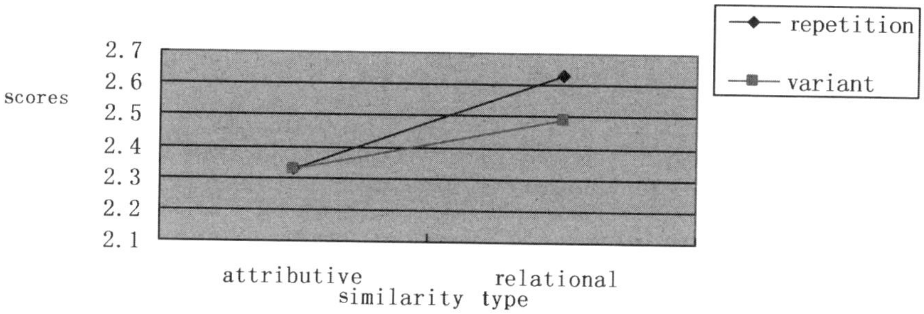

Figure 6. 12 Mean rating scores in the similarity judgment task in the learning phase of Exp 3b

See table 6. 9 for the univariate measures anova summary of mean latency in the similarity judgment task for the learning plase of Exp 3b.

Table 6. 9 Univariate measures anova summary of mean latency in the similarity judgment task for the learning phase of Exp 3b.

source	type III sum of squares	df	mean square	F	sig.
similarity type	1 584. 133	1	1 584. 133	0. 009	0. 923
learning type	5 904 316. 033	1	5 904 316. 033	34. 610	0. 000
similarity type * learning type	201 556. 033	1	201 556. 033	1. 181	0. 279

续表

source	type III sum of squares	df	mean square	F	sig.
error	1.979E7	116	170 595.942		
total	4.075E8	120			

a. R Squared=.236(Adjusted R Squared=.216)

As shown in Table 6.9, the univariate measure anova on the latency data revealed a significant effect of learning type, $F_{(1,\ 116)}=34.610$, MSE=5 904 316.033, $p<0$. As indicated in Table 6.8, collapsing across different similarity types, the mean latency found in the repetition group($M=1\ 561.5$ ms, i.e., the mean of 1 524 and 1 599) was significantly faster than that observed in the variant topic group($M=2\ 005$ ms, i.e., the mean of 2 050 and 1 960). No significant effect was obtained either in similarity type, $F_{(1,\ 116)}=0.009$, MSE = 1 584.133, $p=0.923$, or in the interaction between similarity type and learning type, $F_{(1,\ 116)}=1.181$, MSE=201 556.033, $p=0.279$.

See table 6.10 for the univariate measures anova summary of mean rating scores in the similarity judgment task for the learning plase of Exp 3b.

Table 6.10 Univariate measures anova summary of mean rating scores in the similarity judgment task for the learning phase of Exp3b

source	type III sum of squares	df	mean square	F	sig.
similarity type	1.514	1	1.514	10.110	0.002
learning type	0.157	1	0.157	1.148	0.308
similarity type * learning type	0.129	1	0.129	0.864	0.355
error	17.375	116	0.150		
total	736.538	120			

Table 6.10 presents the univariate measure anova on the similarity judgment rating scores. The results indicated that there was a different pattern of main effects in the rating scores as in the latency. There was a significant effect of similarity type, $F_{(1,\ 116)}=10.110$, MSE=1.514, $p=0.002$. As indicated in Table 6.8, collapsing across different learning type, the mean score found in the relational similarity group ($M=2.56$, i.e., the mean of 2.63 and 2.49) was significantly higher than that

observed in the attributive similarity group(M=2.33, i.e., the mean of 2.33 and 2.33). No significant effect was obtained either in learning type, $F_{(1, 116)}$ = 1.048, MSE=0.157, p=0.308, or in the interaction between similarity type and learning type, $F_{(1, 116)}$=0.864, MSE=0.129, p=0.355.

6.3.2.4.2 Results in the testing phase

Only correct responses in the lexical decision task were recruited for further analyses. Data from 3 subjects who got accuracy rate less than 80 % were removed. Response times beyond 2.5 standard deviations were considered outliers and removed prior to analyses, resulting in an elimination of 6.2 % of all the correct responses. The descriptive statistics for the mean response times and accuracy rates are shown in Table 6.11, and the univariate measures anova summary of mean latency in the lexical decision task for the testing phase of Exp 3b are shown in Table 6.12.

Table 6.11 Descriptive data gained in the lexical decision task in the testing phase of Exp 3b

	attributive similarity						relational similarity					
	repetition			variant topic			repetition			variant topic		
	RT	ACC	N	RT	ACC	N	RT	ACC	N	RT	ACC	N
literal target	576	97.2	28	579	95.2	29	559	93.6	30	641	93.7	30
metaphorical target	574	94.8	28	561	93.9	29	550	95.2	30	611	93.4	30
unrelated control	564	94.5	28	553	94.6	29	541	94.5	30	609	92.3	30

* RT(in ms) ACC(%)

Table 6.12 univariate measures anova summary of mean latency in the lexical decision task for the testing phase of Exp 3b

source	type III sum of squares	df	mean square	F	sig.
within-subjects target	30 617.883	2	15 308.941	9.825	0
target * learning type	5 696.273	2	2 848.137	1.828	0.163
target * similarity	1 473.408	2	736.704	0.473	0.624
target * learning type * similarity	93.552	2	46.776	0.030	0.970
error(target)	352 143.909	226	1 558.159		
between-subjects learning type	86 666.851	1	86 666.851	6.547	0.012

续表

source	type III sum of squares	df	mean square	F	sig.
similarity	24 364. 008	1	24 364. 008	1. 840	0. 178
learning type * similarity	127 900. 478	1	127 900. 478	9. 662	0. 002

The overall results from the three-factor analysis of variance (similarity type, learning type, and target type) using subjects as a random factor are reported first. As shown in Table 6. 12, there was no significant main effect of word pair similarity type on target lexical decision time, $F_{(1,\ 113)} = 1.840$, MSE = 24 364. 008, $p = 0.178$. As indicated in Table 6. 11, pairwise comparison indicated that, collapsing across all conditions of learning types and target types, subjects responded equally fast in the attributive similarity condition(M=568 ms, i. e., the mean of 576, 574, 564, 579, 561 and 553) and in the relational similarity condition(M=584 ms, i. e., the mean of 559, 550, 541, 641, 611 and 609). The main effect of learning type reached significance, $F_{(1,\ 113)} = 6.547$, MSE = 86 666. 851, $p = 0.012$. Collapsing across conditions of similarity type and target types, responses were significantly faster in the repetition condition(M=560 ms, i. e., the mean of 576, 574, 564, 559, 550, and 541) than in the variant topic learning condition(M = 592 ms, 579, 561, 553, 641, 611 and 609). The main effect of the within-subject factor, i. e., target type was also significant, $F_{(2,\ 226)} = 9.825$, MSE = 15 308. 941, $p < 0$. Collapsing across various conditions of learning and similarity type, responses to literal targets were significantly slower(M=588 ms, i. e., the mean of 576, 579, 559, and 641) than to the abstract metaphorical targets(M=574 ms, i. e., the mean of 574, 561, 550, and 611) and to the unrelated targets(M=566 ms, i. e., the mean of 564, 553, 541, and 609).

The interaction between target type and similarity type was not significant, $F_{(2,\ 226)} = 0.473$, MSE = 736. 704, $p = 0.624$; the interaction between target type and learning type was not significant either, $F_{(2,\ 226)} = 1.828$, MSE = 2 848. 137, $p = 0.163$. The three way interaction between target type, learning type and similarity type did not reach significance either, $F_{(2,\ 226)} = 0.030$, MSE = 46. 776, $p = 0.970$. However, the interaction between learning type and similarity type reached significance, $F_{(1,\ 113)} = 9.662$, MSE = 127 900. 478, $p = 0.002$. Collapsing across three types of target words, the results showed that when studying through repetition of the same topic and vehicle pairs, reaction times were faster for the relational pairs(M=550 ms, i. e. the mean of 559, 550 and 541) than for the attributive pairs (M=571 ms i. e. the mean of 576, 574 and 564); whereas when studying through processing the same topic with variant vehicles, the pattern of the reaction time got converted, i. e., reaction time were slower for the relational pairs(M=619 ms, i. e. the mean of 641, 611 and 609) than for the attributive pairs(M=564 ms, i. e. the mean of 579, 561 and 553).

The anova on the ACC rate yielded a significant main effect in similarity type, $F_{(1, 113)}$ = 4.383, MSE=0.014, p=0.039, and a marginally significant main effect in learning type, $F_{(1, 113)}$ = 3.509, MSE = 0.011, p = 0.064. The main effect of target type didn't reach significance, $F_{(2, 226)}$ = 1.318, MSE = 0.003, p = 0.270. The two-way interaction between target and similarity didn't reach significance, $F_{(2, 226)}$ = 2.087, MSE=0.004, p=0.126. The two-way interaction between learning type and similarity didn't reach significance, $F_{(1, 113)}$ = 0.087, MSE = 0.000, p = 0.768. The two-way interaction between learning type and target didn't reach significance either, $F_{(2, 226)}$ = 0.069, MSE = 0.000, p = 0.933. The three-way interaction effect between similarity type, target type and learning type also failed to reach significance, $F_{(2, 226)}$ = 1.814, MSE=0.004, p=0.165(see Figure 6.13).

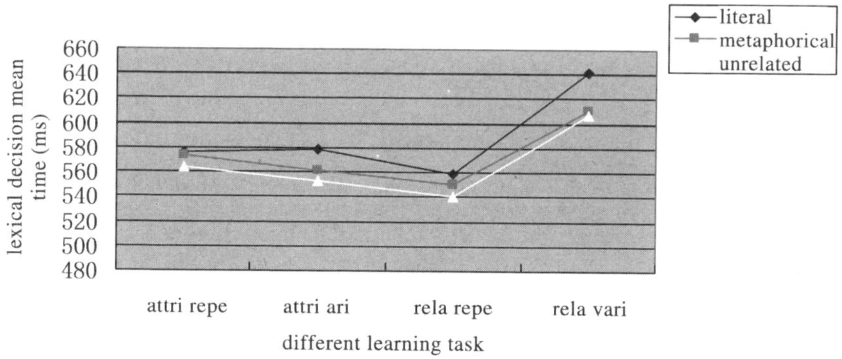

Figure 6. 13 Mean reaction time(in ms) in the lexical decision task in the testing phase in Exp 2C

Notes: attriRepe: attributive, repetition; AttriVari: attributive, variant topic
RelaRepe: relational, repetition; RelaVari: relational, variant topic

More importantly, given the expected variability between subjects in the lexical decision tasks, the study was designed to allow the experimental hypotheses to be tested within subjects through several planned comparisons. As shown in Figure 6.13, different patterns of priming effects in the lexical decision tasks after different learning tasks were detected. In the attributive, repetition learning condition, the response time for the literal, metaphorical and unrelated targets were statistically close (M=576, M=574 and M=564 respectively), $F_{(2)}$ = 1.557, MSE = 1 206.048, p=0.220. However, when the same vehicles were learned through pairing with various topics, response time for the literal targets (M = 579) were marginally significantly longer than those for the metaphorical targets(M = 561), $t_{(28)}$ = 1.871, p=0.072, and significantly longer than those for the unrelated control targets (M=553), $t_{(28)}$ = 2.797, p = 0.009. When the same vehicles were learned through pairing repeatedly with the same topics which provide relational similarity, the literal targets (M = 559) were significantly more slowly responded to than the unrelated controls (M=541), $t_{(29)}$ = 2.537, p=0.017; and the metaphorical targets(M=550) fall midway between the two conditions with no significant difference, $t_{(29)}$ = 1.015, p=0.323 and $t_{(29)}$ = 1.405, p = 0.171 respectively. When the same vehicles were learned through pairing with various topics which provide relational similarity(e.g., boss, enemy, competitor-shark), the literal targets(M = 641) were significantly more slowly responded to than the metaphorical targets(M=611) and the unrelated control targets(M=609), $t_{(29)}$ = 3.124, p=0.004 and $t_{(29)}$ = 2.018, p=0.053 respectively.

Several one-way anovas were performed to test possible differences between subjects when responding to the same target type. The result showed that for the literal targets, there was significant difference among the four conditions, $F_{(3)}$ = 7.361, MSE=38 513.387, p<0. Pairwise comparison showed that response time to the literal target words in the relational, variant topic learning task(M=641ms) were significantly slower than in the other three learning styles which varied nonsignificantly(M=559 ms, M=579 ms, M = 576 ms). Similar pattern of priming effect was also detected in the metaphorical targets, the results showed that there was significant difference among the four learning types, $F_{(3)}$ = 3.782, MSE=20 857.746, p = 0.013. Pairwise comparison showed that response times to the metaphorical target words in the relational, variant topic learning task ($M = 611$ ms) were significantly slower than in the other three learning types($M=550$ ms, $M=561$ ms, $M=574$ ms). The systematicity of this pattern in the relational, variant topic learning task was further confirmed in the unrelated control targets, for which the response time ($M = 609$ ms) in the relational variant topic learning task were also significantly slower than those for the other learning style ($M=541$ ms, $M=553$ ms, $M=564$ ms).

6.3.2.5 Discussion

This section of discussion work is delivered with focus on the statistical findings obtained both in the learning phase and the testing phase. In order to fully interpret the findings, data from the two phases are also analyzed in a combined fashion when necessary.

6.3.2.5.1 On the learning phase

For the latency time in the similarity judgment task, there emerged two major findings. First, results in the learning phase concerning the significant main effect of learning types indicated that when the vehicles were presented with various topics, it would take more time to interpret and judge the similarity degree between the two terms. The author thinks that this finding is unsurprising. In the repetition learning condition, each vehicle term was presented with the same topic for three times. Such repetition would definitely leave some trace on the subjects' short-term memory, which would lighten the cognitive load in judging the commonality between the two terms. Second, the nonsignificant main effect of similarity type showed that interpreting both attributive similarity and relational similarity were equally cognitively demanding in terms of the amount of the consumed processing time. This finding was rather contradictory to our original theoretical prediction. Previous studies provided evidence showing that attributive similarity and relational similarity play qualitatively distinct roles in determining the categorical inclusion form of a metaphorical assertion. Recall that relational similarity has usually been considered to be "more abstract" "deeper" or "more diverse" in meaning interpretation (see Section 4.2), it should be noted, however, that this conclusion has been mainly drawn on the basis of off-line empirical evidence. This kind of off-line evidence was mainly focused on the final outcome of interpretation, neglecting the on-line processing. The findings revealed by the present study demonstrated that such kind of depth or abstractness in the meaning did not necessarily involve more processing time. That is to say, the experimental difference may merely lie in the outcome of interpretation, but not in the processing itself.

With regard to the similarity rating scores, there was one major finding. The significant main effect of similarity type (see Table 6.8 and Figure 6.12) indicated that word pairs with relational similarity, no matter whether learned in a repeated fashion or a variant-topic fashion, were always rated as holding more similarity than those with attributive similarity. This finding was in line with previous studies which indicated that relational metaphors were interpreted as deeper or of more diversity in meaning (Utsumi, 2007). Although relational similarity dose not involve perceptual sensicality, it is greater in the "amount" of similarity than attributive similarity. Numerous studies (Gentner and Markman, 1997) indicated that human had the natural cognitive ability in detecting more rule-based abstract commonality among feature ones, and that abstract commonality takes the upper hand over mere perceptually feature clusters in categorizing process.

A combined interpretation of the findings both in the learning phase of the present experiment and Exp 1 leads us to the conclusion that the qualitative difference between relational similarity and attributive similarity can only be interpreted as acceptable in terms of their "outcomes" rather than their underlying processing mechanisms. Extending this finding to the notion of metaphorical categorization, it can be concluded that relational similarity differs from attributive similarity only in that they convey different senses of similarity in terms of the interpretation outcomes. No existing on-line evidence yet shows that interpreting relational similarity is different from interpreting attributive similarity in terms of their cognitive loads.

6.3.2.5.2 On the testing phase

As the major goal of Exp 3b is to investigate the dynamic induction of the abstract categorical referent in the vehicle, findings revealed in the testing phase are of more crucial interest to the present study. Generally, three central findings were obtained.

Firstly, the statistical results revealed that the gaining of the abstract metaphorical referent in the vehicle was merely reflected through the relative suppression of the literal senses of the vehicle rather than the active activation of the abstract senses themselves. Although the two independent variables (similarity type and learning type) have some priming effect on the activation of the literal and the abstract metaphorical sense of the vehicle, at odds with the author's prediction, these effects are only reflected via the actively suppressed literal senses of the vehicle rather than the activation of the abstract metaphorical sense. Recall that the target word type had a significant main effect, and that the unrelated controls were significantly faster responded to across all the conditions, thus this finding can be taken as indication that the greater strength of the association between the vehicle and the metaphorical sense merely depends on the effort in actively suppressing the literal senses. Or put it another way, comparing with the unrelated control targets, neither the literal targets nor the abstract metaphorical targets were positively primed. In fact, the literal targets and the abstract metaphorical targets differ from each other in that the former were suppressed to a greater degree than the latter. As a result, in the course of metaphor understanding, the abstract metaphorical targets were relatively easier to access than the literal targets.

This finding was partially in line with both Gensbacher et al.'s study (2001) and Exp 1 of the present study, in which it was found that the active suppression mechanism plays a crucial role in language comprehension. More specifically, on the one hand, it is suppression rather than decay that is responsible for the decrease in the activation of the inappropriate meanings of metaphors; on the other hand, such active suppression takes extra cognitive costs. Both of the two points were demonstrated by the present study that, on the one hand, the literal targets were significantly more slowly responded to than the unrelated baseline controls, and on the other hand, after a more cognitively demanding learning task (e. g., the relational similarity and variant topic condition), all the target words, including the unrelated baseline controls, were significantly more slowly responded to. Consequently, in light of Gensbacher's theoretical proposal which asserts that suppression is based on general cognitive mechanism, it can be concluded that the gaining of the abstract metaphorical referents in the vehicle is also part of human general cognition.

Secondly, although similarity type of the learned word pairs failed to exert a significant effect in general, planned comparison results showed that for vehicles that were learned through paring with topics providing relational similarity, no matter through repeated learning or variant topic learning, the literal senses of the vehicle were consistently inhibited, or in Gensbacher's sense, the literal senses of the vehicle probes were actively suppressed as they were getting "more irrelevant". This is consistent with our prediction that in processing the relational similarity between the two words, no matter through repetition of the same topics or variant topics, the abstract metaphorical senses in the vehicle got continuously activated, then the literal target words were negatively suppressed as they were far inconsistent with the priming context which was provided by the learning context.

In contrast, for the vehicles which were learned through paring with attributive topics, there was an interaction between similarity type and learning type. That is, for the repetition condition, there was no significant effect of the negative suppression of the literal meanings, yet for the variant topic condition, the literal targets were negatively suppressed in a fashion similar to the relational similarity fashion, and thus the abstract metaphorical senses of the vehicle would get more salient in comparison with the literal ones. In fact, results from the repeated learning of the attributive similar word pairs are within our prediction in that memorizing the attributive similarity plays little role in the induction of the abstract referents in the vehicle. However, results from the vehicles which were learned through variant topics with attributive similarity were at odds with our original prediction. According to our theoretical hypotheses, when vehicles were learned through pairing with different topics which provide attributive similarity, the literal meanings of the vehicles would get activated and the abstract meanings get suppressed, yet contrary to this, the results showed that a similar priming effect for the literal targets, showing that the literal meanings got actively suppressed.

Although this finding is against our prediction, it is partially in line with Bowdle and Gentner's study (2005). Recall that as we reviewed in Section 6.3.2.2, in Bowdle and Gentner's study which investigated the comparison basis for categorization in metaphor understanding, participants were firstly exposed to sets of novel similes with the same vehicle, e.g., "An acrobat is like a butterfly." and "A figure skater is like a butterfly." Then they were instructed to generate a topic for the statement "________ is like a butterfly." such that it expressed the same meaning as in the previous two similes. In the test phase, participants' expression preference for the metaphor form was measured, e. g., the metaphors form "A ballerina is a butterfly." relative to the simile form"A ballerina is like a butterfly." The results indicated that metaphor preference was greater when participants had been exposed to the vehicle concept than when they had not. These results were taken as support for a dynamic shift from comparison to categorization in metaphor comprehension as the vehicle get more abstractly associated with the metaphor meanings. Both the author's and Bowdle and Gentner's studies showed that experiencing one certain vehicle paired with variant topics providing attributive similarity can result in the abstraction of the vehicle.

These similar counter-intuitive results revealed by the present and Bowdle and Gentner's experiments are very difficult to explain. By revisiting these two studies both theoretically and empirically, the author can figure out two potential explanations. One possible explanation is that both the two studies may have confounded attributive similarity with abstract relational features to some extent. Recall that in our study, we operationally defined attributive similarity according to the extent to which the similarity involves "direct perception", which depends on the five human basic sense modalities(e. g., Barsalou, 1999, 2003), including vision, hearing, touch, smell and taste. The author suspects that some attributively similar topic-vehicle pairs can possibly also have some abstract relational features. For example, in one typical pair used in our study, i. e., lake surface — mirror, it got a below-mean score(=2. 7) in the 7-point scale designed to measure the extent of the involvement of a third argument, showing that it had a weak tendency to evoke relational similarity. However, some more in-depth contemplation will lead us to the finding that similarity between these two words, although mainly depend on physical appearance, may also involve some abstract common relations, which is, lake surface "reflects" physical objects as mirror "reflects" physical objects. The materials used in Bowdle and Gentner's study were suspiciously not free from this problem. In fact, their study did not operationally manipulate the similarity type provided by the topic and vehicle pairs. As the full list of the original experimental materials was not provided, the author suspects that their materials might have contained such topic-vehicle pairs with double-featured similarity.

Besides the nature of similarity, as econd more important potential account for this result is more cognition oriented. That is, man has the innate ability to derive abstract similarity from attributive similarity. Some recent studies posit that conventionally so-termed "attributive similarity" also rely on some relational features. Evidence from developmental studies indicated that the attributive similarity sense ability can give rise to relational similarity sense ability. More abstract understanding of the similarity is based on perception of the attributive concrete world. This notion is in coherence with the embodiment commitment held by cognitive linguistics. That is, human beings understand the abstract concepts in terms of the perception of the concrete world they directly get contact with. People start out relying on overall (mostly perceptual) commonalities to judge similarity between objects, but only shift to appreciating relational similarity, depending on the particular task, as late as 4 years (Blades and Cooke, 1994; Gentner, 2003; Loewenstein and Gentner, 2001, 2005; Rattermann and Gentner, 1998; Smith, 1984) or even 9 ~ 10 years of age (Gentner and Toupin, 1986).

It is also interesting to note that the active suppression of the literal senses in the attributive pairs only occurs to the repeated learning condition. This indicates that the relatively strong association between the vehicle and the metaphorical abstract referent depends on the same abstract schema activated through pairing the same vehicle and various topics.

The third significant finding in this experiment concerns the cognitive load in comparing various kinds of topic-vehicle pairs. Note that after the variant topic learning task that requires comparing relational similar word pairs, the unrelated control baselines were significantly slower responded to than the other three learning conditions. This indicates that such type of learning task is the most cognitively demanding. Recall that the four groups of subjects took part in the same pace of experiment procedure and the same lexical decision task, so the only difference in the four groups is due to the differences in the learning tasks. As a result, the author can attribute the differences in RTs in the testing phase to the learning tasks. This result was within our expectation. On the one hand, relational similarity was more cognitively demanding to derive than attributive similarity even though the two processes consume the same amount of time; on the other hand, the subjects got heavily cognitively loaded when interpreting various pairs of words, without a chance to get access to and retrieve knowledge from memory. After the same duration and relaxation activity, the relational, various topic groups failed to got recovered to the same level as the other three groups, thus in the following testing task, they had significantly slower RTs in the lexical decision task.

6.3.2.6 Summary

All the findings revealed in Exp 3b combinarily verify Sub-H2 pertaining to the core dynamic process of metaphorical categorization, especially in terms of the induction of abstract referent in the metaphor vehicle. First, diachronical learning of topic-vehicle pairs fostered the gaining of the abstract metaphorical referent in the vehicle. Second, the salience of the abstract referent in the vehicle was not due to the activation of the abstract meanings, but rather the relatively active suppression of the literal meanings in the vehicle. Third, experiencing topic-vehicle pairs conveying relational similarity, no matter through mere repeatedly memorizing or multiple activation of the same schema based on various pairs can result in the abstraction of the vehicle. These finding can be accounted for in the framework hypothesized for the present study.

Besides these three findings that speak well for this study's original hypothesis, one counter-intuitive result was also detected showing that deriving the similarity in topic-vehicle pairs that include the same vehicle and various topics which provide attributive similarity could also lead to a significant suppression of the literal meanings in the vehicle, thus resulting in a relative salience of the abstract metaphorical sense in the vehicle. The author provided explanation for this finding mainly on two grounds. First, there might be some confounding effect between relational similarity and attributive similarity due to a failure in experimental material manipulation. Second, a more cognition oriented account may be related to the notion of "embodiment", that is, human beings understand the abstract concepts in terms of the perception of the concrete world they directly get contact with.

6.4 Summary

In this chapter, the author empirically examined research Q2 and Q3 through testing two aspects of Sub-H2 concerning the dynamic aspect of metaphorical categorization both at the micro level and the macro level.

Section 6.2(Exp 2) concerns research Q2, i.e., the relation between structure-mapping and metaphorical categorization at the micro level. The findings indicated that the priming effect for the category target words reached significance in the MAP task wherein the subjects were merely instructed to process the mapping between the structural relations held by the topic and the vehicle, yet without being explicitly instructed to process the category relation. It can be interpreted as evidence that unconscious structure mapping between the analogical relations held by the topic and the vehicle terms leads to the induction of the categorical relation between the topic and the vehicle.

Except for these findings, there was yet an interesting pattern of priming effect observed in the data for the semantically related target words in the CAT task, which can only be interpreted as evidence showing that overtly categorizing two concepts belonging to two distinct conventional categories entails processing relational semantic information in the two terms. This point is distinct from the finding in Green's study which showed that, for conventional categories, the CAT task did not prime the semantically related target words. Combining the results by the present experiment and Green's study, it could be at least tentatively concluded that metaphorical categorization differs from conventional categorization in that the former involves activation of the relational information held by the two concepts being processed while the later does not. To conclude, metaphorical categorization as a dynamic process involves structure mapping of the analogical relations held by the topic and the vehicle.

In Section 6.3(including Exp 3a and Exp 3b), the author empirically sought the answer to research Q3 via testing one aspect of Sub-H2 concerning the dynamic aspect of metaphorical categorization at the macro level. The author proposed that it is structure-mapping and schema induction that underlies the mechanism of metaphorical categorization. Specifically, two major hypotheses have been generally confirmed through Exp 3a and 3b respectively.

The findings in Exp 3a pertaining to the time course of the priming effect on various types of target words indicate that, as predicted by the structure-mapping and schema induction theory, there is a first-matching-later-projecting feature in the time course of the induction of the abstract schematic meanings in the vehicle.

The findings revealed in Exp 3b combinarily verify Sub-H2 pertaining to the core dynamic process of metaphorical categorization, especially in terms of the induction of abstract referent in the metaphor vehicle. First, diachronical learning of topic-vehicle pairs fostered the gaining of the abstract metaphorical referent in the vehicle. Second, the salience of the abstract referent in the vehicle was not due to the activation of the abstract meanings, but rather the relatively active suppression of the literal meanings in the vehicle. Third, experiencing topic-vehicle pairs conveying relational similarity, no matter through mere repeated memorizing or multiple activation of the same schema based on various pairs can result in the abstraction of the vehicle. These findings can be accounted for in the framework hypothesized for the present study.

One counter-intuitive result was also detected showing that deriving the similarity in topic-vehicle pairs that include the same vehicle and various topics which provide attributive similarity could also lead to a significant suppression of the literal meanings in the vehicle, thus resulting in a relative salience of the abstract metaphorical sense in the vehicle. The author provided explanation for this finding mainly on two possible grounds: failure in experimental material manipulation or embodiment in human cognition.

Chapter 7 Study III: duality of metaphorical categorization

7.1 Introduction

Study III (Exp 4) is aimed to examine Sub-H3 (i. e., duality of metaphorical categorization) through investigating potential constraints on the categorical relation between the metaphor topic and vehicle. If hypothesized as schema induction in analogical reasoning (see 4.2.2), metaphorical categorization would involve two distinct albeit related layers of categorization. At the micro level, it involves the establishment of the categorical relation between the topic and the vehicle; at the macro level, it involves the induction of the whole abstract relation in the vehicle. The author argues that the categorization occurring at the micro level can be operationalized as the level of metaphor aptness. At the macro level, the categorical relation between the abstract relation schema and the metaphor vehicle can be operationalized as the level of conventionality, which results from the diachronical association between a certain vehicle and the same abstract relation through repeated use in natural language occurrence①. The author believes that the degree to which a metaphor denotes a category inclusion as it literally asserts depends combinairily on the two layers of categorization.

This experiment took an insight into the duality of metaphorical categorization through investigating the potential factors influencing the category inclusion relation between the topic and the vehicle.To more directly investigate the categorical relation between the topic and the vehicle denoted by the metaphorical form "An x is a y.",

① The operational definitions of aptness and conventionality are discussed in more detail in 7.2.3.

Exp 4 adopted a variant stroopian paradigm① developed by Glucksberg, Gildea, and Bookin(1982) and extended by Keysar(1989) in their landmark studies on metaphor comprehension. In the literature of psycholinguistic studies of metaphor, these stroopian paradigm studies have served as major sources of evidence for the initial stage of metaphor processing. Basically, this technique is based on what is usually termed "metaphor interference effect", i. e., metaphors can interfere with readers' understanding of literal meanings of one assertion, which experimentally indicates that readers have difficulties in rejecting metaphors as "literal category false". Based on these experimental findings, researchers have concluded that what a metaphor denotes is a category-inclusion relation. The author assumes that this conclusion is suspected to be overgeneralized because related studies mainly failed to take variation in metaphors into account. To be specific, previous studies didn't manipulate potential confounding factors, failing to find out that the category inclusion relation denoted by a metaphor is a matter of degree constrained by certain properties of the metaphor itself. Given these considerations, Exp 4 was expected to make some contribution to our understanding of the underlying process of metaphorical categorization through operationally looking into the correlation between metaphor aptness, vehicle conventionality and the stroopian-fashion interference effect.

7.2 Exp 4: conventionality, aptness and stroopian interference effect

7.2.1 Research aim

Exp 4 was aimed to seek the answer to research Q4, i. e., what are the potential constraints on the category inclusion relation between the topic and the vehicle? Operationally, the relation between metaphor aptness, vehicle conventionality and

① In Stroop's classic experiment(1935), words were printed in various colors and people were asked to name the color of the ink instead of reading the words themselves. When color words such as red were printed in any color other than red(e. g., green), people had difficulty in naming "green", indicating that they were experiencing response competition from the involuntary reading of the word "red" itself.

stroopian interference effect in rejecting metaphors as literally false category statement was investigated. Hopefully, this experiment would provide some integrated evidence pertaining to the constraints determining the degree to which a metaphor denotes categorical inclusion relation between the topic and the vehicle, thus sheds light on the underlying process of metaphorical categorization which accounts for the category inclusion relation denoted by nominal metaphors.

7. 2. 2 Design logic and hypothesis

The logic underlying this semantic variant stroopian interference effect experiment is as follows. Since a metaphor has the identical grammatical form with literal category-inclusion statement("An x is a y.") and always has the tension arising from category inclusion and category violation which is essential for "metaphoricity" or "being a metaphor". If a metaphor is spontaneously processed through category-inclusion as what it literally denotes, readers will have difficulty rejecting the metaphor as category-violation, which results in a stroopian-like interference effect. Nevertheless, if a metaphor is directly processed through category-violation, readers will not have difficulty rejecting metaphor as category-inclusion, which results in no stroopian-like interference effect. Taking advantage of the automaticity nature of the stroopian interference effect, Exp 4 was intended to investigate the nature of the relation between the topic and the vehicle without potential contamination from metalinguistic judgment. One specific hypothesis could thus be derived:

According to the proposed duality-categorization of metaphor model, if vehicle categorization(the macro-categorization) and topic-vehicle categorization(the micro-categorization) are the by-products of the induction and activation of abstract schemas in metaphor comprehension, then metaphorical categorization would involve dual processes of categorization. As the micro-categorization and macro-categorization are hypothetically operationalized as aptness and conventionality respectively, our research hypothesis of this experiment is that the degree to which a metaphor denotes category inclusion relation will be influenced by both vehicle conventionality and metaphor aptness.

Technically, the apt andconventional metaphors would have greater stroopian effect, i. e., would take longer time to be rejected as category violation assertions. In contrast, metaphors that are unapt or unconventional would have smaller stroopian effect, i. e., would take shorter time to be rejected as category violation assertions.

7. 2. 3 Method

Participants:32 participants, including 7 males and 25 females, were recruited from the population of undergraduate students at South China Normal University. The ages of these participants ranged from 19 to 22. Participants spoke chinese as their first language, and had normal or corrected-to-normal vision.

Material development: Material manipulation was crucial for the present study, as it had to theoretically define and operationally control the two key variables involved in the core hypothesis of the resent experiment. This section included the following steps which were operationalizing macro- and micro-categorization and the manipulation of aptness and conventionality including aptness manipulation, conventionality manipulation and statistical manipulation.

(1) Operationalization of macro- and micro-categorization

Micro-categorization: Recall that in Section 4. 3. 2, micro-categorization in metaphor is defined as "the small-scale categorization of individual component or argument terms or elements within the larger-scale aligned relational schemas in the process of structural mapping". According to this definition, micro-categorization involves the categorical association between the topic and the vehicle based on the structure-mapping between them, that is to say, the topic and the vehicle can be categorically associated when they are structurally matchable even though they are not perceptually similar. Also take the case "A man is a wolf." for instance, "man" and "wolf" are included in the parent abstract category "CHASER" in that they play similar roles in the abstract structural relation "CHASING". In this regard, the determinant of the categorical relation between the two concepts is not some superficial perceptual similarity, but rather certain important roles underlying certain abstract relations. Recall that in the literature of psycholinguistic study of metaphor, aptness has been generally defined as "the extent to which the metaphor vehicle captures important features of the topic" (Chiappe et al., 2003: 97; Blasko and

Connine, 1993:297; Gong and Zhou, 2011). In this vein, the auther proposes that the micro-categorization echoes with the notion of aptness in that they both denote the degree to which the vehicle describe the important features of the topic which is determined by the common abstract relation.

Macro-categorization: As depicted in Section4. 3. 2, macro-categorization in metaphor is based on the schema induction of the common abstract relation shared by the topic and the vehicle with other objects. The same structural relation, after being repeatedly used with the same vehicle, will be solidified and get associated with the vehicle and become one entrenched sense of the vehicle. Recall that in psycholinguistic studies, vehicle conventionality is generally defined as "the strength of association between a metaphor vehicle and its figurative meaning" (Bowdle and Gentner, 2005; Gentner and Wolff, 1997; Gentner and Bowdle, 2001; Wolff and Gentner, 2000; Giora, 1997, Gong and Zhou, 2011). Also take the "A man is a wolf." for example, the figurative meaning of a vehicle(wolf) actually arises from the relational schema(CHASING) based on structural mapping between the topic and the vehicle(man chases woman as wolf chases sheep). In light of these analyses, we assume that macro-categorization can be operationalized as the strength of the association between the metaphor vehicle and the common abstract relation shared by the topic and the vehicle with other objects. Following the tradition in psycholinguistic study and for the sake of discussion, the author will term this kind of strength as vehicle conventionality.

Before proceeding to manipulate the two factors, it is vitally noteworthy to point out that just as micro- and macro- categorizations, aptness and conventionality are also two independent factors. Given their independence in nature, it is feasible to operationally manipulate the two factors simultaneously. That is, metaphors with the same vehicle definitely have the same level of conventionality, yet metaphors consisting of the same vehicles and yet different topics can have different levels of aptness(e. g., "A rooster is an alarm-clock." vs "A bird is an alarm-clock."). Even novel vehicles may also produce apt metaphors in spite of their relatively weak association with the figurative meaning. Maybe this is why newly created vehicles sound more attractive and interesting. For example, compared with the conventional vehicle "gold mine", the vehicle "diamond mine" is of greater novelty. Nevertheless, the metaphor "The library is a diamond mine." is also apt in asserting that the library provides a huge resource of literature.

(1) Manipulating aptness and conventionality

As argued above, the author justifiably operationalizes micro-categorization, or the strength of the categorical relation between the topic and the vehicle as the level of aptness, and macro-categorization, or the strength of the association between the vehicle and the abstract common structural relation as the level of conventionality.

Materials used in this study were modified metaphors selected from previous metaphor studies, and some of them were created by the writer of the thesis. Most of the materials developing procedures followed Jones and Estes (2006) with some modifications.

①Aptness manipulation: To manipulate aptness, 200 original metaphors selected from previous literature were used as the high apt stimuli (e. g., A rooster is an alarm clock.). And for each metaphor we correspondingly created a low apt stimulus by substituting a less apt topic (e. g., A bird is an alarm clock.). Thus there were 200 pairs of metaphors, with each pair consisting of one hypothesized high apt and one hypothesized low apt version, both of which had the same vehicle. Aptness ratings for all the 400 metaphors were collected on a 7-point scale ranging from 1 (very unapt) to 7 (highly apt). Metaphors scored lower than 3 were considered as unapt, and those higher than 5 were taken as apt. Following previous studies, aptness of a metaphor was defined as "the extent to which the metaphor vehicle captures important features of the topic" (Chiappe et al., 2003: 97; Blasko and Connine, 1993:297).

② Conventionality manipulation: The task of conventionality manipulation falls into two steps.

Conventional property generation: The aim of this property generation task was to identify thetypical property most commonly associated with each vehicle. Both metaphors in a pair (the apt and its unapt counterpart) were presented simultaneously, and the sequence of presenting each pair was counterbalanced between subjects. Each participant generated a single property that was conveyed by those metaphors. For each metaphor vehicle, the most frequently generated property was taken as the one that is conventionally associated with the specific vehicle.

Conventionality rating task: After a property was generated for each metaphor vehicle, another independent group of 20 undergraduates were asked to rate, on a 7-point scale ranging from 1 (very unconventional) to 7 (highly conventional), the conventionality of the most frequently generated property (see above) for each vehicle. Following the procedure used in Gentner and colleagues' studies (e. g., Bowdle and Gentner, 2005; Gentner and Wolff, 1997; Wolff and Gentner, 2001), we defined conventionality as "the extent to which the concept is associated with the figurative meaning". All the rating scores were collected. Metaphors scored lower than 3 were taken as novel ones, and those higher than 5 were taken as conventional ones.

③ Statistical Manipulation: First, from this extensive stimulus norming process we selected 64 pairs of high and low apt metaphors, 32 of which have a novel vehicle and 32 of which have a conventional vehicle. Stimuli were selected so as to be well controlled for aptness and conventionality within each condition, while maximally varying aptness and conventionality between conditions. The conventionality ratings were subjected to an independent sample t-test, and confirmed a significant effect ($t_{(62)} = 26.7$, $p<0$), thus indicating that the conventional vehicles are indeed more conventional ($M = 5.33$, SE = 0.05) than the novel ones ($M = 2.93$, SE = 0.08). Second, to ensure that aptness and conventionality were manipulated simultaneously, the aptness rating scores were subjected to a 2(aptness)×2(conventionality) mixed anova (with conventionality as the between-subject variable and aptness as the within-subject variable). The result confirmed a significant main effect of aptness ($F_{(1,62)} = 987.48$, $p<0$), such that the high apt items ($M = 5.55$, SE = 0.07) are indeed more apt than the low apt items ($M = 2.59$, SE = 0.06). Neither the main effect of conventionality ($F_{(1,62)} = 0.005$, $p = 0.94$) nor its interaction with aptness ($F_{(1,62)} = 0.92$, $p = 0.34$) was significant, suggesting that the manipulation of aptness did not differ appreciably between the novel stimuli and the conventional stimuli. A full list of the materials and their statistical manipulation is presented in Appendix XIV. A list of sample stimuli is presented in Table 7.1:

Table 7.1 A list of sample stimuli and the manipulation of the aptness and conventionality of the stimuli

sentence type			example	conventionality score(SE)	aptness score(SE)	number
metaphoricl categorization	conventional	apt	图书馆是金矿。(e. g., The library is a goldmine.)	5.33(0.05)	5.59(0.13)	32
		unapt	传达室是金矿。(e. g., The janitor's room is a goldmine.)	5.33(0.05)	2.55(0.07)	32
	novel	apt	公鸡是闹钟。(e. g., A rooster is an alarm clock.)	2.93(0.08)	5.49(0.08)	32
		unapt	小鸟是闹钟。(e. g., A bird is an alarm clock.)	2.93(0.08)	2.63(0.09)	32
scrambled categorization			拖鞋是手枪。(e. g., A slipper is a gun.)	—	—	32
literal categorization fillers			水杯是容器。(e. g., A cup is a container.)	—	—	160

Design: A2(conventionality: conventional, novel) ×2(aptness: high apt, low apt) within-subject design was adopted. The dependent variables were response time and accuracy rate.

Procedure: This experiment was conducted on an E-prime program through computer screen presentation. Subjects were run in two groups. The statements were presented one at a time. They were instructed to judge whether the presented statement was literally true or false in terms of categorization statement. Subjects were instructed to read each statement carefully and were informed that response speed and accuracy are equally important. After subjects read the instructions, they were presented with 10 practice trials followed by the 64 experimental trials presented in a random order. Each trial consisted of a fixation "+" presented for 500 ms followed by a blank screen lasting for 100 ms. Upon the removal of the blank, a statement denoting the linguistic form "An x is a y." was presented for 2 500 ms. The subjects were instructed to judge as quickly and accurately as they could whether the sentence constituted a true category inclusion statement. The statement remains visible until the response key is pressed. Response time longer than 2 500 ms was considered as invalid. Upon the key press, there was a blank remaining for 500 ms as trail interval.

Both response time and accuracy were automatically recorded by E-prime software. The procedure for a trail is presented in Figure 7. 1:

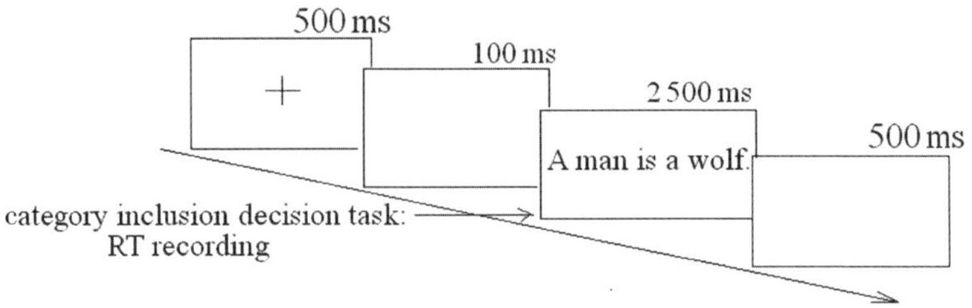

Figure 7. 1 The experimental procedure of Exp 4

7. 2. 4 Results

Only correct responses were recruited for further analysis. The data from 2 subjects who got accuracy rates lower than 80 % were removed. Response time beyond two and a half standard deviations were considered as outliers and were removed prior to further statistical analyses, resulting in elimination of 2. 98 % of all the responses. The statistical work was analyzed by SPSS13. 0. The descriptive statistics for the mean response time and accuracy rates are shown in Table 7. 2:

Table 7. 2 Descriptive data of reaction times(in ms) and accuracy rate(in %) gained in Exp 4

		RT(SD)	ACC(SD)
highly apt	conventional	1 021(35. 6)	93. 5(5. 4)
	novel	986(30. 0)	97. 5(5. 2)
lowly apt	conventional	962(29. 8)	98. 9(3. 9)
	novel	982(36. 6)	97. 3(4. 7)
scrambled		932(28. 1)	98. 4(4. 1)
standard fillers		939(28. 6)	98. 6(4. 4)

Firstly, the overall results of the RTs from the two-factor anova (aptness, conventionality) using subjects as a random factor are reported. There was a significant main effect of aptness on reaction time, $F_{(1, 29)} = 5.31$, $p = 0.029$; collapsing across two levels of conventionality, subjects were significantly faster to judge lowly apt metaphors ($M = 972$) as category mistake than highly apt metaphors

(M=1 004). The main effect of conventionality didn't reach significance, $F_{(1, 29)}$ = 0.80, p = 0.377. The interaction of aptness and conventionality was marginally significant, $F_{(1, 29)}$ = 3.56, p=0.069.

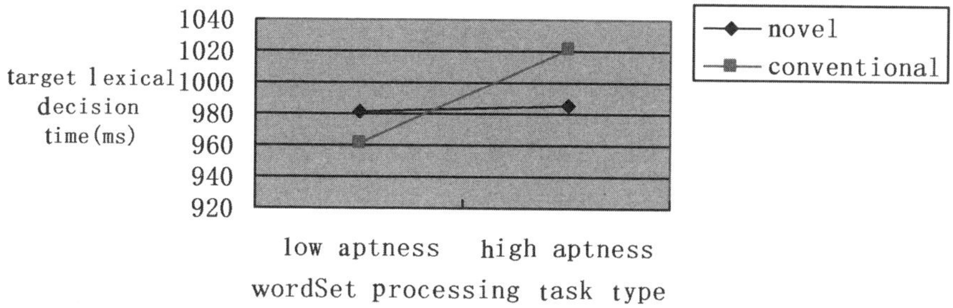

Figure 7.2 Category inclusion relation decision mean latency in Exp 4

Simple effect test revealed a different pattern of conventionality effect when the metaphor was lowly apt than highly apt. As shown in Figure 7.2, at low level of aptness, response time for conventional metaphors (M = 962) and novels ones (M=982) did not differ significantly, $t_{(1,29)}$ = 1.108 , p=0.277. However, when the same vehicles were used with topics which create highly apt metaphors, response time for novel metaphors (M = 982) was significantly faster than conventional ones (M=1 021), $t_{(1,29)}$ = −2.163 , p = 0.039. For novel metaphors, the difference between response time for the ones with lowly apt topics(M=982) and the ones with highly apt topics(M=986) did not reach significance, $t_{(1,29)}$ = −0.179, p=0.860; for conventional metaphors, response time for the ones with lowly apt topics(M=962) was significantly faster than the ones with highly apt topics (M = 1 021), $t_{(1, 29)}$ = −3.242, p=0.003.

Secondly, the overall results of the accuracy rates were subjected to a two-factor anova(aptness, conventionality) using subjects as a random factor. The result showed a significant main effect of aptness, $F_{(1, 29)}$ = 11.15, p = 0.002. The main effect of conventionality didn't reach significance, $F_{(1, 29)}$ = 1.35, p = 0.256. The interaction between aptness and conventionality was marginally significant, $F_{(1, 29)}$ = 6.86, p=0.14. The result generally showed that there was not a trade-off effect between RT and ACC.

Thirdly, to further examine the stroopian effect directly, four independent t-tests were performed on response times between each of the four critical conditions and the baseline condition, i. e., the scrambled category statements. The results showed that only conventional, apt metaphors (M = 1 021) were responded significantly more slowly than the scrambled category statements (M=932), $t_{(1, 58)}$ = 2.025, p=0.047. None of the other three conditions differed significantly from the scrambled condition [respectively, for conventional, lowly apt condition (M = 962), $t_{(1, 58)}$ = 0.773, p=0.443; for novel, low apt condition (M=982), $t_{(1, 58)}$ = 1.119, p=0.268; and for novel, highly apt condition (M=986), $t_{(1, 58)}$ = 1.357, p=0.180].

7.2.5 Discussion

The statistical analyses on the stroopian effect demonstrated that the categorical inclusion relationship denoted by nominal metaphors is a matter of degree constrained by metaphor aptness and vehicle conventionality. Since metaphor aptness and vehicle conventionality, as described in Section 7.2.3, can justifiably serve as the operational indicators of the two layers of metaphorical categorization proposed by this study, the author could conclude that our general hypothesis concerning duality of metaphorical categorization was generally confirmed.

Specifically, metaphor aptness had a significant stroopian effect, yet vehicle conventionality did not. More importantly, there emerged a significant interaction between the two factors. The effect of aptness mainly depended on the factor of vehicle conventionality. Compared with the baseline control condition which consists of scrambled category statements, only the apt conventional condition out of the four experimental conditions was found with significant stroopian effect, that is, only apt conventional metaphors were significantly difficult to be rejected as category violation. Or put it another way, only apt conventional metaphors were more likely to be interpreted as category inclusion statements. This result can be theoretically interpreted as evidence showing that the category-inclusion relation between the topic and the vehicle depends on the satisfaction of two requirements. First, as indicated by metaphor aptness which denotes micro-categorization, the topic and the vehicle have to be structurally matchable. Second, as indicated by vehicle conventionality, the vehicle has to be considerably tightly associated with the abstract relational structure resulting from macro-categorization.

The author assumes that this result speaks powerfully for the major hypothesis of the present study, i. e., metaphorical categorization involves two independent albeit related processes of schema induction. Recall that in the present experiment, the author simultaneously manipulated the levels of aptness and conventionality and thus was able to investigate their separate influences. In this vein, the present research successfully eliminated potential confounding effects detected in previous relevant studies. In this regard, this finding is at odds with Glucksberg's study (2006), in which aptness was taken to sufficiently determine the category inclusion relation between the topic and the vehicle. That is, even newly created metaphors, if apt enough, are processed through category attribution. We assume that this argument can not account for the "beauty" or "sense of creativity" of metaphor, especially in novel ones. It is widely accepted that newly coined metaphors can always convey some sense of "beauty" or "sense of creativity" which is considered to be the result of the tension arising from the cognitive competition in dispelling category violation in metaphor processing (Xu, 2008). Better than Glucksberg's study (2006), our finding can explain two basic observations in metaphor use. First, metaphor undergoes a "life span" from novelty to conventionality, which results from repeated use. Second, aptness is not the sufficient determinant of the category inclusion relation denoted by metaphor. That is to say, besides the structural matching between the topic and the vehicle which is reflected in aptness, the vehicle has to be at a higher level of abstractness, which results from the macro-categorization denoted by vehicle conventionality. As Glucksberg (ibid) didn't simultaneously control aptness and conventionality, the author suspects that the effect of aptness found in their study might be confounded by the factor of vehicle conventionality.

With regard to the role played by vehicle conventionality in determining the category inclusion relation, the findings of the present experiment are also against Bowdle and Gentner's career model (2005) which explicitly asserts that vehicle conventionality sufficiently and exclusively determines the category inclusion relation in metaphor. The author suspects that this assertion is so strong that it fails to capture the role of aptness in metaphor comprehension and even in the course of conventionalization itself. Actually, this kind of suspicion is motivated by such a logical problem: without being aptly used with a range of topics, how is it possible for a metaphor vehicle to be used repeatedly over time by a certain language community and eventually get conventionalized? Indeed, although Bowdle and Gentner (2005) only controlled the level of vehicle conventionality in their study, they detected in a post-test finding that their conventional items ($m = 6.54$ out of 10, $SD = 1.27$) were more apt than their novel items ($m = 4.18$, $SD = 1.68$), which indicated that they had inadvertently confounded conventionality and aptness. In this respect, two crucial statistical results found in the present research can be taken as strong evidence for our hypothesis. First, there was an interaction effect between metaphor aptness and vehicle conventionality. Second, only apt and conventional metaphors got a significant stroopian effect. These two findings can be combinarily taken as good evidence for the duality account of metaphorical categorization proposed by this thesis.

Besides the findings concerning the constraints on metaphorical categorization, another important implication of the present experiment is with regard to the degree to which metaphor denotes category inclusion statement. In this line, the present study offered some implications in terms of the experimental technique in investigating the nature of metaphorical "An x is a y.". As reviewed in Section 3.2.2, existing research have developed several empirical paradigms to investigate metaphorical categorization, including measuring comprehension speed, rating grammatical form preference or even most directly rating the category membership of the vehicle in the topic. Recall that as for the degree of the category inclusion, results revealed by previous studies could merely be interpreted as indicators of a quantitative preference rather than a qualitative distinction. As for the internal validity of the empirical techniques, most of these paradigms based on off-line judging tasks were suspicious of contamination from conscious metalinguistic analysis strategy.

Given these considerations, results from the stroopian paradigm in the present research have at least two advantages over existing relevant empirical studies. On the one hand, by adopting the stroopian paradigm which is considered to be a classical technique for investigating automatic cognitive processing (Stroop, 1935), the present study can eliminate the problem of potential strategic metalinguistic judgment to the utmost extent. On the other hand, through comparing the reaction times of various kinds of metaphorical category statements with the baseline control condition of literal category false statements, this variant stroopian paradigm offers a more operational method to detect to what extent metaphors denote category assertions and the potential constraints on this extent. In the present research, the author found that only apt conventional metaphors have significant stroopian effect. The other three conditions, although took longer time to be rejected as literally false, the difference did not reach significance.

7.3 Summary

In this chapter, we empirically tested the hypotheses of the duality nature of metaphorical categorization through adopting a semantic variant of stroopian paradigm. The central hypothesis is that metaphorical categorization is derived from two layers of schema-induction which is based on structure-mapping between the metaphor topic and the vehicle. The author operationalized the two layers of categorization as aptness and conventionality, which denote the micro- and macro- categorization respectively.

Two important results support our hypothesis emerged:

First, only apt conventional metaphors have significant stroopian effect; the other three conditions, although took longer time to be rejected as literally category false, did not reach significance in terms of the stroopian effect. This indicates that the category inclusion relation between the topic and the vehicle is combinarily constrained by the two factors of aptness and conventionality, which reflect the degree of micro- and macro- categorization respectively.

Second, the category inclusion relation between the topic and the vehicle is merely a matter of degree which is constrained by the associating strength of the two layers of induced schemas.

Besides the two empirical findings, the present experiment, through adopting the stroopian paradigm, also sheds some light on the on-line empirical technique of investigating categorical relation between the topic and the vehicle.

Chapter 8 General discussion

8.1 Summary of the empirical findings

Echoing with the general theoretical framework and the specific research questions raised in the empirical study framework for the present dissertation, there emerge the following four major empirical findings pertaining to metaphorical categorization:

(1) The mediator of metaphorical categorization

Based on a comprehensive review on category and similarity theories, Study I (Exp1) operationalized the definitions of attributive similarity and relational similarity through an "n-place" argument rating paradigm. Through a metaphor-simile grammatical form preference task, Exp 1 investigated the correlation between the "n-place" argument rating scores and the metaphor-simile grammatical form preference to explore the determinant of the category-inclusion form of metaphorical comparisons. The results demonstrate that it is relational similarity rather than attributive similarity that upper-handedly mediates metaphorical categorization.

(2) The core process of metaphorical categorization

The present dissertation argues for a dynamic view of metaphorical categorization. Generally, structure-mapping and schema induction were taken as the underlying mechanisms of metaphorical categorization. To test this basic hypothesis, Study II [Exp2 and Exp 3(3a and 3b)] examined three basic aspects of the core process of metaphorical categorization through three separate albeit related experiments.

Exp 2 tackled the central hypothesis that the structural alignment between the topic and the vehicle activates a common abstract superordinate category which includes both the topic and vehicle as the subordinate categories. Also taking a semantic priming paradigm, Exp 2 discovered that the unconscious structure mapping between the analogical relations held by the topic and the vehicle terms led to the induction of the categorical relation between the topic and the vehicle. Besides this, there was yet evidence showing that overtly categorizing two concepts belonging to two distinct conventional categories entailed processing relational semantic information in the two terms. Combining the results in Exp 2 and Green et al.'s study (2006b, 2008a), it could be at least tentatively concluded that metaphorical categorization differs from conventional categorization in that the former involves activation of the relational semantic information held by the two concepts being processed.

Exp 3, consisting of Exp 3a and 3b, addressed the dynamic nature of metaphorical categorization. Two aspects were explored. Exp 3a examined the time course of the gaining of the abstract categorical referent by employing a semantic priming paradigm. Two major findings in concern were released. First, it was revealed that metaphors conveying relational similarity resulted in a priming effect for the abstract target words, yet the same priming effect was not discovered in metaphors conveying attributive similarity. This finding can be interpreted as evidence showing that metaphorical categorization takes structure-mapping which is based on abstract relational structures as the foundation. Second, the findings pertaining to the time course of the priming effect on various types of target words indicate that, as predicted by the structure-mapping theory, there is a first-matching-later-mapping feature in the induction process of the abstract schematic meanings in the vehicle.

Exp 3b was based on a vitro-diachronical approach, and took an insight into the diachronical nature of metaphorical categorization through testing the historical acquisition of an abstract referent in the vehicle. Three findings of interest emerged. First, diachronical learning of topic-vehicle pairs can foster the gaining of the abstract metaphorical reference in the vehicle. Second, the gaining of the abstract reference in the vehicle results from the relative active suppression of the literal meanings in the vehicle rather than the actual activation of the abstract meanings. Third, experiencing topic-vehicle pairs conveying relational similarity, no matter through mere repeated memorization or multiple activation of the same schema based on various pairs can result in the abstraction of the vehicle. Besides these three findings, one somewhat counter-intuitive result was also detected showing that deriving the similarity in topic-vehicle pairs that include the same vehicle and various topics which provide attributive similarity could also lead to a significant suppression of the literal meanings in the vehicle.

(3) Duality of metaphorical categorization

The present dissertation claims a duality view of metaphorical categorization. That is, the categorical inclusion relation between the topic and the vehicle is formed based on the categorical relation between the two general abstract relations denoted by the topic and the vehicle. Two layers of categorization occur in the course of metaphor processing: at the macro level, an abstract relational category is formed; at the micro level, the individual arguments playing analogous roles in the matched relations get categorically related. Operationally, the justification of juxtaposing the metaphor topic and vehicle in a metaphor which has the same grammatical form of literal category inclusion statement combinarily depends on both aptness and conventionality.

Study III (Exp 4) adopted a stroopian variant paradigm to explore the duality of metaphorical categorization through investigating the factors influencing the categorical conclusion relationship between the topic and the vehicle. We operationally defined the categorical relationship strength at the micro level as the level of metaphor aptness, and the categorical relationship strength at the macro level as metaphor vehicle conventionality. Three important findings supporting this basic hypothesis emerged from Exp 4. First, only both apt and conventional metaphors exerted significant stroopian effect. The other three conditions, although took longer time to be rejected as literally false, did not reach significance in terms of stroopian effect. This result indicates that the category inclusion relation between the topic and the vehicle is combinarily constrained by the two factors of aptness and conventionality which reflect the degree of micro- and macro- categorization respectively. Second, the category inclusion relation between the topic and the vehicle is merely a matter of degree which is constrained by the two layers of categorization. Third, besides the two empirical findings, Exp 4 also sheds some light on the on-line empirical technique of investigating categorical relation between the topic and the vehicle.

8.2 Theoretical reflections and evaluations

8.2.1 Metaphor and fluidity of categorization

Just imagine a world where categories have only strictly rigid boundaries so that "An x is an x." and "A y is a y.". We are not constrained to such a world. That is, we are constantly employing our unique ability to cross the boundaries of the factual world and to deal with category inclusion statements that are "contrary to fact, yet that are on some level true and authentic" (Winner, 1988: 2). In other words, it can sometimes rightly be stated that "An x is a y.". It is exactly such juxtaposition of concepts stemming from divergent categories yet linked by certain similarity that lies at the root of fluidity of categorization. Metaphor is perhaps the most widely recognized phenomenon for an explanation for such fluidity in categorization, since by their very nature they seek to stretch the boundaries of domain description and dynamically establish new ways of determining inter-domain similarity.

The recognition of the role of metaphors in categorization has accompanied the changes in the views for categorization over the past few decades. In the 1940s, categorization was treated as the meeting of two bounded, describable entities. In this traditional view, metaphor is often thought to be outside the purview of classical theories of categorization. Classical theories of categorization have been influenced by the opinions that metaphor, as a form of nonliteral language, is essentially defective or no more than ornamental, even if its use does offer cognitive insights (Percy, 1958). Recent developments have called attention to the complexities of the categorization process and specifically to the fluid, fuzzy nature of the environment. An opposing perspective more recently proposed by this stream of cognitive linguistics is that all language use is preconditioned by metaphor, and that metaphor is fundamental to cognition and is therefore part of the backdrop to category extension and word polysemy (Lakoff, 1987; Lakoff, 1993; Sweetser, 1990; Taylor, 1995).

It has been widely recognized that metaphor plays a crucial role in the fuzzy nature of categorization, and that it is a powerful "cognitive tool", which helps us get hold of and express complex and abstract ideas and even serves to reshuffle or create new pathways of categorization(Lakoff, 1987; Winner, 1988; Veale, 2003a, 2003b, 2006). In this view, metaphor is more than a decorative aspect of language, a substitute for a literal term, and a simple comparison between the topic and the vehicle. This suggests that metaphors are in essence a categorization process and that metaphor-driven categorization and recategorization render the open-endedness of concepts.

Despite the strong claim for the role of metaphor in category extension, extremely few studies have explored the dynamic mechanism underlying the process in which an original category gains a more abstract metaphorical referent and the theoretical framework in which such a dynamic mechanism can be analyzed. Metaphor brings about a change of possible concepts. There are two aspects of the how question pertaining to metaphorical categorization. The first aspect is concerned with the internal structure of the categories which are based on metaphor extension. A majority of past studies on categorization based on retrospective description of some cases were mainly focused on how the extended categories clustered around the core category. These studies were mainly inspired by the pioneers on the prototype theory from various research fields, such as Wittgenstein(1953)(philosophical reflections on the relation between necessary and sufficient conditions and the definition of category); Austin(1961)(relationships among meanings of words; analogy; primary nuclear sense); Zadeh (1965) (study of sets with fuzzy boundaries); Lounsbury (1964) (kinship categories); Berlin and Kay (1969) (color categories as an empirical establishment of wittgenstein's ideas of gradience and centrality);Brown(1958, 1965) (the primary study of basic-categories); and most importantly, Rosch and Mervis (1975) (first providing a general perspective on internal structure of human categories). Two prominent linguistic studies have provided important evidence pertaining to the internal structure of metaphorical categorization. They are Lakoff's analyses on different categories of "mother" (1987: Chapter 2), and Sweetser's systematic research on perceptual expressions, for example "see" (1990). These research theoretically mainly followed the argument of the prototype theory of category, and methodologically followed the retrospective analysis approach. The main conclusions drawn by these studies are: first, the categories are extended dynamically and diachronically; second, there are central or peripheral senses of one item.

The second aspect of the how question of metaphorical categorization is no less trivial yet more neglected by previous studies. That is how these categories are extended. This question exactly renders the theoretical significance of the present dissertation. Specifically, this question involves three issues. First, as similarity is recognized as the mediator for categorization, then what is the nature of the similarity associating the metaphor topic and vehicle? Second, how is the similarity identified? Third, how is the categorical inclusion relation established? The present dissertation provides a unified theory framework in which the above three questions could be more systematically accounted for.

Generally, to tackle the three questions of the second how question of metaphorical categorization, this research seeks to work out our basic hypotheses in the framework of relational similarity theory; for the second and the third question, the author takes a dynamic view of schema induction based on structure-mapping. The author suggests that metaphorical categories are represented via relational descriptions and formed by a process of progressive abstraction through successive comparisons with incoming exemplars. Structural alignment and schema induction play important roles in metaphorical categorization. Based on this viewpoint, the present thesis seeks to explore the fluid nature of categorization by observing how the relationship among categories changes through metaphorical categorization. Building relationships between categories with implicit relational similarity is a dynamic process performed by metaphor language use. The author terms such a process similarity-retrieving and schema-induction to emphasize the dynamic and fluid nature of metaphorical categorization.

More specifically, this account has the following basic assumptions. First, the abstract metaphor vehicle, although eventually stored in the long-term memory, is recreated every time they occur when compared to the incoming metaphor topics. Second, abstract concept formation through metaphorical extensions must be dynamic because it is based on "extensions" of existing concrete concepts. Third, the abstract metaphorical sense acquisition is universal to the whole speaker community in that metaphorical extension(metaphorical categorization) is among the most basic mental activities of human beings. These processes are interesting because they often exploit the latent similarities between domains that have not been explicitly represented in the underlying conceptual structure. To better account for these main ideas, we can tentatively put it in the architecture as shown in Figure 8. 1.

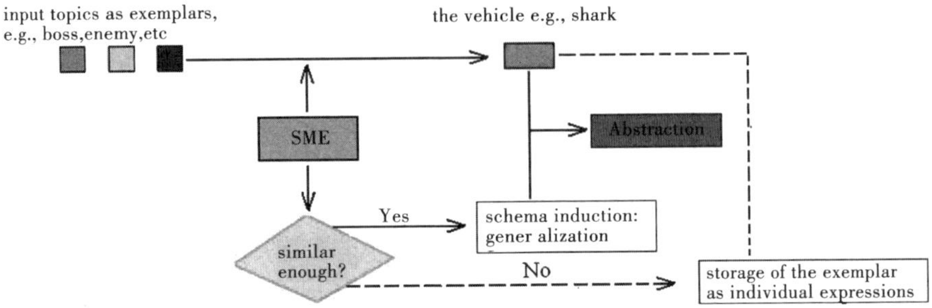

Figure 8. 1 The progressive abstraction model of metaphorical categorization

This book puts forward a progressive abstraction(PA) model to address the fluid nature of metaphorical categorization. Generally, the abstract categorical referent denoted by a metaphor vehicle is a structured description generated by successive comparisons with incoming exemplars provided by the topics. In the course of metaphor use, a set of generalizations and a set of exemplars are maintained. Each is regarded as a separate category. The exemplars are items not similar enough to the existing categories to be assimilated into any of them. As each new exemplar arrives, it is first compared with either the existing concrete vehicle category or the existing generalization(s), through structural alignment which is based on structure mapping engine(SME). If the match is sufficient enough then the topic category is assimilated into the abstract generalization based on the relational overlapping. If no generalization is sufficiently similar, then the topic is compared with each stored exemplar of the vehicle. If the base and target are judged sufficiently similar by the process just described, a generalization process will transform the most promising mapping between the two descriptions into a new generalized description. The generalization algorithm creates a new description by copying the predicate structure in the overlap of the mapping, substituting generic labels for particular entity names but preserving the predicate structure, including the specific predicate names used.

To put it more clearly, we use the metaphorical categorization "The boss is a shark." for a better illustration. As a consequence of being repeatedly compared with different incoming topics to convey similar meanings (e. g., "The lawyer is a shark." "The salesman is a shark." "The enemy is a shark.") , the term "shark" has come to be associated with the category "any creature that is vicious, merciless, aggressive etc.". Once this process of generalization or abstraction has taken place, any further metaphors with "shark" in the vehicle position can be understood as categorization statements. Then instead of interpreting the metaphor by seeking an overlap of attributive properties between the target and base, the author can interpret it as a statement that the target term belongs to the category represented by the vehicle term.

The explanatory advantage of this progressive model resides in two aspects. First, it at least provides a tentative psycholinguistic explanation for the fluidity of categorization by accounting for the dynamic gaining of the abstract meanings in the vehicle. Second, it can account for how metaphor is possible, i. e., how metaphorical category misjuxtaposition is made felicitous.

8. 2. 2 The nature of metaphorical category: relational category

In line with the argument for the dominant role of relational similarity in metaphors, the present study relied on a new school of category theory, namely, the relational category theory. In contrast to entity category such as apple, cup etc., whose category members share perceptual features, relational category refers to a category whose membership is determined by a common relational structure rather than by common features (Gentner and Kurtz, 2001). According to Gentner and Kurtz (ibid.), relational category necessarily involves n-place arguments, and the arguments can unrestrictedly range widely. The author also borrows Gentner and Kurtz's example here. For X to be a bridge, X must connect some other entities or points. A bridge can connect two concrete locations such as two bank or two abstract concepts such as two generations. The instances of a relational category can have few or no intrinsic properties in common with one another.

The relational category view offers some new complementary explanations relevant to categorization theory. There is evidence that humans prefer matches that share common higher-order relations over those that share only object attributes and seek systems of commonalities rather than isolated commonalities when carrying out comparisons(Clement and Gentner, 1991; also see the two case studies reviewed in 4.1.2). This tacit preference for relational structure can address one major challenge in categorization, that is, the role of theory-based knowledge in category formation (Murphy and Medin, 1985; Murphy and Allopenna, 1994; Wisniewski, 1995). For instance, Medin and Shoben(1988) demonstrate that gray clouds are considered more similar to black clouds than to white clouds, but gray hair is considered more similar to white hair than to black hair. It is a relational category that can better account for this phenomenon: gray hair and white hair share a causal relation to aging, whereas gray clouds and black clouds share a causal relation to storms. Another famous example speaking well for this notion is the fact that bats, although share the same salient perceptual features of[+WING] and +[FLY], are categorized as mammals because of the unobvious but theoretically relational properties such as giving birth to live young. Obviously, category judgment in these cases can not be adequately explained via merely perceptual attributes.

Gentner and Kurtz (2001) comment that research on categories have mostly ignored relational categories, and focused mainly on entity categories. For example, early classic empirical research on categories mainly took concrete items such as furniture, vehicles, drinking vessels, fruit and weapons, etc., or abstract entities such as color as the experiment samples(Rosch and Mervis, 1975; Rosch, 1975; Berlin and Kay, 1969; Kay and PMcDaniel, 1978). Despite the relatively minor number of studies in the empirical literature, it is discovered that relational categories play no less important role in human conceptual system and language. For example, informal ratings of the 100 highest-frequency nouns in the British National Corpus (BNC) revealed that about half is relational nouns(Asmuth and Gentner, 2005).

The author assumes that relational category theory can speak very well for metaphorical categorization. Return to the instance of bridge again, when it is metaphorically used, such as in "The seminar is a bridge.", seminar owns its membership in the category "bridge" due to their shared relational structure that holds distinct arguments which although are totally perceptually different. That is, both a seminar and a bridge connect two things: a seminar connects ideas, and a bridge connects two locations.

In addition, the relational category view can also to some extent account for the Invariance-mapping view of metaphor, or the systematicity of metaphor mapping. According to Lakoff and Johnson (1980), one feature of metaphorical mapping is systematicity. For example, in the metaphor "Love is a journey." entities from the topic domain (e.g., the lovers, their common goals, and their relationship) are systematically associated with entities from the vehicle domain (e.g., travelers, destinations, vehicles). Different from the comparison view and the categorization view of metaphor, the relational similarity approach to metaphor comprehension allows for individual novel metaphors to set up extended mappings between the target and base domains, and for these extended mappings to inspire additional novel expressions. Based on the relation, the arguments involved would be systematically aligned, and the key predicates which make up the relation would also be aligned.

It is worthwhile to point out that except for the difference between entity category and relational category in terms of the determinant criteria, the two theories of category also share something in common. That is, like entity category, relational category also has a certain internal structure (Rosch and Mervis, 1975). Internal structure refers to the observation that "categories are composed of a core meaning which consists of the clearest cases (best examples) of the category, surrounded by other category members of decreasing similarity to that core meaning" (ibid: 112). The author claims that the shared relations, which determine the membership of a metaphorical categorization, also have better or worse, central or peripheral examples. Actually, this notion is reflected in the characteristic of "aptness" of metaphor. Recall that in Exp 4 in the current dissertation, the author found that some metaphors can be highly apt and others can be less apt. In light of this argument, we can redefine the notion "aptness" as "the extent to which the metaphor vehicle denotes the relational structure of the topic".

8.2.3 Metaphor-simile distinction revisited

Metaphor and simile are two of the most important tropes. The difference between metaphor and simile seems slight when considered at the most basic linguistic level. That is, they both commonly involve the juxtaposition of two concepts in order to enhance appreciating one of them, differing only in the presence or absence of the hedge-like word "like". The two statements "My boss is a shark." and "My boss is like a shark.", for example, are likely to lead the hearer to the same broad kinds of interpretations about the boss's personality. In spite of their high degrees of syntactic and semantic similarity, the facts that the two do function as distinct linguistic figures of speech and that they are used in different contexts have led many metaphor theorists to consider specifically the relationship between metaphor and simile.

Actually, from the very beginning scholars have been intrigued by the subtle distinction and sameness between metaphor and simile.In Rhetorics(1941), Aristotle associates similes with metaphors, suggesting that, although metaphors should essentially be taken to be nothing more than elliptical similes, they might have greater rhetorical force than similes in certain circumstances: "A simile, as has been said before, is a metaphor differing from it only in the way it is put; and just because it is longer it is less attractive. Besides, it does not say outright that 'this' is 'that', and therefore the hearer is less interested in the idea." (Fogelin, 1988: 27)

This Aristotelian account takes for granted a series of assumptions about the ways in which metaphor and simile function. Firstly, they are not only interchangeable but entirely equivalent. Secondly, longer formulations are necessarily less appealing. Thirdly, direct equation (saying that "this" is "that") is intrinsically more interesting than mere comparison (saying that "this" is like "that"). Metaphors and similes vary merely in their linguistic forms and have no qualitatively different distinctions. Aristotle's influence has been so far-reaching that the same idea is endorsed by many modern scholars as a framework or springboard for the development of their own lines. For example, Miller (1993: 357) sets out an attempt "to defend a version of the traditional view that a metaphor is an abbreviated simile"; and Fogelin (1988: 357) claims that metaphors "differ from similes in only a trivial grammatical way, that is metaphors are similes with the terms of comparison suppressed".

In spite of the strong influence of this view, three recent findings in previous related studies have complicated this equivalent view. First, there is empirical proof that metaphors and similes convey different meanings on the ground that in many cases metaphors create new similarities rather than depending on old ones (Tversky, 1977: 332). Second, certain tension, or some sense of deviation and incongruity is noticeable in novel poetic metaphors especially and even in conventional non-dead metaphors. For example, Ricoeur (1977) claims that a metaphor usually evokes surprise with its unexpected categorical juxtaposition of the topic and the vehicle, thus leading to heightened perceptual involvement and deeper processing, which results in more complex ground relations in a metaphor form than in its corresponding simile form. Third, metaphors often convey more abstract, deeper meanings than similes. As MacCormac (1985) argued that metaphors are more likely to be chosen to evoke consideration of both similarities and differences between the tenor and the vehicle, while similes are used primarily to evoke similarities.

How do these observed distinctions fit into a theory of similarity on which both metaphor and simile theories are based? Previous studies merely focused on the description of the superficial distinction in the outcome of interpretation, but the explanation for the mechanism on which these distinctions rely is relatively inadequate. As this question is central to metaphor studies, the present study can make certain contribution pertaining to the theoretical account of these distinctions. More specifically, what the present dissertation proposes is that metaphors and similes are different in meaning and effect, and that these differences are all due to the fundamental nature of the similarity conveyed by the topic-vehicle pairs. Analyzing in a more general theoretical framework, the author proposes that a metaphor, with a linguistic form of category inclusion, requires the relationship between the topic and the vehicle to be category inclusion. According to our theoretical hypothesis, relational similarity takes a more dominant place in determining categorization than attributive similarity. As a result, an attributive comparison involves the mapping of a shared one-place predicate attribute from the topic to the vehicle, as in "The sun is like an orange.", the sun and the orange are both orange-colored, both round. A relational predicate, on the other hand, involves a secondary association, as in "The sea is like a big aquarium.", both the sea and the aquarium both contain fish and water .

Our finding has the following significant explanatory power regarding the distinctive view of metaphor and simile. It provides a deeper underlying rationale for the observed fact that metaphors and similes are distinct in interpretation outcome and in expressive effect. As Gibb and Wales (1990) point out that metaphors are preferred for abstract vehicles, whereas similes were preferred for concrete vehicles. What accounts for the abstractness in the vehicle has been long unsolved. The notion of similarity as a basic relation in metaphor is old but still appealing. The framework provided by the present dissertation can serve as a tentative explanation for this issue. Also in the relational category analysis framework, as metaphors depend more heavily on relational category and relational concepts (or category) are more abstract in meaning, the abstractness in the metaphor vehicles are thus due to the relationality in them.

8.2.4 Metaphorical vs. conventional categorization: different or equal?

The notion that metaphor is unique dates back to Aristotle. In Poetics, Aristotle (1941) contends that metaphor is "the mark of genius". It differs from normal language in that it is sophisticated. Aristotle's influence has survived for a long time, featuring dominantly many recent views (Grice, 1975; Searle, 1979; Lakoff and Johnson, 1980). On this view, metaphors in the categorical inclusion forms differ from metaphors in the conventional categorical inclusion forms. Deviating from the latter, the former require special processes.

It is this long-standing legacy that led researchers to look for a specific locus for processing of metaphor in the brain. The assumption that it is the right hemisphere (RH) that is specialized in interpreting metaphors seems to date back to Winner and Gardner (1977). Since then, numerous studies have shown greater RH involvement in processing metaphor (Anake, Faust and Kravet, 1998; Gagnon et al., 2003; Kaplan et al., 1990; Kasmerski et al., 2003; Mashal, Faust and Hendler, 2005, 2007; Schmidt, DeBuse, and Seger, 2007; Kacinik and Chiarello, 2007). However, a growing number of research have challenged this traditional RH hypothesis. For example, through using event-related functional magnetic resonance imaging (ER-FMRI), Stringaris et al., (2006, 2007) demonstrated that even conventional English metaphoric sentences (of "An x is a y." type), which took equally long to read in behavioral data recording, recruited the LH (left hemisphere) when the task involved meaningfulness judgments. Compared to literal sentences, deriving meaning from metaphoric sentences activated the left thalamus. In addition, in Lee and Dapretto's study (2006), the results showed that the involvement of the left or right side of the brain depends on the phases of processing. Such findings argue in favor of different processing pathways for literals and nonliterals in the LH. Indeed, most researchers propose that the activation of the left hemisphere might reflect the "open-ended" nature of the metaphors used.

We assume that these conflicting findings could be a consequence of two drawbacks in previous studies. First, previous studies, when investigating the right or left hemisphere bias in metaphor processing, didn't specify different stages of processing. Thus, the final findings could have confounded the hemisphere bias with different phases in processing. Second, previous neurophysiological studies on metaphors did not manipulate the similarity type. As similarity nature is an important determinant of the degree of abstractness in language categorization, the previous studies failed to control a crucial factor influencing neural substrates of metaphor processing.

In this regard, the ERP findings in the present study are of more theoretical significance to the issue whether metaphorical categorization is unique. In the early stage of processing denoted by N400, although different ERP amplitudes indicate that metaphorical category assertions and conventional category assertions rely on different amounts of cognition efforts, the statistically close scalp distributions show that the different category inclusion assertions rely on the same neural resources. In this aspect, such findings cohere with previous studies which indicated no hemisphere bias between metaphorical categories and conventional categories.

More significantly, in the later stage of processing denoted by P600, different ERP amplitudes indicate that metaphorical category assertions and conventional category assertions rely on different amounts of cognition efforts. The statistically distinct scalp distributions between the two types of metaphors with distinct types of similarity demonstrate whether metaphors have a right-hemisphere biased involvement of the brain depends on the nature of similarity. That is, metaphors denoting relational similarity have a right specific engagement of the brain, while such bias is not detected in metaphors denoting attributive similarity. Based on this observation, we can reach the assumption that the confounding results released by previous studies on metaphor may due to their failures in manipulating the similarity type of the experimental metaphors. That is, for the right-hemisphere biased findings, relational metaphors might have been used.

Although there have emerged evidence showing that metaphors with different types of similarity might exert on different parts of the brain, it should be pointed out that such distinctions between different kinds of metaphors can still be accounted for in general language processing frameworks. As discussed in Section 8.2.5, these differences can only speak for the notion that metaphorical and conventional categories may rely on different neural substrates, yet it is still not fully justifiable to conclude that metaphorical and conventional categories are different in nature. This assumption is in coherence with the view that the right hemisphere is not uniquely involved in metaphor processing(Giora et al., 1997, 2002).

Actually, the two types of metaphorical category with distinct similarity together with conventional category have been proposed to be analyzed in the same "similarity space" as termed by Gentner and Markman (1997). According to this model, the contrast among the four categorical assertions investigated in Exp 5 is in fact a continuum, rather than a dichotomy.

As shown in Figure 8.2, the four types of category inclusion statements in the present ERP experiment can be defined in a unified space according to the degree of the overlapping of the relations or attributes shared by the two items in comparison. relational metaphors occur when comparisons exhibit a high degree of relational similarity with very little attribute similarity. In contrast, attributive metaphors share

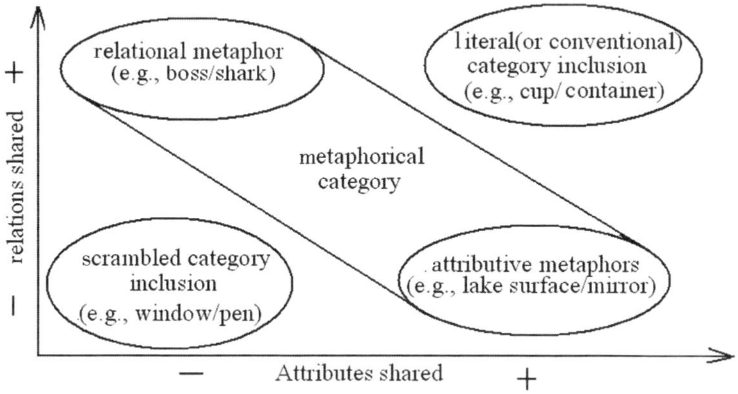

Figure 8.2 Different types of categories interpreted in the similarity space

attributes but little relations. As the amounts of both attribute similarity and relation similarity increase to a certain extent, the comparison shifts toward literal or conventional categorization. When neither relational similarity nor attributive similarity gets overlapped in two items, the comparison of the two items would result in an anomalous comparison, i. e., a scrambled category.

In view of the general language processing frameworks, the author assumes that the findings from the present dissertation generally speak for "the standard pragmatic model" (Grice, 1975; Searle, 1979; Fodor, 1983) instead of "the direct access view" (Gibbs, 1994, 2002; Sperber and Wilson, 1986, 1995). According to the former, initial comprehension of literal and nonliteral language should be identical: it should involve accessing the literal meaning of the utterance first. Recall that in the present study, in the minimal linguistic context (the metaphorical "An x is a y."), the statistically close N400 amplitudes and scalp distributions between the attributive metaphors and the relational metaphors together with the findings in Exp 3a indicated that both the two types of metaphorical category inclusion assertions involved an initial, obligatory, literal stage which is supplemented by an optional stage of adjustment to contextual information, resulting in the derivation of the contextually compatible meaning (demonstrated by different scalp distributions of P600).

Uncontradictoriy, the results also serves as evidence for the graded salience hypothesis (GSH) developed by Giora and her colleagues (Giora et al., 1997, 2002). According to this hypothesis, salient meanings (the concrete attributive feature of the topic and the vehicle) are assumed to be accessed immediately upon encounter of the linguistic stimulus via a direct lookup in the mental lexicon. Less-salient meanings (the abstract relational feature of the topic and the vehicle) will lag behind. Nonsalient meanings (the abstract relational feature of the topic and the vehicle) require extra inferential processes (as indicated by the right hemisphere biased P600 distributions).

In sum, it seems only safe to conclude that metaphorical category in its own right is not unique. The brain is not sensitive to metaphorical or conventional categories as such. Instead, it is sensitive to natures of similarity, which determines remoteness of semantic relationships, open-endedness of a categorical statement.

8.2.5 Philosophical implications for cognitive linguistics

The present study has some significant philosophical implications for modern cognitive approaches to linguistics. One of the basic tenets of cognitive linguistics is what Lakoff terms "the cognitive commitment", the notion is "that linguistic theory and methodology must be consistent with what is empirically known about cognition, the brain and language" (Lakoff, 1990: 40). That is, language is understood as a product of general cognitive abilities, and language ability is not a separate module independent of general human cognitive ability. On this account, language can be studied through methods or approaches which are adopted in studying general cognitive abilities.

The consequences of "the cognitive commitment" follow three philosophical notions in human language: imagination, embodiment, and subjectivism. All the three notions are related to idealism and relativism. Since the enlightenment, the three aspects have been despised in many theories of language, because they are regarded as non-rational, unruly, and idiosyncratic play of ideas, and therefore, unsuitable for scientific research. Nevertheless, in cognitive linguistics, imagination is considered as a basic human cognitive ability and is central to human meaning and rationality. As Johnson (1987: 172) explains, the way we reason and what we can experience as meaningful are both based on structures of imagination that make our experience what it is. We make sense of our less directly apprehensible experiences on the basis of more directly apprehensible experiences.

For decades, linguists have been working on the question what actually constitutes the ability of imagination. Since the recognition of the relation between metaphor and cognition, metaphorical mapping has been considered as one basic imaginative cognitive mechanism①. Because of its theoretical significance, research on metaphor have occupied a central position in cognitive linguistics. One of the major problems that cognitive linguists still face is the question of how to constrain metaphorical mappings. In the tradition of cognitive approach to language study, attempts to constrain the mapping process in metaphorical production and comprehension can be found in Lakoff's "Invariance Principle", i. e. "metaphorical mappings preserve the cognitive topology of the vehicle domain a way consistent with the inherent structure of the target domain" (Lakoff, 1993: 215). The invariance principle is useful in order to constrain the nature of those mappings. That is to say, it is possible to map from the vehicle domain, while having preserved the whole cognitive topology. The only problem with this principle is that it does not show exactly what part of the vehicle domain is consistent with the structure of the target domain.

In view of this problem, the present dissertation from a perspective of psycholinguistics provides a more tangible approach to imagination through a structural view of metaphorical similarity, thus shedding new light on our understanding of the basic principle of imagination. Recall that our hypothetical approach to similarity is derived from empirical findings from other broader research fields such as figure perception (see Section 4. 1). The auther defines linguistic similarity in metaphor in terms of the more general perceptual similarity in figures. Also, as for the invariance principle in metaphorical mapping, our study can serve as a more comprehensive explanation for this phenomenon. That is, the systematicity in structure mapping can constrain that only those relational similarities are recruited for metaphor mapping.

---

① The other mechanism is metonymy, whch is not explored in the present dissertation as it falls out of the scope of the present study.

As for embodiment and subjectivism, our hypotheses on relational similarity in metaphor can also serve as a tentative approach to a better explanation. Specifically, the notion of "relationality" can shed newer light on both the embodiment and subjectivism tenets of cognitive linguistics. The subjectivism tenet is related to the theory of linguistic meaning. Most cognitive linguists reject the objectivist theories of meaning. The term "objectivism" was used by Lakoff(1987) to refer to those theories of linguistic meaning that interpret objective reality as independent of human cognition, as held by montague's theoretical semantics model(Dowty et al., 1981; Cann, 1993). For cognitive linguistics, meanings do not exist independently of the people who create and use them(Reddy, 1993). All linguistic forms do not have inherent meanings in themselves, they act as clues activating the meanings that reside in human minds and brains. This activation of meaning is not necessarily entirely the same for every person because meaning is based on individual experience as well as collective experience(Barcelona, 1997: 9). On this view, mental and linguistic categories are not abstract, disembodied human independent categories. Instead, they are created on the basis of our concrete experiences and under the constraints imposed by our bodies. Human conceptual categories, the meaning of words and sentences and the meanings of linguistic structures at any level, are not a set of universal abstract features or uninterruptible symbols(ibid: 9). Instead, they are motivated and grounded more or less directly in experience, in our bodily, physical, social and cultural experiences because after all, "we are beings of the flesh"(Johnson, 1987: 347).

The present study proposes that the notions of embodiment and subjectivism should be accounted for in the framework of relational similarity in metaphor. Here, what is involved in the relation can be any human being who has active subjective perception or experience. That is, metaphor similarity does not exist objectively in the topic and the vehicle independently of the person who uses the metaphor. Rather, the linking between the topic and the vehicle is embodied in that the user(s) of the language are involved in the construction of the similarity of the two concepts. This actually coheres with the analysis that the metaphor(e.g., "My love is a rose.") depends on something like "I feel about my love as I do about a rose." or "my love does to me what a rose does to me."(compare "the boss does to the employees what a shark does to the small fish.").

As is shown above, the subjectivism tenet of cognitive linguistics can be interpreted in a relational way in terms of the relation between the objects in the world and the perceivers. "The semantic meaning of any word can only be defined in a relational way in that the meanings do not exist independently out in the objective world, but rather in the relationships between the word and the language users." (Sweetser, 1990:1). This argument strongly speaks against the objectivist semantic theory, wherein meaning "is thought of as basically as a relationship between word and world, i. e., between a linguistic form and an object or state of affairs referred to or described by that form" (ibid: 3). According to our relational similarity view, any meaning of one word is dependent on a third involved participant (the speaker) besides the two participants (word and world) proposed in objectivist and formal semantic theory.

In sum, the relational similarity view of the relation between metaphor and categorization has significant implication to basic tenets of cognitive linguistics in that it provides a more reasonable account for the notion of imagination, embodiment and subjectivism.

8.3 Pedagogical reflections and evaluations

8.3.1 Implications for the notion of metaphorical competence

The most direct applicable and pedagogical implication of "metaphorical categorization" is reflected in the notion of "metaphorical competence". Recent years have witnessed much call for the cultivation of the students' "metaphorical competence" in first or second language teaching. These claims have been mainly put forward in the theoretical framework of conceptual fluency (Danesi, 1995, 2003) or communicative language ability (Bachman, 1990; Littlemore and Low, 2006). In both frameworks, the notion of metaphorical competence has been considered as the key to a full mastery of the target language. For example, Danesi (1995) defines metaphorical competence as the ability to comprehend and use metaphors in a given language as used in natural discourse, and claims that such competence is as crucial as the linguistic and communicative competences since it is tightly linked to the ways in which a culture organizes its world conceptually. Littlemore(2008) refers metaphorical competence to the ability of language learners to interpret novel metaphors in the language.

Despite the many disputes over the definition of metaphorical competence, there is one point on which all the branches of studies agree, that is, the mastery of metaphorical competence is an indispensable part of the command of the target language. Although these researchers tell us a great deal about the importance of the command of metaphorical competence in language learning, they fail to provide a comprehensive and consensual view of the nature of such competence, i. e., the cognitive mechanism underlying such so-called metaphorical competence(Lin, 1997, 2004; Gong, 2006; Shi and Liu, 2010). This ignorance may be due to the fact that all the research were defined relatively narrowly as applied-linguistics oriented, and that the underlying cognitive mechanism is of more peripheral interest to the research than the direct goal in pedagogy. Whatever the reason is, the author assumes that if metaphorical competence is of great importance to language learning, an understanding of the cognitive mechanism underlying this competence should be necessarily required for a comprehensive and scientific approach to its cultivation which has always been the research focus of previous studies.

In view of this, the present dissertation, taking a cognitive psychological study on metaphorical categorization, could have some significant implications to the cognitive nature of metaphorical competence. The author assumes that metaphorical competence actually resides in the metaphorical category extension competence. Distinct from previous studies on metaphorical competence conducted by Littlemore, Low(2006) and Danesi(1995), our endeavor basically echoes with the general cognitive approaches to metaphor and categorization(Lakoff and Johnson, 1980). The highly influential contemporary cognitive approach to metaphor defines metaphor as a cognitive process by which "understand and experience one thing in terms of another" (Lakoff and Johnson, 1980:6), and posits that metaphor ability resides in the ability to identify the ground, or similarity conveyed by the metaphor topic and vehicle. Following this argument together with the key findings of the present dissertation, metaphorical competence can be defined as "the competence or ability to understand and experience one thing in terms of another", or in a category research tradition, the competence or ability to "extend the boundaries of conventional categories and accommodate new metaphorical members".

Talking about the old issue in a new vein of terms does not illuminate the basic nature of such competence. So, what cognition is exactly underlying the ability to extend the boundaries of conventional categories? Based on the findings of the present study, the author asserts that metaphorical competence depends on the psychological processes of similarity recognition and analogical reasoning which is based on structure mapping and relational schema induction. More specifically, this argument has the two aspects as unfolded below.

First, as for one aspect of the competence, i. e., "the ability to comprehend and use metaphors in a given language as used in natural discourse" put by Danesi (1995), the author stresses the importance of relational similarity recognition in such competence. Recall that in our study, it was found that metaphor comprehension and use mainly depend on the recognition of relational similarity rather than attributive similarity between the topic and the vehicle. For example, to appropriately comprehend and use the metaphor "A man is a wolf." entails a mental recruitment of the relational similarity shared by the two metaphor items, i. e., man is to woman as wolf is to sheep. Failing to capture such relational similarity will definitely lead to a failure of communication.

Another source of evidence for the relational view of metaphorical competence is from the developmental studies on metaphorical competence. Numerous studies at home or abroad (Feng et al., 2006; Zhou, 2001, 2003; Peng and Zhang, 2009; Thibaut, French, and Vezneva, 2010) consistently revealed that there is a trend in the development of metaphorical competence. That is, children roughly under the age of 7 are more likely to understand a metaphor based on attributive similarity, around puberty or 12 years old, they begin to become more competent in interpreting relational similarity metaphors. Based on these empirical studies, it can be concluded that the trend of the development of metaphorical competence actually relies on the "relational shift" in similarity recognition ability.

The second implication of the current study is concerned with thecharacteristic of creativity in metaphorical competence, i. e., "the ability of language learners to interpret novel metaphors in the language" (Littlemore, 2008; Liu, 2003). Previous studies failed to account for what constitute such creativity in interpreting novel metaphors, especially from a cognitive psychological point of view. In this regard, the findings concerning schema induction and analogical reasoning in the current work on metaphorical categorization could shed some new light on this issue. Recall that in the author's framework, the recruitment of a certain metaphor topic into a vehicle does not merely depend on organized conventional long-term memory, but rather on the induction of the schema which is based on the same relations which exist among a number of discrete elements. This is a process in which partial similarities are observed between concepts so that the characteristics of one of the concepts can be used to shed light on the other (Holyoak, 1984). Analogical reasoning based on schema induction is an important component of higher order cognitive development which is characterized with creativity. Analogy is a conceptual strategy enabling a person to make inferences about novel phenomena, to transfer learning across contexts, and to extract relevant information from everyday learning experiences on the basis of relational similarity.

8. 3. 2 Implications for lexical teaching

A second major pedagogical implication of the relational view of metaphorical categorization put forward by the present study is concerned with lexical teaching. More specifically, by clearly pointing out the dominant role of relational similarity reorganization in metaphorical category extension, our research findings can offer better accounts for two major aspects in lexical teaching. The first is metaphorical polysemy teaching, and the second concerns the abstract lexical teaching. What follow below are some elaborations on these two issues.

The first aspect is concerned with metaphorical polysemy. The studies of metaphorical meanings, especially the semantical changes that deem to take place over time, are the top concern of language teachers and lexicology. It has become popular in cognitive linguistics to use metaphor to explain the links between polysemous meanings of a lexeme(Lakoff and Johnson, 1980; Lakoff, 1993; Rakava, Barcelona, 2005; Sweetser, 1990). Word is understood as polysemous if all its multiple meanings are systematically related. The relation between the different polysemous senses of a word is not arbitrary or random, but motivated. This kind of motivation finds its grounds in our understanding and bodily experience of the world in which we live. A command of these polysemous senses has been considered as an essential part of language learning. Indeed, the Oxford Dictionary of English Idioms (Cowie, Mackin and McCiaq, 1993) states in its introduction that the "accurate and appropriate use of expressions which are in the broadest sense idiomatic is one distinguishing mark of a native command of the language and a reliable measure of the proficiency of foreign learners".

In spite of the wide recognition of the place of metaphorical polysemy inlanguage learning, it is relatively neglected as to what constitute(s) the "motivation" or "systematicity" in metaphorical polysemy extension. Also take the "boss-shark" pair for example, how the two items get semantically related is an important issue in explaining the motivation for category or meaning extension. According to the entity category theory which takes shared perceptual properties as the determining factors in categorization, things are in the same category if and only if they have certain perceptual properties in common. However, multiple senses of a polysemous form do not necessarily seem to share objective perceptual similarity, as the above example show. That is, we can hardly figure out any physical or perceptual commonality shared by boss and shark, thus the sensed relatedness of the two concepts cannot be completely made explicable in terms of a componential analysis of senses. In this sense, metaphorical polysemy has always been problematic to traditional truth-conditional semantics.

In view of the drawbacks of the conditional attributive similarity approach to categorization, the relational view proposed by the present study can be of greater explanatory power. That is, the motivation of the systematic relatedness between metaphorical polysemes can be better accounted for in the framework of relational similarity. As knowing the motivated relatedness of the relationship has been recognized as a key to higher efficiency in lexical learning and teaching, our finding can shed some new light on lexical acquisition by explicitly raising the students' awareness of the relationality of the similarity between the multiple senses of one lexeme(Gibbs, 1999; Boers, 2000; Danisi, 2003).

The second aspect of lexical teaching on which our study can shed light is the issue of relational concept acquisition, which depends more heavily on the notion of relational similarity and less on the notion of metaphoricity. Numerous research have demonstrated that in lexical acquisition, some concepts (e. g., robbery) are more abstract than others(e. g., apple), and thus the former are more difficult than the later to understand or acquire. An increasing number of studies have tried to figure out the true difference between the two types of concepts. Some pointed out that the difference lies in the fact that the former(e. g., robbery) is less constrained and tangible than the latter(e. g., apple). Despite its plausibility, this account is not comprehensive in that the latter (e. g., apple), according to the type hierarchy structure view of knowledge representation(Collins and Loftus; Way, 1991), can also be of high abstractness because it can also represent a "type" (e. g., dog) name which denotes some more concrete exemplars of the type (e. g., different kinds of dogs).

Obviously, to account for the difference in abstractness of the two types of concepts in the type gierarchy structure view is not as convincing as it intends to be. So what can serve as a better explanation? Echoing with one of the key proposals for the present dissertation (see Section 9. 2. 2), the author resorts to the nature of relationality to account for this observation although not all the relational concepts are metaphorical. According to this view, some concepts are more complex in that they involve more logical participants, or "arguments" for definition.For example, robbery as an abstract noun involves three basic arguments (Gentner and Kurts, 2001): Robbery(thief, goods, victim)

Actually, one informal corpus-based study has revealed that half of the top 100 nouns with highest frequency in British National Corpus(BNC) are relational nouns (Asmuth and Gentner, 2005). Besides nouns, the relational view can also account for the relative difficulty in acquiring verbs versus nouns. Numerous studies have demonstrated that verbs are more central and elusive than nouns. For example, developmental studies show that verbs are slower to acquire than nouns (Caselli et al., 1995); poorer in memory than nouns both in recognition and in recall (e. g., Kersten and Earles, 2006); less prone to be borrowed in language contact (e. g., Sobin, 1982); and less stable in translation between languages (Gentner, 1981). Actually, verb learning has been considered as a big challenge for foreign or second language learners. An understanding of what constitute(s) the difficulty is an essential part of the effort to conquer the difficulty.

The author argues that the relational view of similarity and concept can serve as a better account for the distinction between verbs and nouns together with the relative elusiveness of verbs in comparison with nouns. Echoing with the argument for the distinction between relational category and entity category, the author tentatively proposes the propositional analogy shown below: relational categories : entity categories; verbs : concrete nouns.

The fundamental assumption is that although verbs and nouns are distinct due to their different syntactical roles, another equally important source of the difference is their distinct semantic structures. More significantly, the distinct semantic structure could be explained through the notion of relationality proposed in the present study. Relational categories are analogized to verbs in that they semantically take arguments (they are semantically unsaturated) which accounts for the relative complexity of verbs. Also take the verb rob for example, it involves a schematic relational category which is based on the three arguments: rob(thief, goods, victim)

Actually, this argument is in line with the dual-categorization model of metaphorical categorization proposed for the present dissertation. For a better illustration, the author can put forward another analogy: macro-category: micro-category;verb:noun.

Recall that in arguing for the notion of duality in metaphorical categorization (see Section 4. 3. 2 and Chapter 7), the author defined the macro-category as the semantic schema which denotes the relation between two items, and the micro-category as the category relation between the individual participants involved in the relation. As macro-categorization in metaphor is more abstract in that it does not specify the individual participants, thus the specific implication for the metaphorical verbs learning is that, when studying verbs with metaphorical meanings, the teacher can emphasize the more abstract relation denoted by the verb while relatively ignoring the specific entities involved in the relation.

8.4 Summary

In this chapter, the author first summarizes the major empirical findings pertaining to the five key research questions in this study. This was then followed by a delineation of both the theoretical and pedagogical reflections and evaluations of the empirical findings.

Theoretically, this study sheds special light on four important fields.

First, as for the relation between metaphor and categorization, the present study provides a more comprehensive psychological model for the role of metaphor in the dynamic extension of categorization. More importantly, this study can better account for the dynamic process of metaphorical category extension.

Second, regarding the nature of metaphorical category, the author proposes the notion of relational category for a more complementary account. Generally, the author borrows theories from more general cognitive theories of categorization for the notion of relational category. In arguing for the weight on the quality of relationality in metaphorical categorization, the author resorts to the more deeply underlying notion of relational similarity.

Third, this study can shed some special light on the long-existing disputable issue of thedistinction between the two most important tropes, i. e., metaphor and simile. Through arguing for the distinct similarity for metaphor and simile, the present study provides a more cognitively oriented explanatory framework for the qualitatively different account of the relation between the two tropes.

Fourth, the present study enriches our understanding of the distinctions between metaphorical categorization and conventional categorization. The research findings indicate that it is the nature of similarity that determines the uniqueness of the neural substrates of metaphor language. Compared with attributive metaphorical categorization and conventional categorization, relational metaphorical categorization has a right-hemisphere bias. Although there are some differences between various kinds of metaphorical categorical assertions, such differences can be explained in the theoretical framework of general language processing. In light of this, it is still highly risky to conclude that metaphorical categorization is distinct from conventional categorization.

Fifth, the present study has some significant philosophical implications to modern cognitive approaches to linguistics in terms of the cognitive commitment. This generally includes three important respects: imagination, embodiment, and subjectivism. Through schema induction proposed for metaphorical categorization, the author can explain the imagination commitment of cognitive linguistics. Through the notion of relationality in similarity identification, the author can better account for both the embodiment and the subjectivism tenets of cognitive linguistics. In view of this, the present study can also lend some empirical support to the philosophical branch termed as subjectivism.

Pedagogically, this study made two major contributions.

First, it directly shed new light on the important notion of "metaphorical competence". Analyzing in the framework of metaphorical categorization, the author provides a new interpretation of "metaphorical competence", that is, the author redefines "metaphorical competence" as the metaphorical category extension ability which is based on metaphorical categorization. More specifically, such competence mainly relies on the ability to identify the relational similarity conveyed by the metaphor topic and the vehicle.

Second, more practically, our study provides some implications to lexical education in two respects. On the one hand, it can better account for the "motivation" or "rationality" underlying the systematically related senses of metaphor polysemes in the theoretical framework of metaphorical categorization proposed for the current study, thus facilitating the teaching of metaphorical polysemes. On the other hand, through the notion of relationality, the current study can also improve our understanding of more abstract relational nouns and verbs.

Chapter 9 Conclusion

This chapter winds up this dissertation. It first draws conclusions on metaphorical categorization by theoretically summarizing the answers to all the four key research questions depicted in Chapter 4 in a unified research framework (see Section 4.3), then it turns to a discussion of the limitations of this study and some recommendations for further research in related realm.

9.1 Conclusions

The relation between metaphor and categorization has been generally recognized as an important issue with serious theoretical implications in the study of language and cognition. Nevertheless, it is a pity that little attempt has been made to figure out how metaphor works in categorization from a systematically empirical point of view. This pity has been mitigated to a considerable degree by this dissertation which provides a relatively more unified and comprehensive perspective on the underlying metaphorical mechanism in human categorization based on a series of theoretical investigations and empirical experiments. Echoing with the summary of the empirical findings provided in Section 8.1, some concluding remarks can be made on the present study from a more theoretically-oriented perspective.

First, metaphor can be viewed as a way to change the structure of the conventional category hierarchy, or put it another way, metaphor is a complex form of categorical reasoning in which concepts conventionally from one category are mapped onto another category, and resulting in new inferences. The fundamental idea is that a metaphor processing involves an upward search through the category hierarchy for a common superordinate category in which both the topic and the vehicle are included. Such searching process is based on the dynamic induction of a more abstract concept that is more specialized than the common original topic and vehicle and is made the immediate parent of the topic and vehicle concepts.

Second, the dynamic upward search process, which is termed as metaphorical categorization, consists of two sub-processes, i. e., structural mapping and schema induction. More specifically, metaphorical categorization is a mapping between two abstract relations of two situations. Thus the mapped relational commonality or similarity serves as the mediator of metaphorical categorization. The mapping process is actually the relational mapping for further relational alignment in the induction in metaphorical categorization. In metaphorical categorization, a reasoner must first identify the relations that are present within the topic and the vehicle being compared. That is, the reasoner must be able to see how elements relate to each other within each relation. These relations within individual component are actually the conventionalized semantic relations because they usually refer to a conventional way in which two components are related to each other. Take the metaphor "A man is a wolf." again for example, there is a conventionalized semantic relation between the two semantic component elements of the metaphor topic (i. e., "man chases woman"), and there is also a conventionalized semantic relation between semantic component elements of the vehicle "wolf" (i. e., "wolf chases sheep"). Through structural alignment, the two separate types of "chasing" are recruited in a more abstract common relational schema "chasing". That is to say, in order to successfully appreciate a metaphor, a reasoner must comprehend that the two conventionalized semantic relations both represent the same abstract relation.

The abstract relations (e. g., chasing) are higher-ordered in the category hierarchy in that they take more specific, lower-order relations (e. g., "chasing" in the man—woman and wolf—sheep relations) as exemplars. The higher-order relations are abstract in that they do not depend on the specific elements (arguments) of the relations (Blanchette and Dunbar, 2000). Rather, they share commonality at the level of underlying relation. Thus, they can be abstracted from more concrete immediate situations and applied to any specific abstract situations within which the component arguments are related to each other in a similar way. In the present dissertation, we term the abstraction of the relation shared by the topic and the vehicle as the "macro-categorization". As discussed above, the higher-ordered abstract relation depicted in a metaphor does not specify the actual arguments, thus the individual arguments playing analogous roles in the abstracted relation will be enrolled in a higher-order parent category. The present study terms such process in which the specific metaphor topic and vehicle are recruited in a parent category as the "micro-categorization".

Third, as a corollary of the second conclusion, the author assumes that the extent to which a metaphorical "An x is a y." denotes category inclusion relation depends on the two layers of categorization: the macro-categorization level at which the vehicle is associated with specific abstracted relation, and the micro-categorization at which the topic and the vehicle is categorically associated with each other. In the present dissertation, the author operationalizes the association strength in the former level as conventionality and in the later level as aptness. Through simultaneously manipulating the two factors and adopting a strategy-proof experimental technique, the present study investigated the nature of "An x is a y.". The results show that the degree to which metaphorical "An x is a y." denotes categorization inclusion relation takes both conventionality and aptness as the determinants.

9.2 Limitations and recommendations for future research

In spite of our endeavor to give a consistent and unified psycholinguistic account for the role of metaphor in category extension, the present study is by no means immune to many drawbacks in respect of theoretical considerations and methodological manipulations.

First, in this study, in order to eliminate other possible propounding factors, the author narrowly focuses on nominal metaphors which have the same grammatical form as literal category inclusion statements, failing to investigate more complex metaphorical categorizations such as metaphorical compounds, or predicate metaphors with more linguistic contexts.

The second limitation is concerned with the relation between macro-and micro-categorization in metaphorical categorization. In this study the author specified two layers of categorizations in metaphorical categorization, yet failing to provide a clarified account for the relations between the two layers in terms of their processing sequence. That is, the author did not address the question of how categorization at the micro-level interacts with categorization at the macro-level over time as a metaphorical categorization is being constructed. It is likely that any completely serial account of analogy, such as an account in which micro-categorization is completed before macro-level categorization begins, is overtly simplistic. It is more likely that there is a feed-back, feed-forward relationship between categorizations at the micro- and macro-level.

Third, although the present dissertation takes structure-mapping as the basis for metaphorical categorization, it did not go into its underlying mechanism. That is, in spite of the fact that the present paper develops some hypotheses concerning the similarity nature of metaphorical categorization, it fails to provide a tentative account as to how the similarity conveyed by a metaphor is structurally identified and preserved in the process of metaphor comprehension.

The fourth drawback is more empirical. As we know that the ERP studies moredesirably require with-item experimental stimuli, however, due to the extreme difficulty in collecting the same groups of metaphor vehicles which could be used across four experimental conditions, the author resorted to a between-item design. Although the author has manipulated potential factors influencing ERP recordings to the greatest extent, this flaw might still be detrimental to the internal validity of the present study.

In view of the above-discussed limitations, the findings cannot be taken as definitive answers to the questions of this present research. It is the present researcher's hope that the results of this empirically-based study may serve as a step in a better understanding of the relation between metaphor and categorization. A number of areas of research touched upon by the present study are worthy of further pursuing:

First, in this study, in order to eliminate other possible propounding factors, the author narrowly focuses on nominal metaphors which have the same grammatical form as literal category inclusion statements i. e., An x is a y. In future research, we need to broaden our research horizon to include metaphors in more complex contexts or in more diverse forms. For example, in the present study, the author only focuses on nominal metaphors, such as "Time is motion.". Based on our findings, time is included in the category motion in that people experience the passage of time as they see motions. In this sense, the concept "time" gets categorically associated with the concept "motion" in that they both share analogical relations. Nevertheless, in natural language use, the conceptual metaphor is more often used in different kinds of linguistic phrases, such as "Time flies." "We're getting close to Christmas." or "The summer is passing by." A comprehensive linguistic approach to metaphorical categorization has to cover an account for such metaphorical usage. This consideration should be a direction for future related studies.

Second, future related studies should go on to investigate the time-course relationship between the micro- and the macro- categorizations in metaphor processing. One major hypothesis of the present study is that in metaphor processing, the micro-category is formed based on the macro-category, which has been supported by some preliminary evidence found in previous studies. Previous studies have indicated that in within-domain analogies, e. g., hand: glove; foot: sock, the micro-categories respectively including "hand" and "foot", and "glove" and "sock" were formed before the macro-categories including the relations respectively denoting "hand" to "foot" together with "glove" to "sock" were formed. In a metaphorical analogy, the topic and the vehicle do not belong to any shared conventional category, which serves as the basis for metaphoricity. In such condition, it is logically reasonable to assume that the macro-categorization serves as the basis for the micro-categorization. That is to say, the categorical relation between the topic and the vehicle is formed based on categorizing the two analogical relations denoted by the topic and the vehicle. This assumption should be an essential part of the dual-categorization account of metaphor. unfortunately, the present study failed to find any specific evidence concerning this aspect. Further research should be specifically designed to seek more evidence from the perspective of the time-course relationship.

Third, although the present dissertation takes structure-mapping as the basis for metaphorical categorization, it did not go into the underlying mechanism of the structure mapping. It is commonly recognized that a metaphor is a cross-domain mapping(Lakoff, 1993), with each domain composed of a system of objects, object attributes, and relations between objects. A metaphor is considered as a cognitive tool to conceptualize the abstract world rather than just a linguistic trope. The cognitive power in a metaphor exists in the systematic preservation of the structures denoted by the vehicle when mapped to the topic. According to Lakoff's invariance principle, metaphorical mappings preserve the cognitive topology(i. e., image-schema structure) of the source domain, in a way consistent with the inherent structure of the target domain(Lakoff, 1993: 215). The nature of such preservation of the structures has always been essential in metaphor study, yet numerous studies have just pointed out the systematicity nature of the manner of metaphorical mapping without delineating what structures are preserved. Similarly, the present dissertation only developed its studies based on structural similarity as its theoretical framework, failing to provide a deeper investigation into how such structures are retrieved and preserved. Further related studies should go further to this aspect.

Fourth, from a more applied-linguistic perspective, metaphorical polysemes should be further studied. As revealed in the present study, polysemy is considered as the outcome of metaphorical categorization. More study should be conducted to investigate the mechanism in which a concrete term gains a more abstract referent as more understanding of the cognitive basis will definitely shed light on the acquisition of metaphorical polysemes in the foreign language teaching circumstance.

References

[1]ARZOUAN Y, GOLDSTEIN A, FAUST M. Brainwaves are stethoscopes: ERP correlates of novel metaphor comprehension[J]. Brain Research, 2007, 1160, 69-81.

[2]ARIZONAN Y, GOLDSTEIN A, FAUST M. Dynamics of hemispheric activity during metaphor comprehension: Electrophysiological measures[J]. NeuroImage, 2007, 36(1), 222-231.

[3]AUSTIN J. Philosophical Papers[M]. Oxford: Oxford University Press. 1961.

[4]BACHMAN L F. Fundamental Considerations in Language Testing[M]. Oxford: Oxford University Press. 1990.

[5]BARSALOU L W. Ad hoc categories[J]. Memory & Cognition, 1983, 11(3), 211-227.

[6]BARSALOU L W. The instability of graded structure: Implications for the nature of concepts[A]. In U Neisser (Ed), Concepts and Conceptual Development, 1987, 101-140[C]. Cambridge, England: Cambridge University Press.

[7]BARSALOU L W. Perceptual symbol systems[J]. Behavioral and Brain Sciences, 1999, 22(4), 577-609.

[8]BARSALOU L W. Abstraction in perceptual symbol systems[J]. Philosophical Transactions of the Royal Society of London: Biological Sciences, 2003, 358(4), 1177-1187.

[9]BARCELONA A. Clarifying and applying the notions of metaphor and metonymy within cognitive linguistics[J]. Atlantis XIX. 1997, 1, 21-48.

[10] BARCELONA A. Metaphor and Metonymy at the Crossroads: Cognitive Approaches[M]. Berlin and New York: Mouton de Gruyter. 2005.

[11]BARR R A, CAPLAN L J. Category representations and their implications for

category structure[J]. Memory and Cognition, 1987,15(5), 397–418.

[12]BASSOK M, HOLYOAK K J. Interdomain transfer between isomorphic topics in algebra and physics [J]. Journal of Experimental Psychology: Learning, Memory, and Cognition, 1989, 15(1), 153–166.

[13] BEEMAN M, FRIEDMAN R B, GRAFMAN J, PEREZ E, DIAMOND S, LINDSAY M B. Summation priming and coarse semantic coding in the right hemisphere[J]. Journal of Cognitive Neuroscience,1994, 6(1), 26–45.

[14] BEEMAN M. Coarse semantic coding and discourse comprehension [J]. In Beeman M & Chiarello C(eds) Right Hemisphere Language Comprehension: Perspectives from Cognitive Neuroscience, 1998(2), 255–284. Mahwah, NJ: Erlbaum.

[15]BERLIN B, KAY P. Basic Color Terms: Their University and Evolution[M]. Berkeley: University of California Press.1969.

[16] BLACK M. More about metaphor [M]. In Ortony, A (ed), Metaphor and Thought(2nd ed, 19–41). Cambridge, UK: Cambridge University Press.1993.

[17]BLADES M, COOKE Z. Young children's ability to understand a model as a spatial representation[J]. Journal of Genetic P44sychology, 1994, 155(2), 201–218.

[18]BLANK G D. Metaphors in the lexicon[J]. Metaphor and Symbolic Activity, 1988, 3, 21–36.

[19] BLANCHETTE I, DUNBAR K. How analogies are generated: the roles of structural and superficial similarity[J]. Memory and Cognition,2000,28(1), 108–124.

[20]BLASKO D G, CONNINE C M. Effects of familiarity and aptness on metaphor processing[J]. Journal of Experimental Psychology: Learning, Memory and Cognition, 1993, 19(2), 295–308.

[21] BOERS F. Metaphor awareness and vocabulary retention [J]. Applied Linguistics, 2000, 21(4): 553–571.

[22]BOWDLE B F, GENTNER D. Informativity and asymmetry in comparisons[J]. Cognitive Psychology, 1997, 34(3), 244–286.

[23] BOWDLE B F, GENTNER D. The Career of Metaphor [J]. Psychological

Review.2005, 112(1), 193-216

[24]BROWN R. How shall a thing be called[J]? Psychological Review 1958, 65 (1): 14-21.

[25]BROWN R. Social Psychology[M]. New York: Free Press.1965.

[26]BROWN P, LEVINSON S C. Frames of spatial reference and their acquisition in Tenejapan Tzeltal[J]. In L. Nucci(Ed.), Culture, Thought and Development (pp. 2000, 167-197). Mahwah, NJ: Erlbaum.

[27] BUNGE S A, WENDELKEN C, BADRE D, ANTHONY D, WAGNER R. Analogical Reasoning and Prefrontal Cortex: Evidence for Separable Retrieval and Integration Mechanisms[J]. Advance Access publication, 2005,15(3), 239—249.

[28]CANN R. Formal Semantics[M]. Cambridge: Cambridge University Press.1993.

[29]CASELLI M C, BATES E, CASADIO P, FENSON J, FENSON L, SANDED L. A cross - linguistic study of early lexical development [J]. Cognitive Development, 1995,10(2),159-199.

[30]CHAPMAN S. Philosophy for Linguistics[M]. London & Newyork: Taylor & Francis Group.2000.

[31]CHIAPPE D L, KENNEDY J M. Aptness predicts preference for metaphors or similes, as well as recall bias[J]. Psychonomic Bulletin & Review, 1999,6 (4), 668-676.

[32]CHIAPPE D L, KENNEDY J M, CHIAPPE P. Aptness is more important than comprehensibility in preference for metaphors and similes[J]. Poetics, 2003, 31(1), 51-68.

[33]CHIAPPE D L, KENNEDY J M, SMYKOWSKI T. Reversibility, aptness, and the conventionality of metaphors and similes[J]. Metaphor & Symbol, 2003,18 (2), 85-105.

[34]CLARK H. Using language[M]. Cambridge: Cambridge University Press.1996.

[35] CLEMENT C A, GENTNER D. Systematicity as a selection constraint in analogical mapping[J]. Cognitive Science. 1991,15(1), 89-132

[36] CONEY J, LANGE A. Automatic and Atttentional Prosesses in the Comprehension of Unfamiliar Metaphors [J]. Curren Psychology:

Developmental Learning and Personality, 2006,25(2), 93-119.

[37] COLLINS A M, LOFTUS E F. A spreading-activation theory of semantic processing[J]. Psychological Review, 1975,82(6), 407-428.

[38] COULSON S, VAN PETTEN C. "Conceptual Integration and Metaphor Comprehension: An ERP Study[J]." Memory & Cognition, 2002,30(6), 958-968.

[39] COULSON S, VAN PETTEN C. A special role for the right hemisphere in metaphor comprehension? ERP evidence from hemifield presentation[J]. Brain Research, 2007,1146(1), 128-145.

[40] COWIE A P, MACKIN R, MCCIAQ I R. Oxford Dictionary of English Idioms [M]. Oxford: Oxford University Press.1993.

[41] CROFT W. Explaining Language Change: An Evolutionary Approach [M]. Harlow: Longman

Linguistics Library.2000.

[42] CROFT W, CRUSE D. Cognitive Linguistics [M]. Cambridge: Cambridge University Press.2004.

[43] DAVIDSON D. What metaphors mean[A]. IN S.Sacks(eds), On Metaphor, 1977,29-4[C]. Chicago: University of Chicago Press.

[44] DANESI M. Learning and teaching languages: The role of conceptual fluency [J]. International Journal of Applied Linguistics 1995,5(1), 3-20.

[45] DANESI M. Second Language Teaching[M]. A View from the Right Side of the Brain. Dordrecht: Springer.2003.

[46] DOWTY D R, WALL R E AND PETERS S. Introduction to Montague Semantics [M]. Holland: Dordrecht.1981.

[47] FALKENHAINER B, FORBUS K D, & GENTNER D. The structure mapping engine: Algorithm and examples[J]. Artificial Intelligence, 1989, 41(1), 1-63.

[48] FAUST M, MASHAL N. The role of the right cerebral hemisphere in processing novel metaphoric expressions taken from poetry: a divided visual field study [J].Neuropsychologia, 2007, 45(4),860-870.

[49] FRIEDERICI AD, The time course of syntactic activation during language

processing: a model based on neuropsychological and neurophysiological data [J]. Brain and Language, 1995,50(3), 259-281.

[50]FEDERMEIER KD, KUTAS M. A rose by any other name: Long-term memory structure and sentence processing[J]. Journal of Memory and Language, 1999, 41(4), 469-495.

[51]FAUCONNIER G. Mental Spaces[M]. Cambridge, Mass: MIT Press. 1985.

[52]FAUCONNIER G. Mental Spaces: Aspects of Meaning Construction in Natural Language[M].Cambridge: Cambridge University Press. 1994.

[53]FAUCONNIER G, TURNER M. Conceptual integration networks[J]. Cognitive Science. 1998,22(2), 133-187.

[54]FODOR, JERRY, The Modularity of Mind[M]. Cambridge: MIT Press. 1983.

[55] FOGELIN R J. Figuratively Speaking [M]. New Haven and London: Yale University Press. 1988.

[56]FORBUS K D, GENTNER D, Law K. MAC/FAC: A model of similarity-based retrieval[J]. Cognitive Science, 1995, 19(2), 141-205.

[57]GAGNE C L. Metaphoric interpretations of comparison-based combinations[J]. Metaphor and Symbol, 2002,17(3),161-178.

[58] GAGNON L, GOULET P, GIROUX F, & JOANETTE Y. Processing of metaphoric and nonmetaphoric alternative meaning of words after right- and left-hemispheric lesion[J]. Brain and Language, 2003,87(2), 217-226.

[59] GEERAERTS D. Methodology in cognitive linguistics. In KRISTIANSEN G, ACHARD M , DIRVEN R(eds.). Cognitive linguistics: Current Applications and Future Perspectives[M]. Berlin & New York: Mouton de Gruyter, 2006.

[60] GENTNER D. Some interesting differences between nouns and verbs [J]. Cognition and Brain Theory, 1981, 4(2), 161-178.

[61] GENTNER D. Structure - mapping: A theoretical framework for analogy [J]. Cognitive

Science, 1983,7(2), 155-170.

[62] GENTNER D, CLEMENT C. Evidence for relational selectivity in the interpretation of analogy and metaphor. In G. H. Bower(Ed.), The Psychology of Learning and Motivation: Advances in Research and Theory [M], New

York: Academic Press, 1988, 22, 307-358.

[63]GENTNER D, MARKMAN A B. Structure mapping in analogy and similarity[J]. American Psychologist, 1997,52(1), 45-56.

[64]GENTNER D. Why we are so smart. In GENTNER D, GOLDIN-MEADOW S. (eds.), Language in Mind[M]. Cambridge, MA: MIT Press. 2003.

[65] GENTNER D, BOWDLE B F. Convention, form, and figurative language processing[J]. Metaphor and Symbol, 2001,16(3),223-247.

[66] GENTNER D, TOUPIN C. Systematicity and surface similarity in the development of analogy[J]. Cognitive Science, 1986, 10(3), 277-300.

[67]GENTNER D, WOLFF P. Alignment in the processing of metaphor[J]. Journal of Memory and Language, 1997,37(3), 331-355.

[68]GENTNER D, KURTZ K. Learning and using relational categories. In AHN W K, GOLDSTONE R L, LOVE B C, MARKMAN A B. &WOLFF P W(eds), Categorization Inside and Outside the Laboratory [M]. Washington, DC: APA. 2001.

[69] GERNSBACHER M A. Mechanisms that improve referential access [J]. Cognition, 1989, 32(2), 99-156.

[70] GERNSBACHER MA. Group differences in suppression skill [J]. Aging, Neuropsychology, and Cognition, 1997, 4(3), 175-184.

[71]GERNSBACHER M A, KEYSAR, ROBERTSON, The role of suppression in understanding metaphors[J]. Journal of Memory and Language. 2001,45(3), 433-450.

[72] GERNSBACHER M A, JESCHENIAK J D. Mataphoric devices in spoken discourse[J]. Cognitive Psychology, 1995, 29(1), 24-58.

[73] GIBBS R W. Categorization and metaphor understanding [J]. Psychological Review, 1992,99(3), 572-577.

[74]GIBB H, WALES R. Metaphor or simile: psychological determinants of the differential use of each sentence form[J]. Metaphor and Symbolic Activity, 1990,5(4), 199-213.

[75]GIBBS RAYMOND W Jr. The Poetics of Mind[M]. Cambridge Cambridge University Press. 1994.

[76] GIBBS RAYMOND W Jr. A new look at literal meaning in understanding what is said and implicated[J]. Journal of Pragmatics 2002, 34(4): 457-486.
[77] GIBBS R W. Researching metaphor. In L CAMERON , G Low (eds). Researching and Applying Metaphor[M]. Cambridge: Cambridge University Press. 1999.
[78] GICK M L, HOLYOAK K J. Schema induction and analogical transfer[J]. Cognitive Psychology, 1983,15(1), 1-38.
[79] GILDEA P, GLUCKSBERG S. On understanding metaphor: The role of context [J]. Journal of Verbal Learning and Verbal Behavior, 1983, 22(5), 577-590.
[80] GIORA R. Understanding figurative and literal language: The graded salience hypothesis[J]. Cognitive Linguistics, 1997, 7(3), 183-206.
[81] GIORA R. Literal vs. figurative language: different or equal? [J]. Journal of Pragmatics, 2002,34(4), 487-506.
[82] GLUCKSBERG S, GILDEA P, BOOKIN H B. On understanding nonliteral speech: Can people ignore metaphors? [J] Journal of Verbal Learning and Verbal Behavior, 1982,21(1), 85-98.
[83] GLUCKSBERG S, KEYSAR B. Understanding metaphorical comparisons: Beyond similarity[J]. Psychological Review, 1990, 97(1), 3-18.
[84] GLUCKSBERG S, MCGLONE M S, MANFREDI D. Property attribution in metaphor comprehension[J]. Journal of Memory and Language, 1997,36(1), 50-67.
[85] GLUCKSBERG S, MCGLONE M S. When love is not a journey: What metaphors mean[J]. Journal of Pragmatics, 1999,31(12), 1541-1558.
[86] GLUCKSBERG S. Understanding Figurative Language[M]. Oxford: Oxford University Press. 2001.
[87] GLUCKSBERG S. The psycholinguistics of metaphor[J]. Trends in Cognitive Science, 2003,7(2), 92-96.
[88] GLUCKSBERG S. Can Florida become like the next Florida? When Metaphorical Comparisons Fail[J]. Psychological Science, 2006,17(11), 935-938.
[89] GOATLY A. The Language of Metaphor. London: Routledge[M]. 1997.

[90]GOSWAMI U. Transitive relational mappings in three- and four-year-olds: The analogy of Goldilocks and the Three Bears[J]. Child Development 1995,66(3):877-92.

[91]GRAUWE S D, SWAIN A, HOLCOMB P J, DITMAN T, KUPERBERG G R. Electrophysiological insights into the processing of nominal metaphors[J]. Neuropsychologia ,2010, 48(7), 1877-2230.

[92] GREEN A, FUGELSANG J, DUNBAR K. Automatic priming of category concepts in analogy[J]. Memory, Cognition, 2006,7(7), 1414-1421.

[93] GREEN A, FUGELSANG J, KRAEMER D, SHAMOSH N, DUNBAR K. Frontopolar cortex mediates abstract integration in analogy [J]. Brain Research, 2006,1096(1), 125-137.

[94]GREEN A, FUGELSANG J, KRAEMER D, DUNBAR K. The Micro-category account of analogy[J].Cognition, 2008,106(2), 1004-1016.

[95]GRICE H P. Logic and conversation. In P. COLE & J. L. MORGAN(eds.), Syntax and semantics (Vol. 3, pp. 41- 58) [M]. New York: Academic. 1975.

[96]GRICE H P. Further notes on logic and conversation. In P COLE(ed.), Syntax and semantics(Vol. 9, pp. 113-127)[M]. New York: Academic. 1978.

[97]HAGOORT P, HALD L, BASTIAANSEN M, PETERSSON KM. Integration of word meaning and world knowledge in language comprehension[J]. Science, 2004,304(5669), 438-441

[98]HAUN D, CALL J. Great apes' capacities to recognize relational similarity[J], Cognition 2009,110(2), 147-159.

[99]HALL D, WAXMAN S. Assumptions about word meaning: Individuation and basic-level kinds[J]. Child Development, 1993, 64(5), 1550-1570.

[100]HINTIKKA. The Logic of Metaphor: Analogous Parts of Possible Worlds[M]. Dordrecht/Boston/London: Kluwer Academic Publishing. 2001.

[101]HOEKS J C J, STOWE L A, DOEDENS G. Seeing words in context: The interaction of lexical and sentence level information during reading [J]. Cognitive Brain Research, 2004, 19(1), 59-73.

[102]HOLYOAK K J, THAGARD P. Mental leaps: Analogy in Creative Thought

[M]. Cambridge, MA: MIT Press. 1995.

[103] HOLYOAK K J, GENTNER D, KOKINOV B. Introduction: the place of analogy in cognition. In D GENTNER K J, HOLYOAK, B N KOKINOV (Eds), The Analogical Mind: Perspectives from Cognitive Science [M]. Cambridge, MA: MIT Press. 2001.

[104] HOLYOAK K J. Analogy. In HOLYOAK K J. MORRISON, R. G(Eds), The Cambridge Handbook of Thinking and Reasoning [M]. Cambridge: The Cambridge University Publishing House. 2004.

[105] INHOFF A W, LIMA, S D, CARROLL, P J. Contextual effects on metaphor comprehension in reading[J]. Memory & Cognition, 1984, 12(6), 558-567.

[106] JACKENDOFF R. Semantics and Cognition [M]. Cambridge, Mass: MIT Press, 1985.

[107] JONES L L, & ESTES Z. Metaphor comprehension as attributive categorization [J]. Journal of Memory and Language, 2005, 53(1), 110-124.

[108] JONES L L, &ESTES Z. Roosters, robins and alarm clocks: Aptness and conventionality in metaphor comprehension [J]. Journal of Memory and Language, 2006, 55(1), 18-32.

[109] JOHNSON M. The Body in the Mind: The Bodily Basis of Meaning, Imagination, and Reason[M]. Chicago: University of Chicago Press, 1987.

[110] JOHNSON M G, & MALGADY R G. Some cognitive aspects of figurative language: Association and metaphor[J]. Journal of Psycholinguistic Research, 1979, 8: 249-265.

[111] KAAN E, HARRIS A, GIBSON E, & HPLCOMB P J. The P600 as an index of syntactic integration difficulty [J]. Journal of Language and Cognitive Processes, 2000,15(2), 159-201.

[112] KACINIK N A & CHIARELLO C. Understanding metaphors: is the right-hemisphere uniquely involved [J]. Brain & Language, 2007, 100 (2), 188-207.

[113] KAPLAN, JOAN A, HIRAM H. BROWNELL, JANET R. JACOBS, and HOWARD GARDNER. The effects of right hemisphere damage on the pragmatic interpretation of conversational remarks [J]. Brain and Language,

1990,38(2), 315-333.

[114]KAZMERSKI V A, BLASKO D G, & DESSALEGN B G. ERP and behavioral evidence of individual differences in metaphor comprehension[J]. Memory & Cognition, 2003, 31, 673-689.

[115]KAY P & MCDANIEL C K. The linguistic significance of the meanings of basic color terms[J]. Language,1978, 54(5), 610-646.

[116]KERSTEN A W, & EARLES J L. Semantic context influences memory for verbs more than memory for nouns[J]. Memory and Cognition, 2006,26(2), 267-278.

[117] KEYSAR B. On the functional equivalence of literal and metaphorical interpretations in discourse[J].Journal of Memory and Language, 1989, 28 (4), 375-385.

[118]KINTSCH W. The Representation of Meaning in Memory[M]. Hillsdale, NJ: Lawrence Erlbaum Associates, Inc,1974..

[119] KIM A, & OSTERHOUT L. The independence of combinatory semantic processing: Evidence from event-related potentials[J]. Journal of Memory and Language, 2005, 52, 205-225.

[120]KUPERBERG G, CAPLAN D, SITNIKOVA T, EDDY M, & HOLCOMB P. Neural correlates of processing syntactic, semantic and thematic relationships in sentences[J]. Language & Cognitive Processes, 2006a, 21, 489-530.

[121]KUPERBERG G R, SITNIKOVA T, Goff D, & HOLCOMB P J. Making sense of sentences in schizophrenia: electrophysiological evidence for abnormal interactions between semantic and syntactic processing [J]. Journal of Abnormal Psychology, 2006b,115, 243-256.

[122]KUPERBERG G R. Neural mechanisms of language comprehension: Challenges to syntax[J]. Brain Research, 2007a, 1146, 23-49.

[123]KUPERBERG G, KREHER D, SITNIKOVA T, CAPLAN D, & HOLCOMB P. The role of animacy and thematic relationships in processing active English sentences: Evidence from event-related potentials[J]. Brain & Language, 2007b, 100, 223-237.

[124]KUTAS M. & HILLYARD S A. Reading senseless sentences: Brain potentials

reflect semantic incongruity[J]. Science, 1980,207(4427), 203-205.

[125] KUTAS M, & FEDERMEIER K. Electrophysiology reveals semantic memory use in language comprehension[J]. Trends in Cognitive Sciences, 2000, 4 (12), 463-470.

[126] LAKOFF G. Women, Fire, and Dangerous Things: What do Categories of Language and Thought Reveal about the Human Mind [M]. Chicago: University of Chicago,1987.

[127] LAKOFF G. The invariance hypothesis: Is abstract reason based on image-schemas[J].Cognitive Linguistics, 1990, 1(1), 39-74.

[128] LAKOFF G, & JOHNSON M. Metaphors We Live by[M]. Chicago: University of Chicago, 1980.

[129] LAKOFF G. The contemporary theory of metaphor. In Ortony, A. (eds), Metaphor and Thought[M]. Cambridge, Cambridge University Press, 1993.

[130] LAKOFF G, & JOHNSON M. Philosophy in the Flesh——The Embodied Mind and its Challenge to Western Thought[M]. New York: Basic Books, 1999.

[131] LAKOFF G, & TURNER M. More than Cool Reason: A field Guide to Poetic Metaphor[M]. Chicago: University of Chicago, 1989.

[132] LAU E, PHILLIPS C, POEPPEL D. A cortical network for semantics: [de] constructing the N400[J]. Nature, 2008, 9, 920-931.

[133] LEE S S, & DAPRETTO M. Metaphorical vs. literal word meanings: fMRI evidence against a selective role of the right hemisphere[J]. Neuroimage, 2006,29(2), 536-44.

[134] LEECH R, MARESCHAL D. & RICHARD P C. Analogy as relational priming: a developmental and computational perspective on the origins of a complex cognitive skill[J]. Bahavioral and Brain Sciences, 2008,31, 357-414.

[135] LEEZENBERG M. Context of Metaphor[M]. Amsterdam: Elsevier, 2001.

[136] LITTLEMORE J. and LOW G. Metaphoric competence and communicative language ability[J]. Applied Linguistics, 2006, 27(2), p.268-294.

[137] LITTLEMORE J. The relationship between associative thinking, analogical reasoning, image formation and metaphoric extension strategies. In Zanotto,S, M., Cameron, L.,. & Cavalcanti, M .D(eds). Confronting metaphor in Use:

An Applied Linguistic Approach[M]. Holand: John Benjamin Publishing Company, 2008.

[138] LOEWENSTEIN J, & GENTNER D. Spatial mapping in preschoolers: Close comparisons facilitate far mappings[J]. Journal of Cognition and Development, 2001, 2(2), 189-219.

[139] LOEWENSTEIN J, & GENTNER D. Relational language and the development of relational mapping[J]. Cognitive Psychology, 2005,50(4), 315-353.

[140] LOUNSBURY FLOYD G. A Formal Account of the Crow- and Omaha-Type Kinship Terminologies, in Ward H. (ed.), Explorations in Cultural Anthropology: Essays in Honor of George Peter Murdock[J]. New York: McGraw-Hill, 1964,351-393.

[141] LEWIS D. Convention[M]. Cambridge: MIT Press, 1969.

[142] MALGADY R G, & JOHNSON M G. Modifiers in metaphors: Effects of constituent phrase similarity on the interpretation of figurative sentences[J]. Journal of Psycholinguistic Research, 1976,(5), 43-52.

[143] MACCORMAC EARL R. A Cognitive Theory of Metaphor[M]. MIT Press, Cambridge MA. 1985.

[144] MARSCHARK M, KATZ A, PAIVIO A. Dimensions of metaphor[J]. Journal of Psycholinguistic Research, 1983,(12), 17-40.

[145] MASHAL N, FAUST M, HENDLER T. The role of the right hemisphere in processing nonsalient metaphorical meanings: Application of Principal Components Analysis to fMRI data[J]. Neuropsychologia, 2005, 43(14), 2084-2100.

[146] MASHAL N, FAUST M, HENDLER T, JUNG-BEEMAN M. An fMRI investigation of the neural correlates underlying processing of novel metaphoric expressions[J]. Brain and Language, 2007,100(2), 115-126.

[147] MCCLOSKEY M, & CLUCKSBERG S. Natural categories: Well defined or fuzzy sets? [J].Memory & Cognition, 1978,(6), 462-472.

[148] MCCLOSKEY M, & CLUCKSBERG S. Decision processes in verifying category membership statements: Implications for models of semantic memory[J]. Cognitive Psychology, 1979,11(1), 1-37.

[149]MCGLONE M. Concepts as metaphors[M]. In Glucksberg, S. Understanding figurative language. Oxford: Oxford University Press. 2001.
[150]MCGLONE M. What is the explanatory value of a conceptual metaphor? [J]. Language and Communication, 2007,27(2), 109–126.
[151]MCKAY M. The Development and Comprehension of Conventional Metaphors [D]. Unpublished Doctoral dissertation in University of Florida. Accessed at http.www.scnu.library.diss.3864043.cn on Oct 10, 2008. 2004.
[152]MEDIN D L, & SCHAFFER EJ. Context theory of classification learning[J]. Psychological Review, 1978, 85(3), 207–238.
[153]MILLER G A. Images and models, similes and metaphors[A]. In A. Ortony (Ed.) Metaphor and thought (1st ed., pp. 202–250) [C]. Cambridge, England: Cambridge University. 1979.
[154]MILLER G A. Images and models, similes and metaphors[A]. In A. Ortony (Ed.) Metaphor and thought (pp. 357–400) [C]. Cambridge: Cambridge University Press. 1993.
[155]MURPHY G L, & ALLOPENNA P D. The locus of knowledge effects in concept learning[J]. Journal of Experimental Psychology: Learning, Memory, & Cognition, 1994,20(4), 904–919.
[156]MURPHY G L, & MEDIN D L. The role of theories in conceptual coherence [J]. Psychological Review, 1985,92(3), 289–316.
[157] MURPHY G L. Reasons to doubt the present evidence for metaphoric representation[J]. Cognition, 1997,62(1), 99–108.
[158]NAKAMOTO K, & KUSUMI T. The effect of repeated presentation and aptness of figurative comparisons on preference for metaphor forms[M]. Proceedings of the twenty-sixth annual conference of the cognitive science society. Chicago, IL. 2004.
[159]NEELY JH. Semantic priming effects in visual word recognition: A selective review of current findings and theories[A]. In Besner D. & Humphreys G.W. Basic Processes in Reading [C]. Hillsdale, N J: Lawrence Erlbaum Associates, Inc. 1991.
[160]NOSOFSKY RM. Attention, similarity, and the identification–categorization

relationship[J]. Journal of Experimental Psychology: General, 1986,115(1), 39-97.

[161] ORTONY A, SCHALLERT D, REYNOLDS R, ANTOS S. Interpreting metaphors and idioms: Some effects of context on comprehension[J]. Journal of Verbal Learning and Verbal Behavior, 1978,17(4), 467-477.

[162] ORTONY A. Beyond literal similarity[J]. Psychological Review, 1979,86(3), 161-180.

[163] ORTONY A. Metaphor: A multidimensional problem[A]. In A Ortony(Ed.) Metaphor and Thought(2nd edition): 1-16[C]. Cambridge: CAMBRIDGE UNIVERSITY PRESS. 1993.

[164] PALLER KA. KUTAS M. Brain potentials during memory retrieval provide neurophysiologic support for the distinction between conscious recollection and priming[J]. Cognitive and Neuroscience, 1992,4(4), 375-391.

[165] PERRY J. Possible World Semantics [M]. Accessed at http: www. csli. stanford. edu/ jperry/ philpap. On June, 19, 2009. 2008.

[166] POLLIO H, BARLOW J, FINE H, POLLIO M. Psychology and the Poetics of Growth[M]. Hillsdale, NJ: Erlbaum. 1977.

[167] PYNTE J, BESSON M, ROBICHON F H, POLI J. The time-course of metaphor comprehension: An event-related potential study[J]. Brain and Language, 1996,55(3), 293-316.

[168] QUINE W V. Theories and Things[M].Cambridge, Mass: Darvard University Press, 1981.

[169] RAKOVA M. The Extent of the Literal: Metaphor, Polysemy and Theories of Concepts[M]. Palgrave: Macmillan, 2003.

[170] RATTERMANN M J, & GENTNER D. More evidence for a relational shift in the development of analogy: Children's performance on a causal-mapping task [J].Cognitive Development,1998, 13(4), 453-478.

[171] REDDY M. The Conduit Metaphor: A Case of Frame Conflict in our Language about Language [J]. In Ortony, A. (ed.) Metaphor and Thought, 1993, 284-324.

[172] REYNOLD D, & ORTONY A. Some Issues in Measurement of Children's

Comprehension of Metaphorical Language, Child Development[J], 1980, 51, 1110-1119.

[173]RICOEUR P. The Rule of Metaphor: The Creation of Meaning in Language [M]. London: Routledge & Kegan Paul Ltd, 1977.

[174] ROSCH E, & MERVIS C. Family Resemblances: studies in the internal structure of categories[J]. Cognitive Psychology, 1975, 7:573-605.

[175] ROSCH E. Cognitive Representation of Semantic Categories [J]. Journal of Experimental Psychology, 1975,(3):192-233.

[176]ROSCH E, & BARBARA B L. Cognition and Categorization[M]. Hillsdale: Lawrence Erlbaum Associates, Inc, 1978.

[177]RUGG M D, COX, CJC, DOYLE, MC, WELLS, T. Event-related potentials and the recollection of low and high frequency words[J]. Neuropsychologia, 1995, 33(4), 471-484.

[178] SCHMIDT G L DeBuse C J, & SEGER C A. Right hemisphere metaphor processing? Characterizing the lateralization of semantic processes[J]. Brain and Language, 2007, 100(2), 127-141.

[179]SEARLE J. Metaphor. In A. Ortony(Ed.), Metaphor and Thought(1st ed., pp. 92-123)[J]. Cambridge: Cambridge University Press, 1979.

[180]SHINJO M, & MYERS J L. The role of context in metaphor comprehension[J]. Journal of Memory and Language, 1987, 26(2), 226-241.

[181]SLOUTSKY V M. The role of similarity in the development of categorization [J]. Trents in Cognitive Sciences, 2003, 7(6): 246-251.

[182]SMITH L. Young children's understanding of attributes and dimensions: A comparison of conceptual and linguistic measures[J]. Child Development, 1984, 55(2), 363-380.

[183]SLOMAN SA. Feature-based induction[J]. Cognitive Psychology, 1993, 25(2), 231-280.

[184] SPERBER, DAN and DEIRDRE WILSON. Relevance: Communication and Cognition[M]. Oxford: Blackwell, 1986/1995.

[185]STERN J. Metaphor in Context[M]. Cambridge: MIT Press, 2000.

[186]STROOP R. Studies of interference in serial verbal reactions[J]. Journal of

Experimental Psychology, 1935, 18, 643-662.

[187]STRINGARIS A, MEDFORD N, GIORA R, GIAMPIETRO C V, BRAMMER J M, & DAVID S A. How metaphors in.uence semantic relatedness judgments: the role of the right frontal cortex[J]. NeuroImage,2006, 33, 784-793.

[188]STRINGARIS A K, MEDFORD N C, GIAMPIETRO V C, BRAMMER M J, & DAVID A S. Deriving meaning: Distinct neural mechanisms for metaphoric, literal, and nonmeaningful sentences[J]. Brain and Language,2007, 100(2), 150-162.

[189]SHAPIRO S. Philosophy of Mathematics: Structure Ontology[M]. New York: Oxford University Press,1997.

[190]SOBIN N. Texas Spanish and lexical borrowing. In Amastae, J. & Olivares, E. L.,(eds.), Spanish in the United States: Sociolinguistic Aspects, 166-181 [J].Cambridge: Cambridge University Press,1982.

[191] SWEETSER E. From etymology to pragmatics: metaphorical and cultural aspects of semantic structure [M]. Cambridge: Cambridge University press,1990.

[192]TAYLOR J. Linguistic Categorization[M].Oxford: Clarendon Press. 1995.

[193]THIBAUT J P , FRENCH R , VEZNEVA M. The development of analogy making in children: Cognitive load and executive functions [J]. Journal of Experimental Child Psychology,2010,106(1), 1-19.

[194]TVERSKY A. Features of similarity[J]. Psychological Review, 1977,84(4), 327-352.

[195]UNGERER F, & SCHMID H J. An Introduction to Cognitive Linguistics[M]. Harlow: Longman. 1996.

[196]UTSUMI A, & KUWABARA Y. Interpretive Diversity as a Source of Metaphor-simile Distinction[A]. In Proceedings of the twenty-seventh annual conference of the cognitive science society[C]. Italy : Stressa. 2005.

[197] UTSUMI A. Interpretive diversity explains metaphor-simile distinction [J]. Metaphor and Symbol, 2007, 22(4), 291-312.

[198]VAN DE MEERENDONK N, KOLK H H J, CHWILLA D J, VISSERS C T W M. Monitoring in Language Perception [J]. Language and Linguistics

Compass, 2009,3(5), 1211-1224.

[199]VAN DE MEERENDONK N, KOLK H H J, VISSERS C T W M, CHWILLA D J. Monitoring language perception: Mild and strong conflicts elicit different ERP patterns[J]. Journal of Cognitive Neuroscience, 2010,22(1), 67-82.

[200] VAN PETTEN C, & KUTAS M. Interactions between sentence context and word frequency in event-related brain potentials[J]. Memory and Cognition, 1990,18(4), 380-393.

[201]VAN BERKUM J J A, HAGOORT P, BROWN C M. Semantic integration in sentences and discourse: Evidence from the N400[J]. Journal of Cognitive Neuroscience, 1999,11(6), 657-671.

[202] VEALE T. An analogy-oriented type hierarchy for linguistic creativity[J]. Knowledge-Based Systems, 2006, 19(7),471-479.

[203] VEALE T. Dynamic type creation in metaphor interpretation and analogical reasoning [A]. In Conceptual structures for Knowledge Creation and Communication LNAI 2746[C]. Berlin: Springer.2003.

[204] VEALE T. Systematicity and the Lexicon in Creative Metaphor [A]. In Proceedings of the ACL 2003 workshop on Figurative Language[C]. Japan: Sapporo.2003.

[205]VERBRUGGE R R, & MCCARRELL N S. Metaphoric comprehension: Studies in reminding and resembling [J]. Cognitive Psychology, 1977, 9 (4), 494-533.

[206] VEGA MORENO E ROSA. Creativity and convention. The Pragmatics of Everyday figurative Speech [M]. London: John Benjamins Publishing Company. 2007.

[207] WAY E C. Knowledge Representation and Metaphor[M]. London: Kluwer Academic Publishers. 1991.

[208]WISNIEWSKI M. Deep supercooling in woody plants and the role of cell wall structure[A]. In LEE R E JR, WARREN G J, GUSTA L V(eds.) Biological Ice Nucleation and its Applications[C]. Minneapolis, Minn:APS Press. 1995.

[209] WITTGENSTEIN L. Philosophical Investigations [M]. New York: Macmillian. 1953.

[210] WINNER E, & GARDNER H. The comprehension of metaphor in brain-damaged patients[J]. Brain, 1977,100(4), 717-729.

[211] WINNER E. The Point of Words: Children's Understanding of Metaphor and Irony[M]. Cambridge: Harvard University Press. 1988.

[212] WOLFF P, & GENTNER D. Evidence for role-neutral initial processing of metaphors[J]. Journal of Experimental Psychology: Learning, Memory, and Cognition, 2000,26(2), 529-541.

[213] ZADEH L. Fuzzy sets[J]. Information and Control, 1965, 8(3),338-353.

[214] ZHARIKOV S, & GENTNER D. Why do metaphors seem deeper than similes? [A]. In GRAY W D & SCHUNN C D(eds.) Proceedings of the twenty-fourth annual conference of the cognitive science society, 976-981[C]. Fairfax VA: George Mason University. 2002.

[215] 龚玉苗. 隐喻意识与外语词汇教学[J]. 外语界, 2006(01): 40-45;76.

[216] 龚玉苗, 周榕. 隐喻理解的 ERPs 研究述评[J]. 心理学探新, 2009, 29(02): 38-42.

[217] 龚玉苗, 周榕. 隐喻表述范畴隶属关系的影响机制研究[J]. 现代外语, 2011, 34(01): 66-74.

[218] 胡壮麟. 语言·认知·隐喻[J]. 现代外语, 1997(04): 51-52.

[219] 胡壮麟. 认知隐喻学[M]. 北京:北京大学出版社, 2004.

[220] 李　艳. 认知视野中比喻的相似性[J]. 修辞学习, 2007(02): 70-72.

[221] 刘铁铠, 谷化琳. 比喻的相似性与相关性及其感知过程[J]. 四川外语学院学报, 2005(06): 90-95.

[222] 刘雪春. 论比喻的相似性[J]. 修辞学习, 2001(06): 13-14.

[223] 林书武. 国外隐喻研究综述[J]. 外语教学与研究, 1997(01): 14-22.

[224] 林书武. 隐喻研究的基本现状、焦点及趋势[J]. 外国语(上海外国语大学学报), 2002(01): 38-45.

[225] 李佐文, 刘长青. 论隐喻的相似性基础[J]. 河北大学学报(哲学社会科学版), 2003(03): 63-67.

[226] 刘晓明. 意象的逻辑:创造性思维的首要推动者[J]. 自然辩证法研究, 2003(08): 32-36.

[227] 卢　植. 认知与语言——认知语言学引论[M]. 上海:上海外语教育出版

社，2006.
[228]彭宣维，张莎. 比喻认知能力的发展——一项以学龄前儿童为对象的实证研究.外语教学与研究[J]. 外语教学与研究，2009，41(05)：359-364.
[229]钱锺书. 管锥编[M]. 北京：中华书局，1979.
[230]石　磊，刘振前. 隐喻能力研究：现状与问题[J]. 外国语，2010，33(03)：10-16.
[231]束定芳. 隐喻学研究[M]. 上海：上海外语教育出版社，2000.
[232]束定芳. 认知语义学[M]. 上海：上海外语教育出版社，2008.
[233]徐盛桓. 隐喻为什么可能[J]. 外语教学，2008(03)：1-7.
[234]王文斌. 再论隐喻中的相似性[J]. 四川外语学院学报，2006(02)：125-130.
[235]王小璐. 汉语隐喻认知的神经机制研究[D]. 杭州：浙江大学，2007.
[236]王　寅. 认知语言学[J]. 中国外语，2011，8(04)：1；38.
[237]吴世雄，陈维振. 论语义范畴的家族相似性[J]. 外语教学与研究，1996(04)：14-19.
[238]吴世雄，陈维振. 范畴理论的发展及其对认知语言学的贡献[J]. 外国语(上海外国语大学学报)，2004(04)：34-40.
[239]夏国军. 论蒯因的相似性概念[J]. 自然辩证法研究，2010，26(02)：24-29.
[240]周榕. 隐喻认知基础的心理现实性——时间的空间隐喻表征的实验证据[J]. 外语教学与研究，2001(02)：88-93.
[241]周榕. 儿童时间隐喻能力的发展研究.现代外语，(2)：188-197.
[242]钟书能. 生命度——构建语言意义的核心因素[J]. 北京第二外国语学院学报，2008(04)：24-31；39.

Appendices

Appendix I: the questionnaire for the similarity rating in Exp 1

相似性特征调查问卷

性别＿＿＿＿＿ 年龄＿＿＿＿＿

你好！欢迎参加这次调查。本调查旨在考察你对不同词汇之间相似性特征的感知。不同类别的事物之间可能具有某种相似性。相似性具有不同特征，例如在词对"月亮—盘子"中，"月亮"和"盘子"的相似性在于它们都是"圆的"，这种相似性只涉及二者的表面特征，并不涉及与其它事物的某种关系；相对来讲，对于"老板—鲨鱼"来说，"老板"和"鲨鱼"的相似性并非在于二者之间的表面特征，而在于二者分别与其它某种事物之间的抽象关系，如"老板追逐利益就像鲨鱼追逐猎物"或"老板对待员工就像鲨鱼对待小鱼"等。

你需要做的是发挥想象力，对下列各对名词间的相似性进行理解；在7级量表上评定它们之间的相似性与二者本身之外其它事物之间的联系程度。"1"表示它们的相似性与其它事物完全没有关系，"7"表示它们的相似性与其它事物的关系非常紧密。数字从1到7依次表示它们的相似性与其它事物关系密切程度的递增。

请在你认为合适的数字上画"√"。该任务没有时间限制，请认真阅评。

1. 月亮——香蕉 1 _ 2 _ 3 _ 4 _ 5 _ 6 _ 7 _	2. 云彩——棉花 1 _ 2 _ 3 _ 4 _ 5 _ 6 _ 7 _
3. 信念——灯塔 1 _ 2 _ 3 _ 4 _ 5 _ 6 _ 7 _	4. 耳朵——扇子 1 _ 2 _ 3 _ 4 _ 5 _ 6 _ 7 _
5. 虚伪——匕首 1 _ 2 _ 3 _ 4 _ 5 _ 6 _ 7 _	6. 风筝——小鸟 1 _ 2 _ 3 _ 4 _ 5 _ 6 _ 7 _
7. 足球——鸡蛋 1 _ 2 _ 3 _ 4 _ 5 _ 6 _ 7 _	8. 诱惑——陷阱 1 _ 2 _ 3 _ 4 _ 5 _ 6 _ 7 _
9. 理想——翅膀 1 _ 2 _ 3 _ 4 _ 5 _ 6 _ 7 _	10. 棉花——海绵 1 _ 2 _ 3 _ 4 _ 5 _ 6 _ 7 _

续表

11. 太阳——桔子 1 _ 2 _ 3 _ 4 _ 5 _ 6 _ 7 _	12. 蛇虫——麻绳 1 _ 2 _ 3 _ 4 _ 5 _ 6 _ 7 _
13. 湖面——镜子 1 _ 2 _ 3 _ 4 _ 5 _ 6 _ 7 _	14. 历史——警钟 1 _ 2 _ 3 _ 4 _ 5 _ 6 _ 7 _
15. 讽刺——尖刀 1 _ 2 _ 3 _ 4 _ 5 _ 6 _ 7 _	16. 灯光——星星 1 _ 2 _ 3 _ 4 _ 5 _ 6 _ 7 _
17. 蜻蜓——飞机 1 _ 2 _ 3 _ 4 _ 5 _ 6 _ 7 _	18. 时间——良药 1 _ 2 _ 3 _ 4 _ 5 _ 6 _ 7 _
19. 危险——暗礁 1 _ 2 _ 3 _ 4 _ 5 _ 6 _ 7 _	20. 露水——珍珠 1 _ 2 _ 3 _ 4 _ 5 _ 6 _ 7 _
21. 流言——病毒 1 _ 2 _ 3 _ 4 _ 5 _ 6 _ 7 _	22. 大腿——柱子 1 _ 2 _ 3 _ 4 _ 5 _ 6 _ 7 _
23. 面试——栏杆 1 _ 2 _ 3 _ 4 _ 5 _ 6 _ 7 _	24. 月亮——弓箭 1 _ 2 _ 3 _ 4 _ 5 _ 6 _ 7 _
25. 眉毛——月牙 1 _ 2 _ 3 _ 4 _ 5 _ 6 _ 7 _	26. 理想——支柱 1 _ 2 _ 3 _ 4 _ 5 _ 6 _ 7 _
27. 彩虹——桥梁 1 _ 2 _ 3 _ 4 _ 5 _ 6 _ 7 _	28. 心脏——水泵 1 _ 2 _ 3 _ 4 _ 5 _ 6 _ 7 _
29. 头发——干草 1 _ 2 _ 3 _ 4 _ 5 _ 6 _ 7 _	30. 方法——路径 1 _ 2 _ 3 _ 4 _ 5 _ 6 _ 7 _
31. 鼻子——蒜头 1 _ 2 _ 3 _ 4 _ 5 _ 6 _ 7 _	32. 书籍——粮食 1 _ 2 _ 3 _ 4 _ 5 _ 6 _ 7 _
33. 蘑菇——小伞 1 _ 2 _ 3 _ 4 _ 5 _ 6 _ 7 _	34. 草原——地毯 1 _ 2 _ 3 _ 4 _ 5 _ 6 _ 7 _
35. 麦秆——吸管 1 _ 2 _ 3 _ 4 _ 5 _ 6 _ 7 _	36. 信念——灯塔 1 _ 2 _ 3 _ 4 _ 5 _ 6 _ 7 _
37. 皮肤——薄膜 1 _ 2 _ 3 _ 4 _ 5 _ 6 _ 7 _	38. 柳絮——雪花 1 _ 2 _ 3 _ 4 _ 5 _ 6 _ 7 _
39. 家庭——港湾 1 _ 2 _ 3 _ 4 _ 5 _ 6 _ 7 _	40. 舞者——天鹅 1 _ 2 _ 3 _ 4 _ 5 _ 6 _ 7 _
41. 月光——薄纱 1 _ 2 _ 3 _ 4 _ 5 _ 6 _ 7 _	42. 公鸡——闹钟 1 _ 2 _ 3 _ 4 _ 5 _ 6 _ 7 _
43. 毛发——丝绸 1 _ 2 _ 3 _ 4 _ 5 _ 6 _ 7 _	44. 气球——泡沫 1 _ 2 _ 3 _ 4 _ 5 _ 6 _ 7 _
45. 地球——母亲 1 _ 2 _ 3 _ 4 _ 5 _ 6 _ 7 _	46. 老师——园丁 1 _ 2 _ 3 _ 4 _ 5 _ 6 _ 7 _
47. 楼群——丛林 1 _ 2 _ 3 _ 4 _ 5 _ 6 _ 7 _	48. 薄雾——烟云 1 _ 2 _ 3 _ 4 _ 5 _ 6 _ 7 _
49. 奋斗——阶梯 1 _ 2 _ 3 _ 4 _ 5 _ 6 _ 7 _	50. 鱼鳍——翅膀 1 _ 2 _ 3 _ 4 _ 5 _ 6 _ 7 _
51. 阴谋——陷阱 1 _ 2 _ 3 _ 4 _ 5 _ 6 _ 7 _	52. 磨难——风雨 1 _ 2 _ 3 _ 4 _ 5 _ 6 _ 7 _
53. 眼睛——窗户 1 _ 2 _ 3 _ 4 _ 5 _ 6 _ 7 _	54. 短剑——匕首 1 _ 2 _ 3 _ 4 _ 5 _ 6 _ 7 _

Appendix II: result of similarity rating in Exp 1

No.	pairs	rating scores	No.	pairs	rating scores
1.	月亮——香蕉	2.75	2.	耳朵——扇子	1.96
3.	风筝——小鸟	3.13	4.	足球——鸡蛋	2.79
5.	棉花——海绵	2.58	6.	太阳——桔子	3.04
7.	蛇虫——麻绳	3.46	8.	湖面——镜子	2.92
9.	灯光——星星	2.75	10.	蜻蜓——飞机	3.17
11.	露水——珍珠	3	12.	大腿——柱子	2.79
13.	月亮——弓箭	3	14.	彩虹——桥梁	3.17
15.	头发——干草	3	16.	鼻子——蒜头	2.88
17.	草原——地毯	3.33	18.	麦秆——吸管	2.79
19.	皮肤——薄膜	2.71	20.	舞者——天鹅	3.29
21.	月光——薄纱	3.38	22.	毛发——丝绸	3.42
23.	气球——泡沫	2.42	24.	薄雾——烟云	2.83
25.	信念——灯塔	5.63	26.	虚伪——匕首	5.5
27.	诱惑——陷阱	5.29	28.	理想——翅膀	5.38
29.	历史——警钟	5.58	30.	时间——良药	5.08
31.	危险——暗礁	5.25	32.	流言——病毒	5.25
33.	面试——栏杆	5	34.	心脏——水泵	5
35.	方法——路径	5.76	36.	书籍——粮食	5.25
37.	信念——灯塔	5.13	38.	家庭——港湾	5.38
39.	公鸡——闹钟	6.04	40.	地球——母亲	5.21
41.	老师——园丁	5.33	42.	奋斗——阶梯	5
43.	阴谋——陷阱	5.08	44.	短剑——匕首	2.75
45.	楼群——丛林	3.04	46.	柳絮——雪花	3.83
47.	蘑菇——小伞	2.71	48.	眉毛——月牙	3.08
49.	云彩——棉花	3.33	50.	眼睛——窗户	4.92
51.	磨难——风雨	5.08	52.	理想——支柱	5.13
53.	讽刺——尖刀	5.17			

Appendix III: the questionnaire for the grammatical form preference rating in Exp 1

比喻句句法形式倾向性调查问卷

性别________ 年龄________

你好！欢迎参加这次调查。本调查旨在考察你对不同比喻句的感知。比喻分为明喻和隐喻，其中明喻用“像”字表述（如“时间像金钱”），而隐喻用“是”字表述（如“时间是金钱”）。

在下列句子中，你将会看到同一词对分别用明喻和隐喻两种形式进行了表述，这两种表述被分别置于7级量表的两端。你需要做的是1）认真默读并理解这两种表述方式；2）根据第一感觉在7级量表上评定哪种表述更自然、更合适。在下列量表上，“1”表示明喻形式，如“时间像金钱”；“7”表示隐喻形式，如“时间是金钱”。数字越接近1表示越适合用明喻形式，越接近7表示越适合用隐喻形式。

请在你认为合适的数字上画“√”。该任务没有时间限制，请认真阅评。

1. 月亮像香蕉 1____2____ 3____4____ 5____ 6____7 月亮是香蕉
2. 云彩像棉花 1____2____ 3____4____ 5____ 6____7 云彩是棉花
3. 信念像灯塔 1____2____ 3____4____ 5____ 6____7 信念是灯塔
4. 耳朵像扇子 1____2____ 3____4____ 5____ 6____7 耳朵是扇子
5. 虚伪像匕首 1____2____ 3____4____ 5____ 6____7 虚伪是匕首
6. 风筝像小鸟 1____2____ 3____4____ 5____ 6____7 风筝是小鸟
7. 足球像鸡蛋 1____2____ 3____4____ 5____ 6____7 足球是鸡蛋
8. 诱惑像陷阱 1____2____ 3____4____ 5____ 6____7 诱惑是陷阱
9. 埋想像翅膀 1____2____ 3____4____ 5____ 6____7 理想是翅膀
10. 棉花像海绵 1____2____ 3____4____ 5____ 6____7 棉花是海绵
11. 太阳像桔子 1____2____ 3____4____ 5____ 6____7 太阳是桔子
12. 蛇虫像麻绳 1____2____ 3____4____ 5____ 6____7 蛇虫是麻绳
13. 湖面像镜子 1____2____ 3____4____ 5____ 6____7 湖面是镜子
14. 历史像警钟 1____2____ 3____4____ 5____ 6____7 历史是警钟
15. 灯光像星星 1____2____ 3____4____ 5____ 6____7 灯光是星星

16. 蜻蜓像飞机 1____2____3____4____5____6____7 蜻蜓是飞机
17. 时间像良药 1____2____3____4____5____6____7 时间是良药
18. 危险像暗礁 1____2____3____4____5____6____7 危险是暗礁
19. 露水像珍珠 1____2____3____4____5____6____7 露水是珍珠
20. 流言像病毒 1____2____3____4____5____6____7 流言是病毒
21. 大腿像柱子 1____2____3____4____5____6____7 大腿是柱子
22. 面试像栏杆 1____2____3____4____5____6____7 面试是栏杆
23. 月亮像弓箭 1____2____3____4____5____6____7 月亮是弓箭
24. 讽刺像尖刀 1____2____3____4____5____6____7 讽刺是尖刀
25. 眉毛像月牙 1____2____3____4____5____6____7 眉毛是月牙
26. 彩虹像桥梁 1____2____3____4____5____6____7 彩虹是桥梁
27. 心脏像水泵 1____2____3____4____5____6____7 心脏是水泵
28. 头发像干草 1____2____3____4____5____6____7 头发是干草
29. 方法像路径 1____2____3____4____5____6____7 方法是路径
30. 鼻子像蒜头 1____2____3____4____5____6____7 鼻子是蒜头
31. 书籍像粮食 1____2____3____4____5____6____7 书籍是粮食
32. 理想像支柱 1____2____3____4____5____6____7 理想是支柱
33. 草原像地毯 1____2____3____4____5____6____7 草原是地毯
34. 麦秆像吸管 1____2____3____4____5____6____7 麦秆是吸管
35. 信念像灯塔 1____2____3____4____5____6____7 信念是灯塔
36. 皮肤像薄膜 1____2____3____4____5____6____7 皮肤是薄膜
37. 蘑菇像小伞 1____2____3____4____5____6____7 蘑菇是小伞
38. 家庭像港湾 1____2____3____4____5____6____7 家庭是港湾
39. 舞者像天鹅 1____2____3____4____5____6____7 舞者是天鹅
40. 月光像薄纱 1____2____3____4____5____6____7 月光是薄纱
41. 公鸡像闹钟 1____2____3____4____5____6____7 公鸡是闹钟
42. 毛发像丝绸 1____2____3____4____5____6____7 毛发是丝绸
43. 气球像泡沫 1____2____3____4____5____6____7 气球是泡沫
44. 地球像母亲 1____2____3____4____5____6____7 地球是母亲
45. 老师像园丁 1____2____3____4____5____6____7 老师是园丁
46. 薄雾像烟云 1____2____3____4____5____6____7 薄雾是烟云
47. 奋斗像阶梯 1____2____3____4____5____6____7 奋斗是阶梯
48. 阴谋像陷阱 1____2____3____4____5____6____7 阴谋是陷阱

49. 柳絮像雪花 1____2____3____4____5____6____7 柳絮是雪花

50. 楼群像丛林 1____2____3____4____5____6____7 楼群是丛林

51. 短剑像匕首 1____2____3____4____5____6____7 短剑是匕首

52. 眼睛像窗户 1____2____3____4____5____6____7 眼睛是窗户

53. 磨难像风雨 1____2____3____4____5____6____7 磨难是风雨

Appendix Ⅳ: scores for the grammatical form rating in Exp 1

1	月亮——香蕉	1.48	2.	耳朵——扇子	1.89
3.	风筝——小鸟	2.41	4.	足球——鸡蛋	2.78
5.	棉花——海绵	2.85	6.	太阳——桔子	2.78
7.	蛇虫——麻绳	2.33	8.	湖面——镜子	2.33
9.	灯光——星星	2.74	10.	蜻蜓——飞机	2.74
11.	露水——珍珠	2.37	12.	大腿——柱子	2.89
13.	月亮——弓箭	3.07	14.	彩虹——桥梁	3.04
15.	头发——干草	3	16.	鼻子——蒜头	3.11
17.	草原——地毯	3.48	18.	麦秆——吸管	4.33
19.	皮肤——薄膜	4.52	20.	舞者——天鹅	3.89
21.	月光——薄纱	4.04	22.	毛发——丝绸	3.74
23.	气球——泡沫	4.19	24.	薄雾——烟云	4.81
25	讽刺——尖刀	6.96	26.	短剑——匕首	5.63
27.	楼群——丛林	4.41	28.	信念——灯塔	5.07
29.	虚伪——匕首	3.81	30.	诱惑——陷阱	4.85
31.	理想——翅膀	4.48	32.	历史——警钟	5.3
33.	时间——良药	6.04	34.	危险——暗礁	4.85
35.	流言——病毒	4.56	36.	面试——栏杆	4.56
37.	心脏——水泵	3.56	38.	方法——路径	6.04
39.	书籍——粮食	6.26	40.	信念——灯塔	6.7
41.	家庭——港湾	7.07	42.	公鸡——闹钟	5.33
43.	地球——母亲	6.81	44.	老师——园丁	7
45.	奋斗——阶梯	6.52	46.	阴谋——陷阱	6.7

续表

47.	柳絮——雪花	4.3	48.	蘑菇——小伞	3.96
49.	眉毛——月牙	4.11	50.	云彩——棉花	4.59
51.	眼睛——窗户	7.15	52.	磨难——风雨	6.48
53.	理想——支柱	7.59			

Appendix V: metaphorical wordset generating questionnaire in Exp 2

性别 ________ 年龄 ________

你好！欢迎参加这次调查。本调查旨在考察你在隐喻理解方面的想象力。请先仔细阅读下面的介绍，再完成问卷。

隐喻的相似性往往在于本体和喻体与其他事物之间的某种抽象关系，对隐喻的理解往往基于对其他事物及与它们之间的抽象关系的联想。

你需要做的是发挥想象力，对下列各隐喻性词对中的相似性进行理解，在横线上写出你在理解过程中第一个想到的分别与本体和喻体对应的名词。

该任务没有时间限制，也没有对错之分，请认真阅评，谢谢合作！

Appendix VI: metaphorical wordset generating questionnaire for category targets in Exp 2

隐喻结构范畴调查问卷

性别 ________ 年龄 ________

你好！欢迎参加这次调查。本调查旨在考察你在隐喻理解方面的想象力。请先仔细阅读下面的介绍，再完成问卷。

隐喻的相似性往往在于本体和喻体与其他事物之间的某种抽象关系，隐喻的理解往往基于对其他事物及与它们这间的抽象关系的联想。

你需要做的是发挥想象力，对下列各隐喻性词对的相似性进行理解，并基于这种相似性将本体和喻体归入一个隐喻性的抽象的类别。这个抽象的类别可能是具体的名词，如“猎手”，也可能并没有一个具体的名词，在这种情况下，你可以用“动词+者”的方式对这种范畴进行命名，如“追逐者”。在横线上写出一个或两个你想到的描述本体和喻体共属抽象类别的词汇。

该任务没有时间限制，也没有对错之分，请认真阅评，谢谢合作！

Appendix VII: metaphorical wordset generating questionnaire for semantically associated targets in Exp 2

隐喻结构语义调查问卷

性别 ________ 年龄 ________

你好！欢迎参加这次调查。本调查旨在考察你在隐喻理解方面的想象力。请先仔细阅读下面的介绍，再完成问卷。

隐喻的相似性往往在于本体和喻体与其他事物之间的某种抽象关系，隐喻的理解往往基于对其他事物及与它们这间的抽象关系的联想。

你需要做的是发挥想象力，对下列各隐喻性词对的相似性进行理解，并基于这种相似性将本体和喻体归入一个隐喻性的抽象的类别。这个抽象的类别可能是具体的名词，如“猎手”，也可能并没有一个具体的名词，在这种情况下，你可以用“动词+者”的方式对这种范畴进行命名，如“追逐者”。在横线上写出一个或两个你第一个想到的描述本体和喻体共属抽象类别的词汇。

该任务没有时间限制，也没有对错之分，请认真阅评，谢谢合作！

Appendix VIII: critical metaphorical wordsets and their corresponding targets used in Exp 2

	wordset			target	
			semantical	categorical	unrelated
1.	历史 现实	镜子 面孔	映射着	警戒者	挖掘着
2.	友谊 朋友	桥梁 路人	连接着	联结者	迷茫者

续表

3.	信念 人生	灯塔 航船	指引着	指引者	发展着
4.	胸怀 意见	大海 河流	接收着	包容者	观看者
5.	方法 目标	路径 目的地	通达着	联结者	争论者
6.	教师 学生	园丁 花草	培养着	培育者	争取着
7.	理想 人生	翅膀 小鸟	依托着	承载者	书写着
8.	家庭 家人	港湾 船只	庇护着	保护者	实施着
9.	书籍 精神	粮食 身体	填充着	营养者	封锁者
10.	公鸡 世界	闹钟 黎明	唤醒着	提醒者	询问着
11.	地球 人类	母亲 子女	供应着	供养者	轮流着
12.	虚伪 真相	面具 面目	隐藏着	遮盖者	贩卖者
13.	忠言 错误	良药 疾病	改进着	修正者	寄送着

	semi-scrambled for CAT task		semi-scrambled for SEM task		semi-scrambled for MAP task	
1.	硬盘 小鸟	鼠标 书本	大树 小鸟	鼠标 书本	大树 小鸟	猎人 动物
2.	台灯 果汁	海浪 汽水	台灯 员工	海浪 船帆	台灯 员工	海风 船帆
3.	苹果 狮子	银行 大象	苹果 香蕉	银行 大象	苹果 香蕉	银行 金融
4.	树林 现实	饭店 未来	树林 现实	饭店 酒菜	地球 月亮	饭店 酒菜

续表

5.	小刀 电视	水杯 空调	小刀 铅笔	水杯 路人	小刀 铅笔	池塘 青蛙
6.	委屈 飞机	地板 火车	委屈 人生	地板 拖把	拖把 电视	地板 拖把
7.	麻雀 枪炮	鸽子 夸奖	弓箭 枪炮	大海 夸奖	弓箭 枪炮	鸽子 翅膀
8.	床单 社会	被子 护士	懒惰 社会	医生 护士	父亲 儿子	医生 护士
9.	海滩 苍蝇	电脑 蟑螂	海滩 椰林	电脑 牲畜	海滩 椰林	窗户 风暴
10	天空 桌子	水泵 椅子	天空 白云	水泵 拖鞋	天空 白云	轮船 舵手

	fully-scrambled	
	for all tasks	
1.	老虎	砖瓦
	钢笔	烟囱
2.	狮子	娱乐
	篮球	玻璃
3.	球衣	叔父
	童年	地板
4.	书本	桔子
	源泉	地板
5.	高塔	朋友
	窗户	乌云
6.	苹果	兔子
	敌人	球拍
7.	汽车	蒸汽
	市场	庙宇
8.	公鸡	蜻蜓
	床单	西瓜
9.	海军	香蕉
	人类	飞机

Appendix IX: metaphor pairs and their similarity rating scores in Exp 3a

	attributive pairs	scores	relational pairs	scores
1.	风筝——小鸟	2. 45	理想——小鸟	6. 05
2.	荒地——沙漠	2. 9	孤独——沙漠	4. 86
3.	湖面——镜子	2. 43	历史——镜子	4. 57
4.	灯光——星星	2. 67	希望——星星	4. 57

续表

5.	露水——珍珠	2.44	爱心——珍珠	5.05
6.	彩虹——桥梁	2.5	友谊——桥梁	4.34
7.	山路——阶梯	2.45	教育——阶梯	3.57
8.	气球——泡沫	3.04	空想——泡沫	6.05
9.	薄雾——烟云	2.22	历史——烟云	6.27
10.	短剑——匕首	3.11	虚伪——匕首	4.59
11.	鱼鳍——翅膀	3.67	梦想——翅膀	6.68
12.	楼群——丛林	3.87	学派——丛林	5.65
13.	矮墙——栏杆	3.9	面试——栏杆	7.05
14.	田螺——蜗牛	3.89	时间——蜗牛	5.31
15.	纱布——滤网	3.45	考试——滤网	5.76
16.	坚石——钢铁	3.74	意志——钢铁	6.98
17.	大厅——舞台	4.19	生活——舞台	6.5
18.	飘带——彩虹	4.12	希望——彩虹	6.68
19.	蘑菇——雨伞	3.34	法律——雨伞	4.46
20.	玛瑙——水晶	3.56	真情——水晶	5.28
21.	火球——朝阳	3.65	孩子——朝阳	4.61
22.	李子——苹果	2.54	爱人——苹果	6.24
23.	清茶——美酒	3.96	岁月——美酒	4.8
24.	线团——乱麻	2.56	矛盾——乱麻	7.17
25.	支架——拐杖	2.98	朋友——拐杖	6.98
26.	头套——面具	3.45	谎言——面具	7.61

Appendix X: metaphor pairs and their corresponding target words (with frequency scores) used in Exp 3a

			concrete	score	abstract	score	unrelated	score
1.	风筝 理想	小鸟 小鸟	天空	5.58	奋进	5.32	盒子	5.55
2.	荒地 孤独	沙漠 沙漠	荒凉	5.26	寂寞	4.68	轻松	5.62
3.	湖面 历史	镜子 镜子	平静	4.82	反思	5.69	草地	6.27
4.	灯光 希望	星星 星星	明亮	5.56	激励	5.22	耳机	4.6
5.	露水 爱心	珍珠 珍珠	晶莹	4.83	珍贵	6.47	海滩	4.93
6.	彩虹 友谊	桥梁 桥梁	拱弯	5.58	联系	5.65	麦田	6.51
7.	山路 教育	阶梯 阶梯	升高	4.51	发展	5.01	水杯	6
8.	气球 空想	泡沫 泡沫	圆形	6.06	虚无	6.78	课桌	6.65
9.	薄雾 历史	烟云 烟云	朦胧	5.31	神秘	4.98	商店	5.67
10.	短剑 虚伪	匕首 匕首	锋利	5.81	伤害	5.54	天空	6.32
11.	鱼鳍 梦想	翅膀 翅膀	浮力	5.06	追求	4.86	高楼	5.61
12.	楼群 学派	丛林 丛林	众多	5.31	复杂	4.65	地毯	4.88

续表

13.	矮墙 面试	栏杆 栏杆	界限	4. 84	阻碍	4. 98	银行	5. 63
14.	田螺 时间	蜗牛 蜗牛	圆形	4. 98	缓慢	6. 56	卡片	4. 56
15.	纱布 考试	滤网 滤网	洞隙	6. 14	选拔	6. 45	爬山	5. 81
16.	坚石 意志	钢铁 钢铁	坚硬	6. 89	坚定	5. 31	全面	5. 69
17.	大厅 生活	舞台 舞台	宽阔	5. 96	精彩	4. 87	凉爽	6. 19
18.	飘带 希望	彩虹 彩虹	长条	5. 64	美好	6. 4	饥渴	5. 44
19.	蘑菇 法律	伞 伞	圆顶	5. 2	庇护	4. 6	迅速	6. 45
20.	玛瑙 真情	水晶 水晶	晶莹	5. 94	真诚	5. 16	暖和	4. 65
21.	火球 孩子	朝阳 朝阳	圆形	5. 21	希望	4. 48	紧张	5. 21
22.	李子 爱人	苹果 苹果	圆形	4. 89	珍重	5. 09	鼠标	5. 27
23.	清茶 岁月	美酒 美酒	清香	4. 89	积淀	5. 27	短信	6. 21
24.	线团 矛盾	乱麻 乱麻	错乱	6. 11	复杂	4. 71	纸张	5. 32
25.	支架 朋友	拐杖 拐杖	支撑	5. 36	协助	5. 65	朗读	6. 09
26.	头套 谎言	面具 面具	遮盖	5. 11	虚伪	6. 54	笔记	5. 22

Appendix XI: materials used for the learning phase in Exp 3b

		本体		喻体			本体		喻体
1	风筝 理想	飞机 希望	蜻蜓 未来	小鸟 小鸟	16	坚石 意志	肌肉 军队	合金 团结	钢铁 钢铁
2	荒地 孤独	废墟 仇恨	戈壁 恐惧	沙漠 沙漠	17	大厅 生活	广场 政治	田间 人生	舞台 舞台
3	湖面 历史	墙壁 朋友	天空 评论	镜子 镜子	18	飘带 希望	衣裳 美梦	礼花 未来	彩虹 彩虹
4	灯光 希望	眼神 激励	火苗 智慧	星光 星光	19	蘑菇 法律	花朵 关系	云朵 人脉	伞 伞
5	露水 爱心	雨滴 童心	牙齿 善良	珍珠 珍珠	20	玛瑙 友谊	玻璃 爱情	玉石 真情	水晶 水晶
6	彩虹 友谊	木板 人缘	天桥 亲情	桥梁 桥梁	21	火球 少年	红球 事业	顶灯 梦想	朝阳 朝阳
7	山路 教育	陡坡 婚姻	梯田 留学	阶梯 阶梯	22	狼狗 商人	狗熊 老板	狐狸 男人	狼 狼
8	气球 空想	气泡 股市	水泡 房价	泡沫 泡沫	23	清茶 岁月	泉水 婚姻	甘露 生活	美酒 美酒
9	薄雾 历史	轻纱 记忆	焰火 往事	烟云 烟云	24	线团 矛盾	毛发 局势	布条 思路	乱麻 乱麻
10	短剑 挖苦	矛头 讽刺	尖刀 辱骂	匕首 匕首	25	夜晚 交易	深洞 真相	夜空 阴谋	黑幕 黑幕
11	鱼鳍 梦想	机翼 学习	风筝 理想	翅膀 翅膀	26	炊烟 财富	大雾 权势	蒸汽 梦想	浮云 浮云
12	楼群 学派	书架 社团	货仓 社会	丛林 丛林	27	头套 谎言	浓妆 虚伪	口罩 假意	面具 面具
13	矮墙 面试	栏杆 要求	篱笆 文凭	门槛 门槛	28	支架 老师	长棍 父母	鹿角 爱人	拐杖 拐杖
14	田螺 时间	海螺 进展	号角 思维	蜗牛 蜗牛	29	李子 爱人	梅子 情人	梨子 儿女	苹果 苹果
15	土包	凸起	草垛	坟墓	30	纱布	丝巾	窗纱	滤网

Appendix XII: four lists of materials for four conditions of learning in Exp 3b

For condition 1: attributive similarity, repetition

性别 ________ 年龄 ________

你好！欢迎参加这次调查，本调查旨在考察你在语言理解中的想象力。下列各词对中的两个词之间具有某种相似性，请理解两词之间的相似性，并在横线上写出你能联想到的最能表达该相似性的一个词汇，该词汇的词性没有限制，可以是名词、动词、或形容词等。词对有重复，对于重复的词对也可发挥想象力填写不同的词汇。

请认真填写，稍后还有相关的语言实验。

风筝——小鸟________	气球——泡沫________	清茶——美酒________
荒地——沙漠________	薄雾——烟云________	线团——乱麻________
湖面——镜子________	短剑——匕首________	夜晚——黑幕________
灯光——星光________	鱼鳍——翅膀________	火球——朝阳________
露水——珍珠________	线团——乱麻________	狐狸——野狼________
彩虹——桥梁________	纱布——滤网________	支架——拐杖________
山路——阶梯________	坚石——钢铁________	李子——苹果________
气球——泡沫________	大厅——舞台________	纱布——滤网________
薄雾——烟云________	风筝——小鸟________	蘑菇——雨伞________
短剑——匕首________	荒地——沙漠________	玛瑙——水晶________
鱼鳍——翅膀________	支架——拐杖________	灯光——星光________
楼群——丛林________	李子——苹果________	露水——珍珠________
矮墙——门槛________	纱布——滤网________	彩虹——桥梁________
田螺——蜗牛________	山路——阶梯________	风筝——小鸟________
彩虹——桥梁________	飘带——彩虹________	荒地——沙漠________
坚石——钢铁________	蘑菇——雨伞________	湖面——镜子________
大厅——舞台________	玛瑙——水晶________	炊烟——浮云________
飘带——彩虹________	火球——朝阳________	头套——面具________
蘑菇——雨伞________	狐狸——狼________	薄雾——烟云________
玛瑙——水晶________	清茶——美酒________	短剑——匕首________

火球——朝阳______	楼群——丛林______	鱼鳍——翅膀______
狐狸——野狼______	矮墙——门槛______	山路——阶梯______
清茶——美酒______	田螺——蜗牛______	气球——泡沫______
线团——乱麻______	夜晚——黑幕______	田螺——蜗牛______
夜晚——黑幕______	炊烟——浮云______	坚石——钢铁______
炊烟——浮云______	头套——面具______	大厅——舞台______
头套——面具______	湖面——镜子______	飘带——彩虹______
支架——拐杖______	灯光——星光______	楼群——丛林______
李子——苹果______	露水——珍珠______	矮墙——门槛______

For condition 2：attributive similarity，variant topics

性别 ________ 年龄 ________

你好！欢迎参加这次调查，本调查旨在考察你在语言理解方面的想象力。下列各词对中的两个词之间具有某种相似性，请理解两词之间的相似性，并在横线上写出你能联想到的最能表达该相似性的一个词汇，该词汇的词性没有限制，可以是名词、动词、或形容词等。词对有重复，对于重复的词对也可发挥想象力填写不同的词汇。

请认真填写，稍后还有相关的语言实验。

风筝——小鸟______	眼神——星光______	尖刀——匕首______
荒地——沙漠______	雨滴——珍珠______	风筝——翅膀______
湖面——镜子______	木板——桥梁______	货仓——丛林______
灯光——星光______	气泡——泡沫______	篱笆——门槛______
露水——珍珠______	轻纱——烟云______	玉石——水晶______
彩虹——桥梁______	矛头——匕首______	顶灯——朝阳______
山路——阶梯______	机翼——翅膀______	云朵——伞______
气球——泡沫______	书架——丛林______	窗纱——滤网______
薄雾——烟云______	栏杆——门槛______	天空——镜子______
短剑——匕首______	玻璃——水晶______	梯田——阶梯______
鱼鳍——翅膀______	红球——朝阳______	广场——舞台______
楼群——丛林______	狗熊——野狼______	口罩——面具______
矮墙——门槛______	泉水——美酒______	布条——乱麻______
田螺——蜗牛______	飞机——小鸟______	号角——蜗牛______
纱布——滤网______	废墟——沙漠______	礼花——彩虹______
坚石——钢铁______	衣裳——彩虹______	蜻蜓——小鸟______

大厅——舞台________	花朵——雨伞________	戈壁——沙漠________
飘带——彩虹________	肌肉——钢铁________	火苗——星光________
蘑菇——雨伞________	丝巾——滤网________	牙齿——珍珠________
玛瑙——水晶________	墙壁——镜子________	天桥——桥梁________
火球——朝阳________	陡坡——阶梯________	水泡——泡沫________
狼狗——野狼________	甘露——美酒________	焰火——烟云________
清茶——美酒________	浓妆——面具________	合金——钢铁________
线团——乱麻________	长棍——拐杖________	田间——舞台________
李子——苹果________	梅子——苹果________	鹿角——拐杖________
支架——拐杖________	毛发——乱麻________	梨子——苹果________
头套——面具________	海螺——蜗牛________	狐狸——狼________

For condition 3: relational similarity, repetition

性别 ________ 年龄________

你好！欢迎参加这次调查，本调查旨在考察你有语言理解方面的想象力。下列各词对中的两个词之间具有某种相似性，请理解两词之间的相似性，并在横线上写出你能联想到的最能表达该相似性的一个词汇，该词汇的词性没有限制，可以是名词、动词、或形容词等。词对有重复，对于重复的词对也可发挥想象力填写不同的词汇。

请认真填写，稍后还有相关的语言实验。

理想——小鸟________	希望——星光________	友谊——水晶________
孤独——沙漠________	爱心——珍珠________	少年——朝阳________
历史——镜子________	友谊——桥梁________	法律——雨伞________
希望——星光________	空想——泡沫________	岁月——美酒________
爱心——珍珠________	历史——烟云________	矛盾——乱麻________
友谊——桥梁________	挖苦——匕首________	生活——舞台________
教育——阶梯________	梦想——翅膀________	希望——星光________
空想——泡沫________	学派——丛林________	爱心——珍珠________
历史——烟云________	面试——门槛________	友谊——桥梁________
挖苦——匕首________	友谊——水晶________	教育——阶梯________
梦想——翅膀________	少年——朝阳________	学派——丛林________
学派——丛林________	希望——彩虹________	面试——门槛________

面试——门槛________	岁月——美酒________	时间——蜗牛________
时间——蜗牛________	理想——小鸟________	意志——钢铁________
考试——滤网________	孤独——沙漠________	老师——拐杖________
意志——钢铁________	希望——彩虹________	爱人——苹果________
生活——舞台________	法律——雨伞________	理想——小鸟________
希望——彩虹________	时间——蜗牛________	孤独——沙漠________
法律——雨伞________	考试——滤网________	历史——镜子________
友谊——水晶________	历史——镜子________	空想——泡沫________
少年——朝阳________	教育——阶梯________	历史——烟云________
爱人——苹果________	生活——舞台________	挖苦——匕首________
岁月——美酒________	谎言——面具________	梦想——翅膀________
矛盾——乱麻________	老师——拐杖________	考试——滤网________
老师——拐杖________	爱人——苹果________	意志——钢铁________
谎言——面具________	矛盾——乱麻________	谎言——面具________

For condition 4：relational similarity，variant topics

性别 __________ 年龄 ________

你好！欢迎参加这次调查，本调查旨在考察你在语言理解方面的想象力。下列各词对中的两个词之间具有某种相似性，请理解两词之间的相似性，并在横线上写出你能联想到的最能表达该相似性的一个词汇，该词汇的词性没有限制，可以是名词、动词、或形容词等。词对有重复，对于重复的词对也可发挥想象力填写不同的词。

请认真填写，稍后还有相关的语言实验。

理想——小鸟________	激励——星光________	辱骂——匕首________
孤独——沙漠________	童心——珍珠________	理想——翅膀________
历史——镜子________	人缘——桥梁________	社会——丛林________
希望——星光________	人脉——雨伞________	文凭——门槛________
爱心——珍珠________	记忆——烟云________	真情——水晶________
友谊——桥梁________	讽刺——匕首________	梦想——朝阳________
教育——阶梯________	学习——翅膀________	阴谋——黑幕________
空想——泡沫________	社团——丛林________	招聘——滤网________
历史——烟云________	要求——门槛________	评论——镜子________

挖苦——匕首________ 爱情——水晶________ 留学——阶梯________
梦想——翅膀________ 事业——朝阳________ 政治——舞台________
学派——丛林________ 未来——彩虹________ 假意——面具________
面试——门槛________ 婚姻——美酒________ 思路——乱麻________
时间——蜗牛________ 希望——小鸟________ 思维——蜗牛________
考试——滤网________ 仇恨——沙漠________ 军队——钢铁________
意志——钢铁________ 美梦——彩虹________ 未来——小鸟________
生活——舞台________ 关系——雨伞________ 恐惧——沙漠________
希望——彩虹________ 生活——美酒________ 智慧——星光________
法律——雨伞________ 比赛——滤网________ 善良——珍珠________
友谊——水晶________ 朋友——镜子________ 亲情——桥梁________
少年——朝阳________ 婚姻——阶梯________ 进展——蜗牛________
爱人——苹果________ 儿女——苹果________ 往事——烟云________
岁月——美酒________ 虚伪——面具________ 团结——钢铁________
矛盾——乱麻________ 父母——拐杖________ 人生——舞台________
老师——拐杖________ 局势——乱麻________ 爱人——拐杖________

Appendix XIII：materials used in the testing phase in Exp 3b

	prime vehicle	concre-tetarget	abstract target	unrelated control	filler vehicle	filler target
1	小鸟	飞翔	奋进	盒子	通知	道获
2	沙漠	干旱	寂寞	轻松	鼠标	靠罗
3	镜子	平静	反思	草地	眼泪	寻植
4	星光	明亮	激励	耳机	参考	境翻
5	珍珠	晶莹	珍惜	海滩	水平	转穿
6	桥梁	拱弯	联系	麦田	安排	东举
7	阶梯	台阶	发展	水杯	心理	跳黑
8	泡沫	圆形	虚无	课桌	食品	狂屏
9	烟云	朦胧	神秘	商店	荷花	都怀

续表

10	匕首	锋利	刻薄	天空	美女	派处
11	翅膀	追求	高楼	羽毛	商品	副超
12	丛林	复杂	地毯	众多	考试	村缕
13	门槛	要求	银行	界限	相片	类慢
14	蜗牛	缓慢	卡片	圆形	皮肤	泡载
15	坟墓	消亡	重要	隆起	来源	料凝
16	钢铁	坚定	全面	坚硬	字典	短刚
17	舞台	精彩	凉爽	宽阔	台灯	极盖
18	彩虹	美好	饥渴	长条	废纸	刺凯
19	雨伞	庇护	迅速	圆顶	保姆	旺抛
20	水晶	真诚	暖和	晶莹	部门	双庞
21	朝阳	紧张	红色	希望	铅笔	滴络
22	恶狼	耳环	长牙	狡猾	展品	坠般
23	美酒	短信	清香	积淀	少年	掉创
24	乱麻	纸张	错乱	复杂	厨房	胡码
25	黑幕	纸篓	昏暗	秘密	丝袜	春肯
26	浮云	热情	天空	虚无	键盘	史汤
27	面具	笔记	遮盖	欺骗	民族	底附
28	拐杖	朗读	支撑	协助	梳子	数持
29	苹果	鼠标	圆形	珍重	目标	丰率
30	滤网	爬山	洞隙	选拔	森林	潘始